Praise for *How to Make You[r]*

Praise for *Making the Most of Your Money NOW*

"The *Joy of Cooking* of personal finance. It provides the basics in just about any area you can think of—from what you should consider about money when you are in your 20s to what to do with your investments once you have retired—and presents simple, straightforward recipes outlining the fundamentals of how to accomplish your goals."

—*The New York Times*

"I found myself racing through this gigantic compendium because it was engagingly written and full of useful information."

—*The Washington Post*

"A financial management bible, updated . . . Jane Bryant Quinn has been teaching all of us how to better manage our money—for the better part of three decades."

—*MarketWatch*

"A practical tour de force from the maven of money. This is simply the best handbook for managing personal finances that I have ever seen."

—Rosabeth Moss Kanter, Harvard Business School,
author of *World Class*

"The class book for practical financial advice—encyclopedic in scope and written with clarity and style."

—Burton G. Malkiel, author of
A Random Walk Down Wall Street

"No one is smarter about money—or easier to read or clearer or more conscientious—than Jane Bryant Quinn."

—Andrew Tobias, author of
The Only Investment Guide You'll Ever Need

ALSO BY JANE BRYANT QUINN

Making the Most of Your Money NOW:
The Classic Bestseller Completely Revised for the New Economy

Making the Most of Your Money

Smart and Simple Financial Strategies for Busy People

Everyone's Money Book

How to Make Your Money Last

THE INDISPENSABLE RETIREMENT GUIDE

Jane Bryant Quinn

SIMON & SCHUSTER PAPERBACKS
New York   London   Toronto   Sydney   New Delhi

This publication contains the opinions and ideas of its author. It is sold with the understanding that neither the author nor the publisher is engaged in rendering legal, tax, investment, insurance, financial, accounting, or other professional advice or services. If the reader requires such advice or services, a competent professional should be consulted. Relevant laws vary from state to state. The strategies outlined in this book may not be suitable for every individual, and are not guaranteed or warranted to produce any particular results.

No warranty is made with respect to the accuracy or completeness of the information contained herein, and both the author and the publisher specifically disclaim any responsibility for any liability, loss or risk, personal or otherwise, which is incurred as a consequence, directly or indirectly, of the use and application of any of the contents of this book.

Simon & Schuster Paperbacks
An Imprint of Simon & Schuster, Inc.
1230 Avenue of the Americas
New York, NY 10020

Copyright © 2016, 2020 by Quinn Works

This Simon & Schuster trade paperback edition January 2020

SIMON & SCHUSTER PAPERBACKS and colophon are registered trademarks of Simon & Schuster, Inc.

For information about special discounts for bulk purchases, please contact Simon & Schuster Special Sales at 1-866-506-1949 or business@simonandschuster.com.

The Simon & Schuster Speakers Bureau can bring authors to your live event. For more information or to book an event, contact the Simon & Schuster Speakers Bureau at 1-866-248-3049 or visit our website at www.simonspeakers.com.

Manufactured in the United States of America

10 9 8 7 6 5 4

Library of Congress Cataloging-in-Publication Data is available.

ISBN 978-1-4767-4376-9
ISBN 978-1-9821-1583-8 (pbk)
ISBN 978-1-4767-4378-3 (ebook)

To all my grandchildren—
the next generation coming up

Hallee, Elias, Dana, Jesse, Tyler, Maisy,
Hudson, Kai, Riley, Juno, and Dion

Contents

Introduction to the Second Edition

I started this book because my head was popping with questions about the life phase we call "retirement." After decades of working, we're finally free—but free to do what? A whole generation is reinventing itself as it moves away from the role of earner toward the new status of "engaged and interested citizen, retired."

There are no guarantees. In the four years since this book first appeared, laws and the economy have taken some sudden turns. If you're younger than Medicare age, you're newly worried about health insurance. Attacks on the ACA (Obamacare) have raised its price, forcing thousands of midlife, middle-income people back into the world of the uninsured. If you're seeking help when managing your retirement savings, your adviser no long has to be a "fiduciary"—that is, an adviser who truly puts your financial interests first. (Chapter 2 tells you how to find real fiduciaries among the "advisers" who now pretend to be.) Due to relaxed regulations, it's also easier to sell "safe, high-interest" investments because "safe" is what's on people's minds. (You know they're not "safe," don't you?)

Amid these changes—emotional and financial—we have to find our footing. We may be free of the workaday world, but what will our lifestyle look like and how are we going to pay for it? None of us knows how many years we have ahead—20? 30? More? Last year, I lost my mother; she was 103—sharp almost to the end.

Centenarians are rare, but our lengthening life expectancies continue to surprise us. On average, you'll reach your mid- to late 80s. More than one in three women and one in five men will live past 90. We have every reason to worry that our money will run out before we do. Many of us stay on the job well past traditional retirement age, not just because we like the work but because we need our salaries, too.

The way you look at your finances changes as you move from preretirement to your postretirement years. While you're still working, you focus on accumulating a comfortable pile. You might have a dollar target in mind. More likely, you're saving whatever you can, aiming every year for "more." You're paying down debt (I hope) and focusing on investments that can make your money grow.

That flips when you enter retirement's door. Suddenly, you have to take the money you've saved and turn it into a reliable income for life—not knowing how long your life is going to be. How do you do that? How large can your income be?

In a perfect world, you'll work on this question well before you leave your job. The answer will tell you when (and whether) you can afford to quit. In this imperfect world, however, you might not have planned for retirement, or might have been pushed into it unexpectedly. You'll need to figure out, *now*, how to manage with what you already have. Modest spenders can live on Social Security and, if they're lucky, a pension, dividends, interest, and perhaps a temporary or part-time job.

Often, however, that's not enough to pay the bills. You'll have to supplement your income with regular withdrawals from your savings and investments. These withdrawals amount to "homemade paychecks," landing in your bank account just the way your working paychecks did. If you're married, the paychecks have to cover the cost of two life spans as well as any emergency need for cash.

What kind of standard of living can you afford? Will you have to look for another job? And how do you stretch your savings to make the money last?

When I started asking those questions for myself, I looked around for information. There isn't much. I found books and websites on how to invest but practically nothing on how to prudently parcel your money out. If you take too little from savings, you're depriving yourself of some of the comforts that you worked for. If you take too much, you'll go broke.

I did find plenty of bad advice from financial firms and their salespeople (a.k.a. "advisers," "financial consultants," and brokerage firm "vice presidents"). I was shocked when I looked at the menu of so-called "safe" and "guaranteed" investments we're being offered. They're loaded with hidden costs and risks. Maybe the firms are unscrupulous, maybe just careless. Either way, people like us—with savings that we need to both hoard and spend—are walking around with targets on our backs. We are where the money is and, believe me, they're coming for it, or trying to.

Fortunately, important and objective research is currently being done on ways of creating reliable incomes for life. I've spoken to the key players and gathered their findings here. What surprised me— really surprised me—is how simple a retirement income plan can be. So simple that you can manage the investments and withdrawals yourself. If you'd rather not, I found several new sources of high-level help at rock-bottom costs. You don't have to pay big commissions and fees to get good advice.

I also learned a lot by talking with practically everyone I met about the retirement decisions they're making for themselves. Often, they were leaving money on the table because they hadn't heard about their alternatives. Social Security benefits topped this list. I found people taking it at age 62—not because they had to but because it was there. They had no idea how much their monthly benefit would increase if they waited a few years to collect. If you're married and each of you has a Social Security account, you might be able to adjust your claiming dates to collect even more.

Then there's the question of what percentage of your retirement savings to put into stocks (or, rather, stock-owning mutual funds— the best bet for you and me). Some savers were so spooked by the near collapse of the financial system in 2007 and 2008 that they still invest only in bonds and insured certificates of deposit (CDs). But even if you can live on today's fixed-interest rates, what will that income be worth in purchasing power as the years go by?

There's a lot of research linking the percentage you hold in stocks to the size of the sustainable income you can withdraw from your savings for life. Having read it, I've come to think of retirement investing as being split in half. For the first half—the next 10 years or so—holding part of your money in safe or low-risk CDs or bond mutual funds makes a lot of sense. You need a reliable source of cash in case stock prices decline. But to fund the second half of retirement— starting 10 or 12 years from now—you'll need to own investments that grow. American and international business, as a whole, has succeeded wonderfully over time (with occasional hiccups). We can share in that growth without breaking a sweat by buying and holding just two or three well-diversified stock-owning mutual funds. When you do this, you'll still be an "income investor." Future capital gains create spendable income just as interest and dividends do.

For prudent cash withdrawals from your retirement savings, the standard advice has been to take 4 percent of the total in the first year and add a dollar increment for inflation in each subsequent year. But 4 percent is too much if you own only bonds and CDs. And it's perhaps too little when part of your money is invested for growth. You don't have to make a wild guess about how much of your savings you can afford to spend. There are recipes. Who knew?

While working on this book I changed my mind about a few things. For example, I developed a new respect for immediate-pay annuities that convert a lump sum of savings into an income for life.

They offer a higher monthly income than you can prudently withdraw from investments that you manage yourself. (Don't confuse "immediate-pay" with the annuities that promise lifetime benefits. "Lifetime benefit" annuities are on my "no" list due to high costs and misleading sales. It's all explained in Chapter 6.)

Another example—I learned a new use for reverse mortgages. These loans against home equity are often a poor deal for people in later age, especially for those who have almost run out of cash. But if you take the loan earlier, in the form of a credit line, you can use it to increase the size of your monthly income. The credit line grows every year, which gives you a nice hedge against inflation.

A homemade paycheck isn't intended to cover everything. You need it only to fill the gap between your retirement expenses and your other sources of income, such as Social Security, pension, rents, part-time work, and whatever. Figuring out that gap is the entryway to sound retirement planning. Don't feel bad if you have to trim your expenses so as not to take too much from your savings every year. Almost everybody trims whether they confess it or not. After the trims, however, I've often found people scrimping too much—piling up extra savings "just in case." This book's cash withdrawal strategies can help you spend as well as save. Peace of mind is finding a way of life that works.

Every personal situation is a little different. Some people focus their plans on retiring at a certain age—anywhere from 45 to "never." Some get a buyout offer at 55 and wonder whether they can afford to take it. Some are pushed into retirement unexpectedly, through illness or job loss, and find that money is short. Some have retired already and need a clearer look (or a second opinion) on how to handle their money now. I've ranged over all the major financial questions I can think of, including health and life insurance. Inevitably, products and options will change in the future, but in my reporting, I sought general principles that will stand the test of time.

The biggest thing I learned, after digging into this subject for several years, is the significance of our sense of self as we approach or enter this change of life. We need to find a new way of being—a fresh identity, different passions and pastimes, and a deeper involvement with family, community, and friends. We're not on the shelf (yet!). We have lots to contribute and the time to find our place. What gives us this freedom of mind and action is having an income that we're sure will last for life. This book was written to help you build it. After that, adventure calls.

Jane Bryant Quinn
New York City

The Joy and Challenge of Life After Work

Now that you can do whatever you want, what do you want to do?

Retirement challenges us like nothing else. We have to reinvent our lives. One day we're part of the vast American workforce—living by the clock, attacking new projects, and focusing our minds and skills. The next day we can sleep until noon if it pleases us. Then we bound out of bed, free at last, ready for coffee and lunch and . . . what?

Successful retirement—whenever it occurs—turns out to be work of another kind. The future now is almost as blank a slate as it was when you were 18 and wondering what was going to happen to you. Fifty years later, you're fortified with knowledge and experience but with no place to take it. You might have a partner in life, children, grandchildren, status in your community, and a dog that loves you. Still, you have seven days a week and 52 weeks a year to fill. No sane human being can watch that much television or play that much golf. Maybe you'll be able to stay at work well past normal retirement age, perhaps with shortened hours. But the last day of work can't be held off forever. You need an action plan to transition into this new phase of life.

You also need a financial plan to make the most of the income and savings that you have available. That's what most of this book is about. "Money can't buy happiness," they say, but it sure can buy food, shelter, heat, phone service, streaming movies on all our new devices, and gas for the car. A little extra buys plane tickets, ball games, concerts, and long-term peace of mind. It's hard to be happy if you're always worried about the bills. Learning how to stretch your available income and rightsize your life are the first steps toward retiring well. Even if retirement seems far away, steps you take now—to save and invest—can greatly improve your standard of living when your paycheck eventually stops.

But before I talk money, I'd like to talk about the nonfinancial challenges of life after full-time work. They're huge and, for most people, unexpected. We fling ourselves into leisure as if a grand vacation lay ahead. But permanent vacations can get pretty boring. When we were working, we had a sense of accomplishment and a place in the world, even if—at the end—we couldn't wait to quit. Now, having shut that door, we need another place. What are we retiring *to*?

Eventually, when you look back on your transition from work to retirement, you'll think of it as perhaps the most creative period of your life. Most of us still need an active sense of social worth. But instead of getting it from a workplace, ready-made, we have to make it ourselves. The challenge is to discover new interests, new places, and new friends. Your weeks should fill up again with projects, meetings, entertainments, family visits, and events—activities you choose yourself, to gladden your days and give purpose to your life. You'll probably take on these projects at a leisurely pace. You won't want to be busy every minute. But neither will you want to look at a daily calendar that's blank.

It takes time to move from the worker role to the role of engaged individual citizen. How long the transition takes will depend on your personal initiative and will. The faster you can bury the old "workplace you" and rise to a new "liberated you," the more content you're going to be.

Not everyone moves into retirement willingly. You might lose your job and spend some unhappy weeks or months rehashing that stressful time. Your health (or your spouse's health) might be dicey, which, for now, completely occupies your mind. The departure from work might have been so sudden that you had no time to prepare emotionally.

Widows, widowers, and the divorced face similar problems. They've been forcibly "retired" from married life and now face their own blank slates.

No matter how you get there, you (and your partner, if you have one) will have to figure out how to build another life. The questions will be the same for everyone.

Who are you, anyway?

For so much of our lives, we identify ourselves with our jobs. "I'm a lawyer." "I'm a teacher." "I'm an operations manager." "I work for IBM." Those who have young children might also say "I'm a mother" or "I'm a father." Our jobs and family responsibilities give us meaning. When we quit, or the children grow up, there's an instant loss of status that few of us are truly prepared for. We're in a new role—that of citizen-retiree. It's an empty vessel until we fill it up.

What are you going to do with the rest of your life?

A 3G retirement (golf, gossip, and grandchildren) isn't always enough, cute as the grandchildren are. Most retirees today are vigorous, mentally alert, and eager to jump into something active and interesting. We have skills, smarts, and dreams. At work, we were accomplishing stuff, even if we got tired of it. As parents, we had the critical job of raising responsible adults. But what are we accomplishing now? Loss of meaning and purpose throws some retirees into depression, even those who thought they couldn't wait to start a leisured life. If you spend your hours in front of a laptop or TV set, you're likely to—quite literally—bore yourself to death. You'll need all your imagination and energy to discover a new role.

Where will you find friends?

When you worked, you made social contact simply by doing your job every day. You had people to chat with or complain about, customers to call on, and lunches with colleagues. When your job ends, however, your workaday friends are likely to fall away. You need to get out of the house and do things, not just for fun and intellectual interest but for the social companionship, too. Women are better at this than men, but it can be a challenge for both.

THE FIVE STAGES OF RETIREMENT

The gerontology researcher Robert Atchley studied the transition from working life to leisure. Retirement, he said, is a process, not an event. Some people hustle through the stages. Others take months, even years, to reach serenity. The better you manage the first stage, the faster your progress is likely to be.

Stage 1: Preretirement. You gradually disengage from work. You're still doing your job, but your imagination moves ahead. You talk with friends about their own plans for life after work and ask retired friends what they're up to now. You put together a budget to see if, and when, you can afford to leave your paycheck behind. If you're married, you have many talks with your spouse about how you each expect retirement to work—your hopes and fears, where you'll live, what you'll do with your time, whether you'll both retire at the same time and, if not, what the expectations will be. You think about what you might do next. If you hope for part-time work, now's the time to start making the contacts. There might be a project you can do for your current employer or others in your business. If you're being laid off, do your best to think about your next life, not your past one. You're not "unemployed" (bad place), you're "semiretired" (better place). Forward is your only choice.

Stage 2: The Honeymoon. You're free! No more deadlines or office stress. You'll do some of the things you've been meaning to get to—clean the closets, paint the porch, take a trip. If you already have a lot of interests, you might step up your engagement with them. If you've led a high-pressure work life, you might simply rest with your feet up, read, go fishing, take walks, or watch ball games. Assuming that your retirement was planned, you're happy, happy, happy with your decision. Your honeymoon can last for many months, provided that you're moving quickly toward your other interests. But it might last only a week or two if you have nothing to do and nowhere to go.

Stage 3: Disenchantment. Gradually, your days come to seem a little bit empty. You feel a loss of status, if you identified strongly with your job. To the younger, working world, you're obsolete. Even if you retired gladly, your new activities might not be as fulfilling as you'd hoped. You see fewer people and feel more isolated, especially if your spouse or partner is still working. You might notice that money is going out the door faster than you planned. "I'm failing at retirement," one friend told me gloomily.

If you retired specifically to do something else, such as starting a business or taking up teaching, you might skip Stage 3 or pass through it pretty quickly. Ditto if you're an outgoing person who loves discovering new things. If not, disenchantment might catch you by surprise and slow down your adjustment. You're not so eager to get out of bed and can't figure out how to spend your afternoons. You join a club or half try to volunteer for a local organization but it doesn't work out. If your health is poor, you might come to feel that your life is effectively over. You're just taking up space. For some, Stage 3 might last a year or more while you obsess over what you "used to be."

Stage 4: Reorientation. It dawns on you how bored (and boring) you've become. Emotionally, you're finally ready to advance. Some retirees will go back to work. For the rest, it's like retiring all over again but with a more realistic eye. You take stock of your income and expenses and rightsize your life financially. You evaluate your experiments with new activities and start to engage more deeply with the one that interests you the most. One is all you need; others will come along. So will friends, who, like you, have retired and are looking for people to pal with. Your lingering work-life persona is finally being put to bed. You feel yourself growing into your new role.

Stage 5: Stability. You've got it together. You're finding new purpose and feeling productive again. You're happy (or at least satisfied) with your life and are living within your means. Along with new interests, you've discovered ordinary pleasures, such as browsing in a library or taking walks with a friend. Some retirees get to this stage pretty quickly—in fact, directly from the honeymoon. Others take years. You'll know you've arrived when all your thoughts are forward-looking and your days feel full.

MAKE YOUR PLAN: IT'S LIBERATING!

The transition from work to "freedom" is harder than most of us realize until we get there. It starts with clearing the old stuff out of your head—your work, routines, and expectations of status. They get in the way of your life ahead. Post-work, you can do anything that's within your budget and physical capabilities.

When your calendar is blank and you're wondering what to do, it seems natural to start a list.

You might begin by asking yourself what makes you happy—not only today but what made you happy in the past. It might be something you haven't done for 30 years. Never mind. Write it down. You're trying to capture anything—specific activities, experiences, relationships—that once put a smile on your face.

From there, branch out to everything you've ever thought of doing. No idea is trivial. Maybe you'd like to improve your tennis or golf. Read all of Charles Dickens. Research your family's roots. Get a puppy and train it. Learn woodworking. Take cooking classes. Take dance classes. Join a singing group (or start one). Join a weight-loss group or exercise class. Learn photography, including the art of editing photos digitally. Teach Sunday school. Take music lessons, maybe on an instrument you used to play before you got so busy. Join a bridge group. Join a chess club. Give parties. Learn another language. Walk a long mountain trail. Learn local history. Run for local office or join a political campaign team. Start a website to share your professional expertise. Join an investment club. Get more involved with your place of worship. Start a local newsletter. Coach sandlot baseball. Throw pots. Paint. (President George W. Bush started painting lessons when he left office.) Volunteer for a worthy cause. Start (or join) a protest group. Go fishing. Tie flies for people who fish. Create gardens for yourself and your friends. Become a local tour guide or docent in a museum. Make beautiful holiday and birthday cards. Learn computer skills. Sign up for Skype or use the FaceTime app so you can talk to your children and grandchildren long distance, free. Run a charity fund drive. Make jewelry. Breed cats. Become a discount coupon maven. Join a yoga class. Sort the family photos and put them online. Attend local concerts and lectures. Write your autobiography. Have regular dinners with friends. Spend quality time with your spouse or children. Join AmeriCorps, for civic opportunities. Teach English as a second language. Start a wine-tasting group. Try out for a local amateur theater production or offer to paint scenery. Find a bird-watching pal. Travel—be it cruises, visits to children, group tours, or day trips to interesting places near your home. Restore furniture or an old car. Manage garage sales for neighbors. Et cetera, et cetera, and so forth. If you move to a retirement community, a wide range of attractive activities usually comes with the contract.

You might enjoy going back to school. Some retirees work toward college or advanced degrees, others audit courses. A school near you might offer extension courses to adults (type "Lifetime Learning Institute" into your search engine for local opportunities). Free or low-fee college courses are available online: Scroll through the offerings at edX.org, Coursera.org, Udemy.com, and Udacity.com as well as the online courses from Harvard, Dartmouth, Yale, Duke, the University of California, Berkeley, and others (for a long list of what is available, go to MOOC-list.com). Some courses are live; you have to be at your laptop at certain hours and complete assignments (although not necessarily submit to tests). Others let you listen to lectures whenever you want.

Finally, make a list of your skills. Are you good with your hands or with computers? Do you know finance? Can you organize groups? Create marketing campaigns? Work well with children? You have a lot to offer your community that it can use. A focus on skills can help direct you to volunteer groups that would be thrilled to have you. Businesspeople might join a local SCORE (Service Corps of Retired Executives), an organization that helps small businesses get started or expand. Financial people might assist a nonprofit with its books, investments, and fund drives, or study to be a financial planner with an emphasis on retirement prep. Those who drive a mean hammer might volunteer with a local Habitat for Humanity. If you're good with people, you might become a health or social service aide. A skills list helps you assess job prospects, too.

You might not find your next life's work immediately—a delay that risks dumping you, grumpily, into the depressive Stage 3. But keep trying things out. One of them will click.

To get yourself moving, set up an engagement calendar—one of those month-at-a-glance hanging calendars or the calendar on your laptop or phone. Put something useful or interesting into your schedule every day. It might be work around the house (sort out the garage, repair the screens), ordinary errands (shopping, doctor's appointment), community activities (club meetings, volunteer days), hobbies (consult your "makes me happy" list), or personal enrichment (reading, study). You might undertake weekly mini-explorations of nearby towns—to visit a new park, a small museum, a used-book store. It takes as little as one activity, plus normal chores, to structure your day. Something you have to do (or want to do) that gets you up in the morning. On some of your days, puttering works, too.

Regular activities also have the virtue of bringing you new friends as well as renewing relationships with friends who weren't also business colleagues. As often as possible, your calendar should include things you do with other people rather than things you do alone. If you like playing Scrabble or backgammon, find a challenging partner rather than spend hours playing anonymously online. If you like to walk, find a walking partner. Cooks might find a cooking partner.

Have I mentioned exercise? One of the best things you can do for yourself is to join a gym, even if (like me) you've resisted exercise all your life. A vigorous workout greatly improves your general health, appearance, and well-being. It holds down doctor bills, takes off pounds, and keeps your joints and muscles moving. Exercise classes are also great opportunities for socializing. Instead of grumbling about the office you can grumble about your abs.

If you're not yet online, a world awaits you. From your laptop, iPad, or iPhone you can follow the news, communicate with family and friends, plan a trip, take a free online college course, research any subject that interests you, find answers to medical questions, follow your investments, shop, get book recommendations, nail the bargain plane tickets sold to people who can travel at the last moment, and find a vacation condo to rent for a month. For travel with a purpose, check the opportunities at RoadScholar.org (formerly Elderhostel). An Internet search for "senior travel" will turn up organizations such as Senior Cycling and ElderTreks. These and similar groups offer adventurous trips in the United States and abroad—always with a good mattress and bathroom at the end of the day. We're past the age of going "scout."

THE WORLD OF THE SEMIRETIRED

For some, volunteering and leisure time interests aren't nearly enough. You spent your life working and miss the buzz. Doing part-time work or starting a home business is a terrific transition from full-time work to, eventually, full-time leisure. It's also the answer for people who need income to tide themselves over to their Social Security checks.

Some companies hire their own retirees for consulting or project work, but don't limit yourself to the sort of thing you did before. People, organizational, communication, mechanical, carpentry, sales, or management skills are transferable to many types of businesses and nonprofits. Active volunteering might lead to a paid job at the institution. Many seniors work in retail. PatinaSolutions.com and YourEncore.com connect businesspeople and professionals with firms in need of consulting help. The health professions are seeking recruits, especially people interested in working with the elderly. Local vocational schools offer short-term training for a wide variety of jobs. Online hiring halls such as Craigslist.com and SeniorJobBank.org list opportunities nearby. Locally, follow your interests: gardeners might find part-time work at a nursery they patronize, tinkerers at a hardware store.

Anyone who wants a job has to be computer literate. Small shops might welcome you with only a printed resume, but larger employers expect to receive job applications by email. If they're interested, they'll turn to the Web to learn more about you. Older professionals and businesspeople, in particular, should post their resumes and personal profiles on LinkedIn.com and set up a Facebook page. The managers who do the hiring—almost certainly younger than you—will check them just to see if you understand modern communications. If you're not on the Web, you're invisible.

Alternatively, you might start your own business. I can't find good numbers on how many retirees do so, but a 2009 "recareering" study done by the Urban Institute for AARP gives you a hint. Of people in midlife who retired from their previous jobs and changed careers, about 31 percent say they went from working for other people to working for themselves.

Finding the right business idea takes time. Again, turn to lists. Write down lots of ideas, no matter how far-out they seem. Test them against your interests, abilities, and professional or social contacts, then winnow them down. A high percentage of retirement businesses take advantage of the knowledge and connections that the retiree already has. If your mind is a blank, I recommend a search of SideHusl.com. It lists some 300 websites offering money-making opportunities, along with an evaluation of how much you're likely to earn and how well workers are treated.

Many good books have been written about starting and running a small business. You might find a course for entrepreneurs at your local community college or the business school at a nearby university. There you'll learn not only from the teachers but from other business owners who are taking classes, too. Legal, sales tax, bookkeeping, and similar unfamiliar issues become manageable when you talk with people who have solved them.

One warning before you launch: Have a plan B. What will you do if the business doesn't work? You can probably afford to lose a small investment, but don't endanger your home or wipe out your retirement savings. Always look ahead to what you'll be doing for the rest of your life.

RETIREMENT FOR TWO

Talk, talk, talk, talk, *talk* to each other. That's what every financial planner tells me that couples need to do when retirement first springs to mind. Single people need to think only about themselves when making plans. Couples, however, are making a dual decision. Are you both ready for retirement? If so, what next? If you both work and one of you isn't ready to quit, how will you handle the relationship? How will a homemaker feel when his or her partner is suddenly home all day? How will the new retiree feel if the partner cheerfully leaves every morning for work?

Spouses or partners often assume that they both see retirement the same way and that's not necessarily so. When they start talking, they might be surprised—pleasantly or otherwise—by what the other thinks. For example, a husband might expect his working wife to retire when he does, when in fact she's perfectly happy with her job. A wife at home might think her husband should work a few more years so they can accumulate more savings. Each spouse might have a different dream about where and how to live. One partner might have secretly run up debt that now has to be confessed.

These can be rough conversations if your differences are large. Somehow you need to get to the same page. The quality of your retirement will depend not only on finding new things to do but on developing new ways of living with each other.

Retirement gets simpler when both members of a working couple quit at the same time. You can travel when you want, make daytime social plans, share household chores and projects, or move somewhere else. A vibrant retirement life means keeping each other excited about what's happening every day.

If only one of you retires, however, you need to develop some ground rules. For example, the spouse or partner at home will typically take on more household chores. (When my late husband retired, our son took him into the laundry room and said, "Dad, this is a washing machine.") In return, the spouse at work should try to find more evening and weekend time for things you can do together. Most importantly, the spouse at home shouldn't pressure the working spouse to quit. If you pout long and hard enough, you might get your way, but your spouse won't be a happy partner down the road. Why should a wife give up her work to husband-sit (or vice versa)? As the retired spouse, you should make your own schedule, find your own friends, get your own life, even take your own trips. Eventually, your partner will be ready for leisure, too.

A full-time homemaker is in a different position. She (it's usually a she) has reinvented her life since the day she "retired" as an all-day parent. She might have gone to work full- or part-time or deeply involved herself as a volunteer. Her days have structure—shopping, cleaning, friends, hobbies, meetings, exercise, walking the dog. The last thing she needs is a crabby husband demanding to be entertained or ordering her around the way he ordered subordinates at work. On the other hand, she can't pretend that he isn't there. Talk, talk, talk about it. You're entering this new life together. A husband's free time, shared with his homemaker wife, can help her get out of a rut that she hadn't noticed—charting new directions for you both.

Not everyone can expect a bouncing, lively retirement life. Your health, or your spouse's or partner's health, might be poor. But even folks with limitations find positive ways to spend their time—connecting with friends, playing cards, learning things on the Internet, taking short day trips.

Whatever your situation, happiness lies in letting go of the past. All that matters now is who you are in the moment. Retirement is an adventure, demanding all of your creativity and force. So keep experimenting and dare to be glad. No one but you can invent your new life.

2

Rightsize Your Life

You're never afraid to open your bank statement when you're living within your means.

You've cashed your last paycheck. The jig is up. Whatever assets you've earned or accumulated—Social Security, pension, savings, investments, home equity—are all you've got, now and forever. Can they support you comfortably for the next 25 or 30-plus years? If you think so, are you sure? If not, what are you going to do about it?

The questions are the same if you're still at work. You're covering your expenses now, but what will your budget look like when your work life ends, as eventually it will? Can you afford to retire soon, or should you wait? It's time for a financial scan.

Before you start this exercise, take a deep breath. You'll be juggling your personal dreams and priorities as well as your budget. New questions will present themselves, perhaps forcing some changes you hadn't foreseen. If, on your first try, you can't bring your income and expenses into balance, put the numbers aside and tackle them again tomorrow or next week. You'll need time for the pieces to fall into place. And they will. Sooner or later, everyone figures out an acceptable way of living commensurate with income. You won't be turned out, fainting, into the street.

I wish there were some quick rules of thumb for making retirement money decisions. Good rules exist for the young and middle-aged: live on less than you earn, increase the amount of money you save every year, stay out of debt, use tax-favored retirement accounts, and invest for the long term. All the rest is ruffles.

When you leave the workforce, however, universal maxims go out the door. Every person and couple is unique. Your financial choices depend on such things as your health, your age when you left work, whether you're married or single, your spouse's or partner's age and health, whether you have a pension, how good your health insurance is, how much (or little) you've saved, how much planning you've done, whether your retirement was voluntary or forced, whether one of your kids (or a parent) needs financial help, how much debt you're carrying, how you feel about investment risk, whether you can (or want to) work part-time, and how easy (or hard) it is to match your spending to your means.

Managing your spending is key. Nothing matters more to the financial success of your retirement. The stock market isn't going to save you if you're burning through cash. You can search for better investments later if you want. But first, pay attention to rightsizing your life.

Rightsizing means finding that happy place where the annual income you expect for the rest of your life matches (or exceeds) your annual cost of living. That's not always easy to do or, if you're a big spender, to accept. But once you've achieved that balance—emotionally as well as materially—you will find yourself at peace. You'll know that you can afford your life.

Some people save enough money, or have large enough pensions, so that their habits don't have to change very much after they retire. But let's face it: that's rare. Most retirees find that their income falls short, so they need, at minimum, some nips and tucks. Making cuts is absolutely normal. Your friends are in the same boat even if it's not obvious.

Nipping and tucking might not make your priority list at first. You'd like to maintain your lifestyle, take more trips, and maybe fulfill a dream, such as buying a boat. We all want to live as richly as we can while we still have our health, even if we're dipping a little more into savings than is prudent.

That approach can work fine for the first year or three, provided that you're spending discretionary money and have an actual plan to cut back—maybe sharply—in your later years. The plan is essential. Otherwise, you're flying blind.

For a few, rightsizing means a substantial change in the way you live, such as selling your house right now and renting an apartment. That's a tough decision, but the numbers don't lie. The sooner you reorganize your life and stop the leakage from your savings accounts, the faster you'll find your way to peace of mind. Life is full of pleasures that don't cost a lot, and few pleasures are greater than feeling financially safe.

GETTING TO SAFETY IN FOUR AMAZINGLY LOGICAL STEPS

When preparing for retirement, we tend to focus on a number: "If I have $250,000 [or $100,000, or $750,000, or $1 million] in savings," we say, "I can afford to retire." The number is nice, especially if you reach it, but it's not the point—or not entirely the point. What matters is the amount of annual income that your savings can reasonably provide you with, for life. That dollar amount plus any guaranteed income such as Social Security defines your standard of living. Your task is to fit your spending to whatever money you have.

Assembling a budget will take a little time. You'll need to develop real numbers for your annual expenses, sound estimates of your expected income from savings, and a list—true to your feelings—of your priorities in life. You'll probably be making choices that you haven't faced before. "It was eye-opening," a friend said, who read this book in draft and worked through the planning process herself. "I was able to sit down with my husband and have an unemotional spending conversation based on actual fact."

Here are the four steps to creating a dependable retirement spending plan:

Step 1: If you haven't retired yet, start by figuring out how much you're spending now (unless you have a black belt in budgeting, you probably don't know). Go back over your checkbooks, bank statements, and credit cards and add up what it cost you to live over the past 12 months. Then subtract the expenses connected with work. That includes such things as commuting costs, lunches, office clothing, take-home dinners because you didn't have time to cook, subscriptions to industry websites and publications, and dues to professional groups. Subtract the contributions you've been making to retirement plans, and the taxes you're paying for Social Security and Medicare. Add to your budget whatever it will cost to buy a Medicare plan or private health insurance. Those with credit card debt should add the cost of an accelerated repayment plan.

If you have already retired, calculate what you're spending currently, including taxes. You need to find out if it's more than you can afford over the number of years you are likely to live.

Step 2: List the annual salary-type income you can expect (or are receiving) as a retiree. That includes such things as Social Security, pensions, income from an annuity you currently own, rental income, any royalties, trust income, and so on. Don't count any income from interest and dividends; it's covered under Step 3.

Step 3:   Add up the current value of all your financial assets—savings, retirement accounts, mutual funds, stocks, bonds.[1] Assume that you're going to spend 4 percent of the total on living expenses. For example, for every $100,000 you have in savings and investments, you can allocate $4,000 this year toward your bills. At this rate of withdrawal, plus an annual inflation adjustment, your savings should last at least 30 years. (I talk about the 4 percent assumption in Chapter 8. You might not decide on 4 percent, but for budgeting purposes it's a reasonable place to start.) This calculation assumes that your interest and dividend payments are reinvested.

Step 4:   Add the 4 percent of your financial assets to your total salary-type income and subtract an estimate for income taxes. What remains is roughly the amount you can safely spend each year without running out of money. Don't worry about inflation at this point in your budget making. You're looking for a reasonable budget in this year's dollars.

Married couples should do this retirement calculation three ways—once for you as a couple and once for each survivor, if the other spouse dies first. After the first death, the survivor's guaranteed

---

1   Don't include the value of your home equity or the market value of any real estate investments. Unless you sell or take a reverse mortgage (Chapter 10), your real estate isn't available to pay your daily bills.

income will decline because he or she will lose one of their two Social Security checks (Chapter 3). The amount received from a private pension might drop, too, depending on the choices you make when you leave the job (Chapter 5). There might be a life insurance payout. If so, add it to your financial assets and assume that the survivor will start by spending 4 percent of the proceeds.

If your income—as a single, a couple, or a widow or widower— exceeds your expenses, relax. You can spend more, give more to charity, or leave more to your kids. Move ahead to the chapters on ways of tapping your capital comfortably.

If there's a gap between your retirement income and expenses, don't worry. This is the puzzle that everyone eventually solves. The options are clear: Work longer (if you can) and put more money into your retirement fund. Or reduce your expenses to the level of income you have. That's it. You can try to raise the return on your investments by taking extra market risk. But if your bets fail, you'll be in even more trouble. Manage your spending first.

Even if you're fine as a couple, you should make budgetary changes if your projections show that one of you (typically a wife) would struggle if left alone. Perhaps more life insurance would fill the income gap. Or you could cut expenses now in order to build up more savings for the future. If the chief breadwinner—say, the husband—puts off retirement for a few years, he will not only receive a higher Social Security check, he'll leave his wife a higher survivor's benefit if he dies first.

Sometimes the gap between income and expenses is so large that nips and tucks won't do. If you can't (or don't want to) work longer, the best solution is usually to change the place you live. A house is a money pit, even if there's no mortgage. By slashing those costs and moving to a condo or rental apartment, you'll probably be able to keep up your spending on all the smaller things that give spice to life. If you're already a renter, look for a smaller apartment. You might also sell one of two cars, or sell both cars and rely on buses, taxis, and ride-hailing services. A few adventurous people even go abroad to live.

If you're still deciding whether to retire, try living for a year on the amount of income you'll have when your paycheck stops. If you hate it, you might decide to stay on the job for the next couple of years and save money like mad.

If you have already retired and are spending more than 5 percent of your capital this year, that's a trumpet call. An alarm bell. An elbow in the ribs. The time has come for a serious look at your options.

Married couples—whatever their situation—need to make retirement and spending decisions together. That takes many conversations, not always easy ones. You might each be amazed to learn that you have different views on how and where to live and what you can or cannot do without. One or both of you might be blind to the need for budgeting because it challenges your hopes or makes you feel "poor" (even though you're not).

Again, it's time for lists. Each of you should write down the things that are most important to your personal happiness, even if it means giving up something else. For example, you might want to stay in your home, move to a condo but stay in your community, move to a warmer place, live near a golf course, live near the kids, keep your club memberships, keep a vacation house, take frequent trips, help your grandchildren, or whatever. Pin down their costs and set them against your expected retirement income. Working with real numbers helps partners face facts, set priorities, and negotiate compromises. Things lower on your lists might not make the cut.

Early on, you don't know how much you're actually going to spend on your retirement life. You have estimates, but it takes daily living to prove them out. You might find yourself dipping into savings more than you intended, which means that your budget needs another scrub. Alternatively, you might spend less than you expected, suggesting that you can afford more recreation or a newer car. Keep reassessing the numbers, year by year. They'll tell you what to do.

EIGHT SPECIAL SITUATIONS

Eight items can't be shoehorned neatly into the budget process:

Real estate. There are various ways you can use your home equity to close a gap between your retirement income and expenses. You might take a reverse mortgage with a credit line. You might sell the house, add the proceeds to your investments, and rent an apartment. You might sell, buy something cheaper, and put the remaining money into investments or cash reserves. Tapping home equity usually isn't part of the first budget conversation but swings into play if your current finances don't add up.

If you're holding real estate as an investment, for income or capital gains, consider how long you'll want to keep it. During your early retirement years, you'll still have the energy to be a landlord. If you have a vacation home, you might even decide to live there for a while and get renters for your larger home. But as time goes by, dealing with tenants and upkeep will get harder. Plan on selling the properties at some point and adding the proceeds to your savings and financial investments. (For real estate investing, see Chapter 9.)

Health care. Base your budget forecast on the amount you're spending currently on routine drug and medical expenses, including dental and vision care. That amount won't change much unless your health takes a turn for the worse (or better!). Redo your budget if you find that you are regularly spending more. What you can't budget for are unexpected and serious illnesses that require long stints of home health care (mostly uninsured) or put you on a lifetime regimen of absurdly high-cost prescription drugs. You also can't budget for political changes that reduce or eliminate your access to health insurance. For these potential costs, your current savings and investments become your medical reserve.

You can beef up your savings by deciding to spend a little less than 4 percent of your retirement nest egg. That creates a health-care cushion. But remember: In your older age, your discretionary spending will inevitably fall, giving you extra dollars to spend on health. For more on the cost of health insurance and choosing coverage, including long-term care insurance, see Chapter 4.

Debt. Owing money can be a killer for retirees. Today's retirees are more likely to be carrying debt, and a higher level of debt, than past generations. Of non-mortgage debt, about one-quarter of borrowers traced it to unemployment, according to a 2012 study of middle-income adults sponsored by AARP. One-quarter borrowed to help relatives, such as unemployed children, grandchildren in college, and elderly parents. The rest of the debt arose from the normal run of emergencies, both household and medical. If you're still working and in the retirement-planning stage, consider using your income to wipe out consumer debt rather than add more to savings. The return on investment by banishing debt equals the interest rate you pay. For example, cleaning up an 18 percent credit card gives you an 18 percent return on your money, guaranteed. By contrast, savings accounts are paying zip. You'll find consumer debt much tougher to repay once your paycheck stops.

If you've already retired, you might look for part-time work to help erase your debt or tap your savings to double up on payments. Don't use your individual retirement account, however. That comes with a tax cost. If you're making substantial money gifts to kids and grandkids, quit. Assuming they're good people (what else?), they'll be grateful for past gifts and understand your new circumstances. Your priority now is protecting your own older age.

Mortgage debt is a different story. Only about half of older people now enter retirement with a paid-up home. If you're one of them, congratulations—a mortgage-free house confers real peace of mind. If you're part of the other half, however, don't tap into tax-deferred savings to pay off your loan. Treat your mortgage as one of the ordinary expenses that you budget for. If interest rates are low, you might even refinance into a 30-year loan to reduce the amount that you have to pay each month.

Caretaking. If you're working and your spouse (or parent) falls seriously ill, your first impulse might be to quit and become a caregiver. But approach this decision carefully. It might make financial sense for you to keep your job and hire a home health aide to help your spouse during the day. Having a salary will provide you with extra income and perhaps extra savings from continuing contributions to a 401(k). You'll keep building your personal Social Security account. Finally, escaping from the house will ease the stress of being a caregiver, which is healthy for both of you. As you look ahead, consider the likely progress of your spouse's disease. What will you need in the way of equipment? Should your home be modified, and what will that cost? Should you move to a modern apartment without stairs? Is a nursing home or assisted living in the cards, and when might a transfer occur? If you have long-term care insurance, what will it cover and for how long (Chapter 4)?

Helping your children. In a perfect world, your money belongs to you alone. It doesn't belong to your kids. You raised them, educated them, and set them free to make their way in the world. Their standard of living lies in their own hands. Whatever money you've saved should go toward making your retirement as pleasant as you'd hoped. You're not obliged to send your grandchildren to college.

Now let's talk about real life. If one of your children stumbles—through job loss, illness, divorce—what are you going to do? Most parents don't say "Tough luck" and shut the door except in extreme cases (estrangement, persistent drug addiction, and so forth). You're probably going to help, even if reluctantly and even if your financial adviser says no. That might mean a tighter budget and a less carefree retirement than you'd hoped. Bring the child into your budget planning right away so that he or she understands how much you reasonably can afford to do and for how long. Take the same tack with a recent college graduate working hard in a low-paying job or trying to make it in the arts. You might volunteer some temporary help. As part of the deal, the child should have an active plan for becoming independent, soon.

If your child is simply overspending and turning to your wallet for help, "No" should come pretty easily. An able kid normally doesn't belong on your payroll. You might provide some stopgap help, but you'll do the child a favor by insisting that he or she figure out an affordable life.

A special-needs child is another matter and beyond the scope of this book. For information on sources of help, turn to special-needs websites, your school district, your state's Medicaid program, and the federal Supplemental Security Income program. Nonprofit organizations such as The Arc or the National PLAN Alliance can help with life insurance and special-needs trusts.

As for legacies, they're strictly optional. Some parents want to leave money to their kids and are willing to budget for it. Others plan to spend their hard-earned savings during their lifetimes. Either one of these perspectives works for me. Kids of well-to-do parents tend to expect a legacy. If you intend to spend it, or most of it, make that clear.

Special purchases. At some point within the next five years, you will probably need a new car. You might want to take one or two trips. Perhaps you intend to add a downstairs bedroom to your house to make it more convenient for your older age. The money you'll need for these kinds of expenditures should be set aside in a bank account, money market mutual fund, or short-term bond fund so it's there when you make the decision to act (see Chapter 9). Don't include this savings account in your budget calculations. Budgets are solely for everyday expenses. Savings are for the large cash expenses that you can foresee.

A much younger spouse. When there's a significant age difference between the spouses, your life planning has to adapt. You each should expect to stay at work longer, to build up a larger pot of savings. Your investments should lean more heavily toward stocks for long-term growth. For budgeting purposes, you might plan on withdrawing just 3 percent of your assets in the first year of retirement (plus annual inflation adjustments) to extend your savings over 40 years or more. Each of you should buy more life insurance—on the older spouse, to help support the younger one if he or she is left alone; on the younger spouse, to help pay for the older one's health-care needs in case the younger spouse dies first. You can buy 15- to 20-year term insurance even at 65 if your health is good (see pages 344 to 345). If you have a company pension, don't take the lump sum unless your spouse is already well provided for. Instead, take the maximum joint-and-survivor option (see page 140). It will pay your surviving spouse 100 percent of your pension for life. Finally, do your best to ensure that the younger spouse will always have health insurance. With luck, that spouse will be safely covered through his or her workplace. If not, you might have to work longer than age 65 to keep your spouse on your own company's plan. If the older spouse goes on Medicare, there should be a cash reserve to cover the younger spouse's individual health insurance premiums, although access to coverage may depend on whether the ACA (Obamacare) survives and in what form.

An inheritance. How should you budget if you're expecting an inheritance? Best advice: Budget without it (yes, dear adult children, I'm talking to you!). Don't count on that money to bail you out. You can't be sure how much you'll get after your parents' health-care bills are paid or how long you'll have to wait for it (more people are living into their 90s; our family enjoyed birthday parties for my mother right up to 103). If one of your parents enters into a second marriage with someone younger, part of his or her money might be set aside, directly or in trust, for the new spouse's support. You might not inherit until after your stepparent dies. (Don't begrudge a stepparent who made your parent happy!) Base your retirement budget on your own resources. Any inheritance should be gravy.

WHAT IS YOUR HEDGE AGAINST THE RISK OF FUTURE INFLATION?

So far, you've figured out a spending plan that meets your needs today. But in most years, prices are likely to go up. With as little as 2.5 percent inflation, you will need 28 percent more income 10 years from now to buy the same things you are buying now. With higher inflation you'll need even more. Where will that extra income come from?

Part of the inflation problem will take care of itself. As you get older, you will most likely spend less, in inflation-adjusted terms. A study by David Blanchett, head of retirement research at Morningstar Investment Management, found that retirees reduced their consumption by an average of 1 percent a year. Some of those are forced cuts, by people who retired on a small budget. But even people with substantial savings buy less. You don't need more household "stuff," you aren't as pressed to keep up with the Joneses as you were when you worked, you have more time to bargain hunt, and later in life you travel less. Your personal consumption costs will probably rise by less than the inflation rate.

Nevertheless, you'll need to plan for at least some additional money each year. Where will it come from?

Your Social Security is adjusted annually for inflation. So are federal government pensions, veterans' benefits, and some state and local pensions. But those are the only increases that are automatic. You have to achieve every other "raise" yourself. In Chapter 6, you can read about creating your own private pension by using some of your savings to buy an annuity. Chapter 8 shows you how to plan your withdrawals from savings so you can raise your income every year by the inflation rate. Chapter 9 helps you diversify your investments for long-term growth. Chapter 10 suggests a way of using a reverse mortgage to increase your income every year. Figuring out how to handle potential inflation is a critical part of your retirement plan. If your income is fixed or dependent on low-rate savings, such as certificates of deposit, your standard of living will gradually drop.

IF YOU DON'T WANT TO DO THE MATH YOURSELF . . .

You can get a *very* rough cut of the maximum you can afford to spend from two online calculators: T. Rowe Price's Retirement Income Calculator and Fidelity Investments' Retirement Income Planner. You enter your income and assets and get back a proposed monthly allowance that, theoretically, could last for life. The calculators give different results, but they're in the same ballpark. (You have to register in order to use them but you don't have to become a customer.)

After that, you need to get serious. Many retirement planning questions have more than one answer. You need to test one set of possibilities against another to see how the alternatives play out. If you have only a couple of choices to make, you'll probably do fine on your own. But for complex and multiple choices, I don't recommend flying solo. God hasn't made enough erasers, yellow pads, hand calculators, or websites for you to work this out alone. If you make mistakes, you might endanger your standard of living in your older age.

Fortunately, God is making more fee-only Certified Financial Planners (CFPs), and I highly recommend that you seek their advice. At this stage of life, it's the best investment you can make. Not necessarily for the money management, I should add. You could do fine with an automated robo-adviser that sets up and executes sound investment strategies in seconds, and at minimal cost. Similarly, some terrific, well-diversified mutual funds are charging zero, or nearly so (see page 271). The help that's worth paying for is the good judgment and ongoing, personal advice you can get from an honest and experienced financial planner. All CFPs have passed a set of rigorous exams on financial planning. That puts them a giant step ahead not only of robos but of the "advisers" (formerly known as "stockbrokers") who are trained mainly in selling products to earn sales commissions and fees.[2]

My recommendation is that you work with a *fee-only* CFP.[3] They are *fiduciaries* (see page 34). They don't sell financial products or take sales commissions—a big plus. They might charge by the hour or at flat rates for specific services, providing advice that you can execute yourself. If you want them to manage your money and help you plan for the future, you'll pay a fixed annual retainer or a fee that's typically 1 percent (or less) of your assets under management. Costs are disclosed in writing, up front. All CFPs provide financial planning services. Fee-only CFPs use low-cost investments to execute your plan. Among other things, you should expect them to project your income and expenses into the future, under various inflation assumptions; encourage you to develop realistic spending plans (read: budgets); evaluate the various types of pension plan distributions you're offered; discuss tax-friendly ways of rolling over money or

---

2 Not that you'll find many "brokers" anymore. Instead, they call themselves "wealth managers," "financial consultants," "investment planners," et cetera—hiding the fact that they're salespeople.

3 As of October 1, 2019, CFPs are required to be fiduciaries, on orders from the CFP Board of Standards, which issues their certificates. However, they still can earn various types of fees for selling expensive products favored by their firms, so we'll have to wait and see how effective that new rule will be.

company stock held in 401(k)s; explain the risks and types of various investments; help you allocate your assets among stocks, bonds, and cash; advise you on prudent ways of turning your savings into a life-time income; and suggest ways of handling special responsibilities, such as a disabled child. Best of all, fee-only planners will spark a long and careful discussion about your personal values and goals and how you hope to live during the retirement phase of life. That's what should drive the financial decisions you're going to make.

Be sure that your CFP is a real fee-*only* financial planner, not a financial salesperson in disguise! CFPs who take sales commissions and similar fees bill themselves as "fee-*based*" planners or advisers. They still have a stake in the types of products they sell—perhaps favoring fixed-income "living-benefit" annuities (yes, high fees for you, high commissions for them), mediocre mutual funds that are pushed by their firm, or expensive managed investment accounts. If annuities or mutual funds make sense for you, low-cost versions are available.

It might appear that fee-based planners and advisers cost you less. Fees might be waived if you buy annuities or other packaged financial products. Insurance agents (rechristened "financial life managers" or "wealth managers") might claim (falsely) that you're paying no fees or commissions (because "the annuity company" is paying). They might say they're "on salary," so get no special benefits from the products they sell.

Don't be fooled. Planners, advisers, brokers, and insurance agents who work for firms that allow commissions always earn more by selling their firms' most profitable products, whether they're called "commissions" or not. This includes "managed accounts"—no com-mission but 1 percent a year plus the (high) cost of the underlying investments. You're probably paying more than you think and often for inferior advice. Financial salespeople who aren't CFPs don't even have the expertise (or take the time) to help you master your bud-get, think through your personal goals, and match your goals to the money and lifestyle decisions you make. They keep their jobs only if they sell, sell, sell.

A fee-only planner, by contrast, will almost certainly save you money—first, because your life goals, your spending, and your savings will be aligned, and second, because you won't be led into buying expensive products that might not serve you well.

Fee-only planners do have potential conflicts of interest. If they're managing your money for a percentage fee, they might be reluctant to recommend actions that remove large sums of money from your account. For example, they might advise you not to withdraw the cash needed to pay off your mortgage or oppose buying substantial cash-value life insurance policies or annuities, even if they'd work for you. But those temptations fade in the face of the daily temptations beckoning commissioned brokers, advisers, and CFPs. Besides, fee-only planners might very well tell you to pay off the mortgage if it makes sense and you can afford it.

There's one limitation to be aware of. If annuities are appropriate (Chapter 6), a fee-only planner might not be able to provide them because most of these products currently carry sales commissions. Fortunately, new, low-cost and commission-free products are coming onto the market. The best planners will research them, and, if prudent, advise that you buy.

What if you've been working with a fee-based or commissioned adviser, paying the fees and commissions, and are happy with the results? The comfort factor is important, so by all means stay there. An adviser who's also a CFP should be taking the time to discuss your personal goals as well as your investments. You're probably paying more than you have to for financial products and might not be getting the best advice. No matter, if you're gaining peace of mind.

But if you're uncertain about a product that the adviser recommends, want a second opinion, or don't yet have an adviser, jump to the fee-only planning world.

There's one group of commissioned salespeople to treat with

special caution: those who claim to be some sort of "senior specialist." There are more than 50 different "senior" designations—strings of impressive initials strung after the salesperson's name. They purport to show that he or she is "chartered" or "certified" or "accredited" for retirement planning due to some special course of study. Mostly, the designations are no more than marketing tools that these salespeople paid for, with little or no serious study. They should actively repel you.[4]

Three designations, however, are based on a rigorous curriculum, according to retirement income expert Wade Pfau of the American College of Financial Services in King of Prussia, Pennsylvania. For income planning, you can feel comfortable if your adviser's business card says that he or she is a Certified Retirement Counselor (CRC), Retirement Income Certified Professional (RICP), or Retirement Management Advisor (RMA). You're also good with a Chartered Advisor for Senior Living (CASL), whose focus includes broader issues, such as health care and estate planning. But these credentials should be in addition to, not in place of, the Certified Financial Planner (CFP) designation. Fee-only planning is the foundation on which specialties can be built.

There are four online networks for fee-only CFPs. To find local firms, just enter your zip code. If you don't like your choices or no one is local, almost all of the firms will serve long-distance customers by Web, Skype, FaceTime, phone, pigeon:

- *The Garrett Planning Network (GarrettPlanningNetwork.com).* Its members typically focus on people with average incomes and assets. They charge by the hour for planning and financial advice, although some of them manage money for a fee. They're

---

4   Also be wary of advisers "accredited" by the U.S. Department of Veterans Affairs. The VA throws its vets to the wolves by approving practically anyone who asks, scamsters included.

especially helpful for single-purpose advice, such as saving for college or creating a retirement savings plan. Any planner who manages money should be a Registered Investment Adviser,[5] so ask about that. All Garrett planners are fiduciaries.

- *The National Association of Personal Financial Advisors (napfa.org).* NAPFA planners tend to work with people who have an above-average net worth. They'll help you develop a financial plan for your retirement if that's all you want. They'll also help with small-business and estate planning, as well as other needs. They manage money for a fee, focusing on investments with low costs. The lower the cost, the higher your returns can be. NAPFA planners are all fiduciaries.
- *The Financial Planning Association (onefpa.org).* The FPA includes commissioned salespeople as well as fee-only planners. When you make a zip code search, open the box that says, "Compensation Type," and click on "Fee Only." (Note that an adviser who works for a brokerage firm or insurance company is never a fee-only planner, even if he or she claims to be.) You want a planner whose website states that he or she is a fiduciary at all times, for all your transactions.
- *The XY Planning Network (xyplanningnetwork.com).* This group of planners specializes in the needs of Generations X and Y. In general, that's people in their 40s and early 50s. They're all NAPFA members, hence fiduciaries.

At each of these websites, your zip code entry produces a list of fee-only planners in your area. Add to your list any fee-only advisers that your friends recommend. Check their websites to learn

---

5   Registered Investment Advisers (RIAs) are registered with the federal Securities and Exchange Commission or state securities office and are entitled to give individual investment advice.

something about their backgrounds and the kinds of services they offer. If they manage money, go to AdviserInfo.sec.gov to read the Investment Adviser Public Disclosure form (IAPD) that they file with the Securities and Exchange Commission. The IAPDs include Part 2 of their ADV ("adviser") form, which discloses, among other things, their educational background, fees, how much money they manage, their investment methods, whether they're truly fee-only (do they sell any financial products?), and any regulatory actions against them.

Once you've done your homework, call or email two or three of them, introduce yourself, and tell them a bit about what you need (retirement income planning? 401(k) advice? money management? tax planning? everything?). If it feels like a fit, make a personal appointment.

Your first visit to a fee-only adviser should be free. The planner should ask about you, your family, your goals, and your assets (don't hide anything; if you do, it will skew the advice you get). You want to hear about the planner's background, education, financial training and investment methods, the kind of expertise the office offers, how the planning process works, and whether he or she has other clients like you (teachers? civil servants? medical professionals? small business owners?). Ask how the planner is paid (Registered Investment Advisers have to give you the SEC-required ADV form, which discloses any commissions and fees). Get the phone numbers of clients you can call—and make the calls. You'll be surprised by what you can find out. It's also useful to visit at least two planners to get a feel for how different offices work. NAPFA.org offers a useful tool called Financial Advisor Diagnostic (go to "Consumers," then to "Consumer Resources" on its Home page). It lists the questions to ask potential advisers, then tells you what the answers show.

One other source of help: big mutual-fund groups that offer low-cost, fee-only financial planning and money management services. For more on these options, see page 297.

THE NEW FIDUCIARY MUDDLE

No matter where you turn for advice, that person should act as your *fiduciary*. Fiduciaries are sworn, by law, to put your financial interests ahead of theirs. It's called a "duty of care." They don't choose high-cost financial products when the same or similar products can be had for less. They eliminate financial conflicts of interest, to the extent possible, and draw your attention to any that remain. Ideally, they don't take sales commission or "revenue-sharing fees" (a.k.a. kickbacks) as rewards for selling the products of particular financial companies. They'll give you a clear and written list of all the fees they charge. Fee-only planners are generally Registered Investment Advisers and RIAs are always fiduciaries. As of last year, all CFPs are supposed to be fiduciaries, but how that works out remains to be seen.

Unfortunately, real fiduciaries now have to contend with what I call fake fiduciaries. The fakes exist thanks to new rules promulgated last year by the Securities and Exchange Commission and strongly backed by the financial industry (which should tell you something). These rules muddied the waters so much that it's hard to pick the true fiduciaries out of the general swarm.

Starting this year, the SEC is allowing stockbrokers (or "wealth managers" or whatever they call themselves) to advertise that they put your "best interests" ahead of theirs. Those are fiduciary-ish words and may lead you to think that you're dealing with the real thing. But as fee-based advisers (see page 29), they can accept sales commissions as well as a variety of incentive fees for making sales. They can (and will) sell you the firm's own higher-cost products when better-performing ones are available—even though they're not supposed to. Their firms can take kickbacks for selling the annuities or mutual funds of favored companies.

How do they get away with it under the "best interest" rule? Simple. They can deem it in your "best interest" to sell you these products. The SEC says only that they have to disclose all these conflicts of interest in the contract you sign. You're not expected to read the disclosures, let alone understand them (they're written in legalese). But because you've supposedly been told that the broker can give you biased advice, you're presumed to agree that your "best interests" are being served. The U.S. Department of Labor is expected to produce similar rules for advisers dealing with retirement accounts.

What makes things even more confusing is that fee-based planners can wear two hats. In some transactions, they might act as your fiduciary; in others, they'll act as a broker whose duty it is to sell you the expensive (or mediocre) products of the firm. As of June 20, 2020, the firm has to give you a document explaining these different hats. Good luck with understanding it. It's safest to assume that anyone working at a brokerage firm or insurance company is not a true fiduciary. Insurance agents selling fixed-index annuities (see page 173) are never fiduciaries. They're not even held to the slippery best-interest standard. One apparently bright spot is that brokers acting purely as salespeople are no longer allowed to call themselves investment advisers. But they can if they also wear a fiduciary hat.

The pity of it is that investors came close to gaining some legal protection from predatory salespeople. A rule took effect in 2017, requiring advisers to act as fiduciaries when handling retirement accounts. Their duty of care extended to the advice they gave on rolling over your 401(k) to an individual retirement account. They had to disclose all the costs of the proposed IRA investments compared with the cost of staying in your company plan. The result was salutary. Sales of complex high-cost investments dropped. Simple fees began to drive out commission sales.

With the new administration, however, everything changed. The fiduciary standard for brokers and other financial salespeople vanished. The SEC embraced the "best-interest" standard in its place. Some states have created their own fiduciary rules to protect their citizens but they're under legal attack.

So when two advisers each say that they put your best interests first, how can you tell the real fiduciary from the one who can still sell you crappy, high-cost products? (1) Be sure that your investment adviser is an "RIA only," at both state and federal levels. Many RIAs are also registered as brokers and try to hide that fact. The recommendations they make as brokers do not have fiduciary protection. (2) Require the adviser to put in the client agreement that he or she is acting as your fiduciary *at all times*, not just for some of your transactions. Don't accept a claim that "best-interest" is the same thing.[6] (3) Before deciding to roll your 401(k) into an individual retirement account, ask the adviser to put in writing a good-faith estimate of the entire cost of the new investments, including any commissions or fees, compared with the cost of leaving your 401(k) money where it is. A true fiduciary will be charging no commissions. A "best-interest" broker, by contrast, will probably make more general comparisons, touting such things as zippy new investment choices rather than their cost. But are all those choices really better than the funds in your 401(k)? I doubt it. (4) Reject complicated products, such as fixed-index annuities. They're rarely in your best interest, no matter who sells them. (5) Don't drop your guard just because your adviser says, "Don't worry, I always put your interests first." If you don't hear the word, "fiduciary," you're in the world of fakes. And even fiduciaries might have a ton of conflicts of interest. How to tell? In the contract, you'll see a long "disclosure" paragraph that you don't understand. (6) It's illegal for insurance agents to recommend that you quit your 401(k). A securities license is required before giving rollover advice. But agents do it anyway. This law isn't enforced. (7) Remember that you're in charge. It's your money. You make the rules.

---

6   Some salespeople lie. A friend's adviser, an insurance agent, tried to sell her two "investment" life insurance policies and two annuities, all the while claiming, verbally, to be a fiduciary.

However you create your retirement spending plan—by yourself or with help—assume that you'll live a long and active life. Aim for a level of income that will last until you're 95, unless you have good reason to expect a shorter (or longer!) life span. If you're married, assume that your spouse or partner will be long-lived, too. That many years might seem too speculative to plan for, but what if your money runs out when you're 85 and you're still doing yoga? Or, rather, *not* doing yoga because you can't afford it anymore?

Stretching your money over 20- or 30-plus years isn't as hard as you think as long as you start out right. Over time, the number of your purchases will go down. You'll travel less and drive less. You might give up the house and move to an efficient apartment. You'll lose the urge to redecorate the living room. These natural changes will offset rises in consumer prices and medical costs. You can also get more from your assets than you probably think, which is what this book is about.

The great pleasure of rightsizing is that it takes you to a place you can comfortably afford. Never look back. Your life as an engaged and valued citizen is 100 percent ahead.

3

How to Double Your Social Security Income (Well, Almost)

Your payout could be worth as much as $1 million over your lifetime. Are you leaving some of that money on the table?

I love Social Security. It's America's finest retirement plan. Nothing else gives you the same combination of income for life, inflation protection, tax benefits, government-backed payment guarantees, and built-in spouse protection, with no annual investment fee and no market risk.

Every time I list those benefits, I say to myself, "Wow!"

Yet millions of retirees are letting part of their Social Security pensions go to waste. You might be losing hundreds of thousands of dollars, over your lifetime, because you filed for your benefits too soon or didn't check to see if you could coordinate claiming strategies with your spouse. If you're the primary breadwinner, the loss could be especially hard on your spouse if you die first (in most cases, it's wives who are left behind).

What surprises me, especially, is that so many people don't even know about their Social Security options or don't investigate what those options are worth. They take the money and run as soon as they're 62 or maybe 66, having no idea how much money they might be giving up.

The earlier you claim Social Security, the smaller your monthly benefits will be. If you're married, filing early also could lower the income available to a dependent spouse. By filing just a few years later you'll get a much larger lifetime check and your spouse might, too.

Some people have no real choice about when to claim their benefits. If your paycheck stops and you're short of money and savings, you'll need your Social Security benefit—right now—to pay your bills. Your options are effectively closed. Sign up and be happy.

But before making this decision, ask yourself if there are other ways of getting by for three or four years more. It's not written in stone that you have to start your Social Security benefits when you leave your job. Maybe you can take part-time work. Often, it makes sense to use some of your retirement savings to cover the bills for a while, so you can let your government benefits grow.

If I can give you just one word of advice about when to sign up for Social Security, it would be *WAIT.* Here's the compelling arithmetic:

You can claim your retirement benefits as early as age 62. If you wait until your full Social Security retirement age, probably 66, your monthly check will be 33 percent higher. If you wait until 70, your check will be 76 percent higher, compared with what you'd have gotten at 62. Okay, that's not double the income, but it's pretty rich. You're credited with annual cost-of-living increases, too. If you're married and wait until 70 to claim your benefits, you're not only building a larger future income for yourself, you'll leave more income to a surviving, dependent spouse if you die first. There are exceptions: Sometimes married couples can rack up a higher lifetime income if one spouse waits to claim benefits while the other spouse files early, or they both file at full retirement age (see page 61). Maximizing

strategies are available both to one-earner couples and dual earners who each have substantial Social Security records of their own.
When to file depends on your health, your birth year, and how the
numbers work out.

From Social Security's point of view, it doesn't matter when an
individual worker retires. Your benefit is scheduled to last for your
actuarial life expectancy, based on the month you put in your claim.
If you start at 62, the payments are smaller because they're spread
over a longer expected period. If you start at 70, the payments are
higher because you have fewer remaining years. But Social Security
runs on averages. Almost certainly, you will die later, or sooner, than
your "proper" date—*and you don't know which.*

Some people start at 62 even if they don't need the money because
they'd really, really hate to feel like Social Security losers. If they put
off collecting their benefits and died early, they'd feel rooked.

But excuse me—you will actually be dead and not feeling much
of anything about your personal finances. Meanwhile, if you're married, your early retirement may have reduced the monthly Social Security income you left for a dependent spouse. Looked at that way,
your beloved widow or widower is the person being rooked, and you
did the rooking.

Another temptation is to take the benefit at 65, the year you're
eligible for Medicare. How shortsighted is that? If you wait just 12
more months, you can claim a full (and larger) retirement benefit
with a better safety net for your spouse.

The danger today comes not from dying too soon but from living too long and running short of money—especially if your earnings have been above average. Life expectancy for people in the
upper half of the income scale is several years longer than for those
in the lower half. In fact, most of the gains in average longevity
over the past century reflect the longer lives of educated people of
means.

So if you're in good health, I beg you to gamble on a long life, not an early death. Consider waiting until until 70 to collect your Social Security retirement benefits (or, at the very least, 66). If you have already filed for benefits, you can suspend them (see page 77), which starts your future benefit building up again.

You'll think differently if you have a serious illness and don't expect to live to your normal life expectancy. Single people would want to file at 62 to get as many years of of Social Security as they can. The same is true for marrieds, if your spouse has a decent Social Security benefit of his or her own. If your spouse has had little or no earnings, however, you should still consider waiting until 66 or 70 (see page 61 to evaluate your choices). By waiting, you're building a higher, inflation-protected survivor's benefit that will help pay the bills when you're no longer there.

A SCREED AGAINST "BREAK-EVEN AGE"

A common aid, when deciding when to claim benefits, is what's called a "break-even analysis." It supposedly tells you how many more years you have to live in order to make delayed benefits a better choice than claiming now.

As an example, say that you're single and could get $1,500 a month at 62 or $2,000 a month at 66. You might calculate your break-even age as 80, meaning that if you live past 80, claiming at 66 will have been the better strategy. You'll have collected a higher-than-average amount of money over your lifetime. On the other hand, if you die before 80, claiming benefits early will have been the better choice. That is, if 80 is the right age. Break even is a slippery calculation. Using different assumptions, you might get a number like 82. In general, break-even age will be earlier than your life expectancy because of the way the calculators work.

So, now you know your break-even age. So what??? You cannot

know how long you're actually going to live, which makes break even a pretty poor guide for making financial decisions. Maybe you'll last past the magic age and maybe not. You might be in poor health yourself and not expecting a long life. But if you're married, your spouse might live for another 30 years. By taking benefits at 62, you're reducing the check a dependent spouse will get for the rest of his or her life. (You won't be around to hear your spouse grumble, but your kids will.)

Another complaint about break even, if I haven't already complained enough: When you're 62, an age like 80 or 82 might seem impossibly far away. It's easy to think, *No way I'll live that long.* But guess what? You probably will, or your spouse will. Average life expectancy for men in the upper half of the income range runs from 83 to 89 and to 92 for top-earning women. If a married couple reaches 65, the chance that one of you will live until 90 is better than 40 percent. Even if both of you come from short-lived families, that doesn't mean you'll run true to type. So forget about trying to pick a "death age." Base your claiming decisions on your financial goals and circumstances—giving a preference to *WAIT.*

The glory of Social Security lies in its value as longevity insurance. You'll keep getting inflation-adjusted monthly checks even if you live to 120. The larger your Social Security check when you first make a claim, the safer your older age will be.

SOCIAL SECURITY BASICS

Later in this chapter, I'll talk about ways of making the most of your Social Security claiming options. First, however, I have some underbrush to clear away. Surprisingly, for a social program that has protected Americans for more than 80 years, Social Security's workings are not well known. Some retirees—especially married, widowed, or divorced women—are losing money because of simple claiming mistakes. I can't cover every possible way of boosting your benefits (the Social Security handbook has 2,728 separate rules!). But here are the concepts and types of claims that you'll be working with:

Your primary insurance amount (PIA). This is the most important number in your Social Security record. It's the monthly amount you'd receive if you began your retirement benefits at your full retirement age (66 in 2019, gradually rising to 67 in 2027). All the rest of your Social Security benefits, including those due your spouse and survivors, pivot around this central, primary dollar amount. It's based on your highest 35 years of earnings.[1] If you worked for fewer than 35 years, Social Security enters zeros for the missing periods, which pulls your average down. If you work longer than 35 years, that might pull your average up.

If you're still working or haven't yet claimed your benefits, you have an estimated PIA. To learn the amount, call Social Security or check it yourself through your online account or your paper Social Security Statement (see page 46). The estimated benefit assumes that you'll continue to earn money at your current rate.[2] If your pay goes up, your estimated PIA at full retirement age will go up, too. The PIA can shrink if your pay goes down. If you keep working after starting benefits, Social Security will add those earnings to your record. Each year, your benefit will be recomputed, which could lead to a higher check.

Cost-of-Living Adjustment (COLA). When you're on Social Security, you get a cost-of-living increase every year (that is, every year

---

1 Earnings prior to age 61 are adjusted upward to reflect wage inflation.

2 Which will probably be wrong. Social Security may overstate or understate what you might receive, so keep on checking every year.

when inflation is 0.1 percent or more). This is a rare and wonderful gift. Your purchasing power is generally protected no matter how high inflation flies. A few states offer COLAs or partial COLAs with their pensions. But most state and private pensions provide a fixed income that loses purchasing power every year.

Types of benefits. Best known is the *retirement benefit* that pays you a pension for life. *Spousal benefits* go to your husband or wife if they lack sufficient Social Security earnings of their own. Ex-spouses can also make a claim on your account, provided that the marriage lasted at least 10 years. Four types of benefits are available to your family if you die: *survivor's benefits* for your spouse (and qualified ex-spouse); *mother's or father's benefits* for a spouse (or ex-spouse) who's taking care of your child who is under 16 or disabled (the disability has to have started before the child reached 22); benefits for your children if they're under 18 (or under 19 and attending high school), or at any age if they become disabled prior to 22; and *parent's benefits* if you had been paying more than half the support for an aging parent. All these payments receive cost-of-living increases.

Earned-income test. You can collect a paycheck while receiving Social Security benefits. But if you're under full retirement age and earn more than a certain dollar amount in any year, your benefit will be temporarily reduced or suspended. The earnings limit applies to people filing for spousal, family, or survivor's benefits, too.

If you're working and claim at 62 (or any other year before the year you reach full retirement age), your benefit will be reduced by $1 for every $2 you earn over the limit. Starting in January of the year you reach full retirement age, you're docked $1 for every $3 you earn over the limit, up to your birthday month. Once you reach your birthday month, however, there are no more penalties for work. At that point, you can earn as much as you want and still receive your full Social Security benefits.

And here's a surprise—Social Security will gradually repay the money that was withheld during the years you made "too much." When you reach full retirement age, your benefit will be recalculated as if an earnings penalty had never been taken out—so your monthly check will rise, permanently. The money owed will be repaid over your expected lifetime.[3]

If you know that you'll earn more than the limit, tell Social Security in advance so that it can adjust your benefit. Alternatively, you can wait until you file your tax returns and let Social Security discover how much you earned. If it's over the limit, the government will calculate what the reduction should have been and stop sending you checks until it has recovered the amount owed.

Note that only your wages and earnings from self-employment count toward your earnings limit. You can receive any amount of interest, dividends, capital gains, pension income, rents, retirement-plan distributions, and other passive income and still get a full Social Security benefit. If you're married and your spouse is working, his or her earnings don't count, either. Social Security looks only at what you personally bring in. There's one exception, affecting people who are drawing benefits on a spouse's record and are younger than full retirement age: Your benefits as a spouse could be withheld if your spouse earned more than the limit. The earnings limits for 2019 were $17,640 from ages 62 to 65, and $46,900 in the year you reached 66. To find the limit for 2020 and

---

3   There's an exception for a surviving parent taking care of a young child, who takes a mother's or father's benefit and also earns a paycheck. Any money docked from this benefit, due to the earnings limit, is not returned.

later, go to SocialSecurity.gov (or ssa.gov) and put "Earnings Test" into the Search box.

The Government Worker Test. This test affects people with government pensions from a job not covered by Social Security, and who also worked at least 10 years in the private sector. All the Social Security rules theoretically apply to private-sector earnings. But your benefits will be reduced or offset by your government pension. For more on this, see page 82.

Your Social Security Statement. This statement shows your future, estimated Social Security payment at various ages as well as the benefits for your family. You can sign up for it online at ssa.gov/myaccount. If online registration fails, create an account in person by bringing identification to your local Social Security office. Social Security mails paper statements to people 60 and over who are not receiving benefits and have not registered online. (Note that online registration always fails if you put a security freeze on your credit card accounts.) Warning: Sometimes these estimates are incorrect. Don't make any retirement decisions before checking the actual numbers with a Social Security office.

WHAT YOU NEED TO KNOW ABOUT RETIREMENT BENEFITS

Your retirement benefit is the monthly sum you're entitled to receive, based on your personal earnings record. To qualify, you need at least 40 "credits" from jobs that are covered by Social Security, at the rate of up to four credits a year. In 2019, you received one credit for each $1,360 in earnings; for four credits you needed $5,440. That amount rises a bit each year. The dollar amount of your benefit is drawn from your highest 35 years of earnings, adjusted for rising wage levels. If you worked fewer than 35 years, you get a zero for each missing year. That pulls your benefits down. If you work more than 35 years, your benefit might go up. The people least likely to have a Social Security record are those who spend most of their lives outside the workforce—often women who raise children. If you've reached your 50s and aren't sure you're covered, call Social Security. You might find that you need just two or three more years of work to establish your own account. Part-time will probably do. Once you're on Social Security's rolls, you also qualify for free hospital insurance under Medicare.

The magic number—your full retirement age. This is the age when you can claim your primary insurance amount (PIA). No discounts or earnings limits apply. How old you have to be depends on the year you were born. It's 66 if your birthday lies between January 2, 1943, and January 1, 1955. For people born later, full retirement age creeps up by two months every year. For example, if you were born between January 2, 1956, through January 1, 1957, your full retirement age is 66 and four months. It reaches 67 for people born on January 2, 1960, or later.

Early retirement and its cost. You can retire as early as 62, but your benefits will be whacked. Assuming that you were born in 1954 or earlier, you'll get 25 percent less at 62 than you would if you had waited until your full retirement age of 66. If you retire at 64, your benefit will be discounted by 13.3 percent. The early retirement discount gradually increases for those born between 1955 and 1959. Those born January 2, 1960, or later lose 30 percent of their primary benefit if they retire at 62. Those discounts affect your benefits for the rest of your life.

The government pays you to retire late. This is my favorite part of the Social Security law. You get a huge bonus if you start benefits later than your full retirement age. The bonus—called a "delayed retirement credit"—is worth 0.66 percent of your primary insurance amount for each month you delay your claim up to age 70. That's an 8 percentage point gain for each full year. If your full retirement age is 66 and you wait to claim benefits until 70, the size of your monthly check will have increased by 32 percent of your primary insurance amount, plus cost-of-living increases.[4]

You can change your mind about taking retirement benefits. A decision to claim your check early doesn't have to be forever. If you regret taking benefits at 62 and have reached your full retirement age, you can tell Social Security that you want to put your checks on hold. Your account will be suspended and your future benefit will start to build again, earning delayed retirement credits for the years you weren't receiving payments. If your spouse is receiving benefits on your account, those will be suspended, too. See "do-over" and "voluntary suspension," page 77.

WHAT YOU NEED TO KNOW TO COLLECT SPOUSAL BENEFITS

Spouses can claim retirement benefits based on the earnings record of their husband or wife. To qualify as a spouse, you have to have been married for at least one year, although there are exceptions— for example, if you're the parent of your mate's biological child.

---

4   When your full retirement age reaches 67, you'll have fewer months to take advantage of the delayed retirement credits. Still, they'll be a terrific deal. For those born on January 2, 1960, or later, claiming at 70 will increase your benefit by 24 percent of your PIA. If you're married and die first, your surviving spouse gets the benefit of that increase, too.

"Married" means married, regardless of sex.[5] Spousal benefits are also available to people in some legal civil unions or domestic partnerships.

You can get up to half of your mate's primary insurance amount, assuming that he or she has already retired. For example, if the husband's PIA is $2,000, the wife could get up to $1,000. To receive the full $1,000, however, she has to claim at her own full retirement age. If she claims earlier, her spousal benefits will be reduced.

Not every spouse gets this benefit. It's reserved for spouses, usually wives, who didn't work long enough to have their own Social Security account. You also might qualify if your lifetime earnings were small. Social Security will compare your personal benefit—the one based entirely on your earnings—with the benefit you'd get as a spouse. If your personal benefit is smaller, Social Security will top it up to equal the spousal amount (that's called the "spousal supplement"). If your personal benefit is larger than the spousal amount, lucky you. That's what you'll receive. Your working years paid off by providing you with a richer Social Security income than you'd otherwise have had.

Two-earner couples got a surprise in 2015 when Congress abruptly canceled two strategies that they were using to rake in double benefits. You can still use one of those strategies if you were born on January 1, 1954, or earlier (see page 64). That's because Congress grandfathered those who were already eligible. Double benefits won't be available, however, to people born on January 2, 1954, or later.

Nevertheless, playing your cards right as a spouse can still make

---

5   The same-sex marriage rules also apply to veterans' benefits and state and railroad retirement plans, which are beyond the scope of this book. Retirement plans through religious organizations should also recognize same-sex couples if they're subject to federal law regarding retirement benefits or employment discrimination based on sex.

a big difference to the amount you'll receive as a couple over time. I've laid out the claiming rules below. For clarity, I've generally written them from the point of view of a wife filing for benefits on her husband's account. (Social Security is too complicated for unisex writing.) All the benefits work the same way if the husband files on his wife's account or one of a same-sex married couple files on the other's account.

Rule 1:   For you to get a spousal benefit, your husband has to be at least 62 and receiving his own retirement benefit. If he delays his claim (which often makes financial sense), your spousal benefit will be delayed as well. If he suspends his benefit (see page 77), your benefit will be suspended, too.

Rule 2:   For a full spousal benefit, you have to claim at your own full retirement age or later. Your husband's age doesn't matter, nor does it matter that he retired early on a discounted check. The size of your payment depends entirely on how old you are when *you* make the claim.

Rule 3:   If you claim early, your spousal benefit will be reduced. At 62, for example, you'll get 30 to 35 percent less than if you had filed at full retirement age, depending on your year of birth. (There may be instances, however, when it pays to file at 62— see page 62.)

Rule 4:   The size of your potential spousal benefit tops out at your own full retirement age—66 to 67. You get nothing extra by waiting one more year. Your benefit will not increase even if your spouse earned delayed retirement credits. So don't leave money on the table. Spousal benefits should be taken no later than full retirement age.

Big Rule 5:   In most cases, you cannot receive a spousal benefit on your mate's account and later switch to a (higher) retirement benefit on your own account. Similarly, you cannot receive retirement benefits on your own account and later switch to the spousal benefit. That's because, when you put in a Social Security claim, you are "deemed" to be applying for both your spousal and your personal retirement benefit at the same time. Social Security pays you the higher of the two. *Sadly, few couples understand this!* I've spoken with many women who thought they'd applied as spouses, at 62, only to learn that they'd been given their own retirement payments instead, and at a reduced amount. Had they known, they might have delayed their claim, in order to collect a higher retirement check in the future. By the time they discovered what had happened, it was too late. Always ask the Social Security rep which of the benefits you'll receive and what you'd get if you wait a few years more. Then check the rep's numbers against a good software program (see page 78). It's not unusual for reps to make mistakes, and it will almost always be at your expense.

Exception to Big Rule 5: You *can* receive both a spousal benefit and, later, your own retirement benefit if you were born on January 1, 1954, or earlier and file for the spousal benefit at your full retirement age or later. This strategy—called a "restricted application"—works well for couples who each have a substantial Social Security account of their own. See page 64 for details.

Rule 6:   There are special cases where you can receive a spousal supplement even though you've been receiving a personal retirement benefit. For example, say that you're single and started your benefits at 62. Then you got married. After waiting a year, you can apply for a spousal supplement based on your new mate's earnings record, if that will raise the payment you receive. Or say that you retired before your husband did, so your only choice, at the time, was your personal benefit. When he starts claiming retirement benefits, you can apply for the supplement to bring your (lower) benefit up to the spousal level.

Rule 7: You cannot take a discounted personal retirement benefit at 62, then expect to claim a full spousal benefit at 66. Any discount you take for claiming retirement benefits early will affect your spousal supplement, too (but not your survivor's benefit—see pages 53 to 54).

Rule 8: You can *not* get a full spousal benefit *in addition* to your retirement benefit, as many couples believe. It's one or the other. If you're currently receiving benefits based on your mate's earnings, any spousal supplement has already been figured in.

Rule 9: If you're married and each of you has reached full retirement age, you can't both claim spousal benefits on the other's account. One of you has to file for retirement benefits while the other takes the spousal amount.

Rule 10: You can claim full spousal benefits when you're younger than 62 if your husband is on Social Security disability or has begun his retirement benefits and you're caring for his child who's under 16 or disabled. This payment will stop once the youngest child reaches 16 (assuming no disability). When you reapply for spousal benefits, at 62 or later, the normal claiming rules apply. Your check won't be docked for the number of years you claimed benefits as the mother of a young or disabled child.

Rule 11: You will be treated as a spouse even if you're legally separated. But the claiming rules are a little different for couples who aren't together. You won't be able to get spousal benefits on your estranged husband's account until he files for benefits of his own. By contrast, if you were divorced you could claim spousal benefits even if he hadn't retired, provided that he's at least 62, eligible for benefits, the marriage lasted at least 10 years, you're at least 62, and you've been divorced for at least two years. (For more on divorced spouses, see page 56.) If you're separated and have passed the 10-year marriage mark, you should get on the horn to your lawyer and finalize the split. If not, drag out the proceedings until 10 years have passed.

Rule 12: If you married someone who's divorced, the ex can claim full benefits on your spouse's account. This does *not* affect your benefit or your spouse's. You all get exactly the same amount as you would if no ex were involved.

WHAT YOU NEED TO KNOW TO COLLECT SURVIVOR'S BENEFITS

If your wife or husband dies, you're usually entitled to a survivor's benefit. To be eligible, you have to have been married for at least nine months. But there are exceptions—for example, if your spouse died in an accident or while serving in the military.

The size of your benefit depends on the earnings record of the spouse you lost. If you've been receiving spousal benefits, Social

Security will upgrade you to the survivor's benefit, which pays much more. If you've been receiving benefits based on your own earnings, you might—or might not—find that the survivor's benefit is the better deal.

Either way, however, your total Social Security income will decline. That's because when your spouse was alive, you each received a check. When you're left alone, only one check will be coming in. For couples making a long-term financial plan, that's an important point to remember.

The claiming rules for any survivor are gruesomely complex, but here's a general overview.

Rule 1:   A surviving spouse can normally claim benefits starting at age 60 (50, if he or she is disabled). But by claiming before your full retirement age for survivor's benefits, your check will be permanently reduced. The claiming age for full survivor's benefits falls two to four months earlier than the claiming age for full retirement benefits. If it's 67 for retirement, it might be 66 and eight months for survivor's benefits.[6] Claim no later than your full retirement age. There are no extra credits for waiting longer.

Rule 2:   If you claim at full retirement age or older, you can get 100 percent of your deceased spouse's benefit even if you retired early on your own, lower earnings record. All that matters is your age when you make the claim for benefits as a survivor.

Rule 3:   If your spouse retired early, taking a reduced benefit, your survivor's benefit will be based on that reduced amount.

---

6   The age for receiving survivor's benefits gradually rises to 67 for people born in 1962 or later.

Rule 4:   You don't have to choose between taking a retirement benefit (based on your personal earnings) and taking a survivor's benefit (based on the earnings of your spouse). You can get them both—not at the same time but serially, one after the other. That's something that the Social Security rep might not explain. Which benefit to take first will depend on how the numbers work out. See page 68 for examples of how to use this rule to maximize your lifetime income.

Rule 5:   You can claim full benefits at any age if you are caring for the deceased worker's child who is under 16 or disabled. These are called "mother's" or "father's" benefits. If you earn a paycheck, however, your Social Security check might be reduced by the earnings limit as well as by the family maximum (see page 71). Mother's or father's benefits stop when the child is no longer eligible. You can apply for benefits again at 60 or older, under the normal survivor rules.

Rule 6:   If your late spouse died before taking Social Security, the rules are especially complex. Your benefit will be based on how long he or she worked and how old you are when you make the claim. Social Security will tell you what you're owed. Benefits go even to the survivors of workers too young to have spent 10 years in the workforce.

Rule 7:   If your late spouse retired early, Social Security will figure your benefits three ways. You'll generally get the higher of the worker's benefit at the time of death or 82.5 percent of the worker's full retirement amount (assuming you file at your full retirement age). Usually, the latter improves the payment to widows whose spouses retired at 62 or 63. (You don't want to hear about the third calculation. Trust me.)

Rule 8: If you remarry at 60 or later (50, if you're disabled), you have a choice. You can take spousal benefits on the account of your new spouse or survivor's benefits on the account of your late spouse, whichever is higher. If you remarry before 60 (or 50), however, you're not allowed to claim on your late spouse's account. If you have the bad luck to lose your second spouse, you can claim survivor's benefits on either of your late spouses' accounts, whichever is higher. Or stick with your own retirement benefit if it's larger than both.

Rule 9: Survivor's benefits are also available to the young or disabled children of the worker who died and to his or her parents if the worker paid for at least half of their support.

Rule 10: Social Security pays a lump-sum death benefit of $255 to the surviving spouse. If there's no eligible spouse, the money goes to any child (or children) who was receiving benefits based on the worker's account or became eligible to receive benefits when the worker died (see page 72). If no children are eligible, payment is not made.

WHAT DIVORCED SPOUSES NEED TO KNOW

If you were married continuously[7] for at least 10 years and haven't remarried, you're eligible for both spousal benefits and survivor's

---

7   You can divorce and remarry the same person and still be married "continuously" provided that the remarriage occurred no later than the calendar year following the calendar year of the divorce.

benefits based on your ex's earnings record. You get the same amount as you would if the divorce had never occurred. For general information, check the sections on spousal and survivor's benefits above. A few of the claiming rules for divorced people are a little different, however. I've listed them here.

Big Rule 1:   No matter how mad you are at each other, try to let your marriage pass the 10-year mark if you're anywhere close. The right to claim on each other's accounts could be worth a lot of money to each of you in future years. If the final blowup came too soon, consider a legal or informal separation, saving the actual divorce until the marriage is 10 years old.

Rule 2:   You have to wait until at least 62 for spousal benefits even if you're caring for your ex's young child who's disabled or under 16. When you have an eligible child in care, you get the full benefit with no discount for filing early.

Rule 3:   You can claim a spousal benefit even if your ex has not filed for retirement benefits of his own under two conditions: Your ex is eligible to claim benefits now and you have been divorced for at least two years.

Rule 4:   If you've remarried, you can claim spousal benefits only on the record of your current spouse, regardless of your age. If your new marriage also lasts at least 10 years and ends in divorce, you can claim on the record of either ex-spouse, depending on which benefit is higher.

Rule 5:   If your ex-spouse dies, you get a survivor's benefit if your marriage lasted at least 10 years and you have not remarried. If you did remarry, you can normally claim survivor's benefits only on the record of your new spouse, with one exception. If you remarry at 60 or later, you have a choice: Take spousal benefits on the account of your new mate (once the marriage has lasted for at least one year) or survivor's benefits on the account of your ex, whichever is higher.

Rule 6:   You don't have to be in contact with your ex in order to claim benefits on his or her account. But you do need your divorce decree, a document you should never throw away. If you can't find your copy, call your lawyer or go to the vital statistics office in the state or county where the divorce occurred.

Big Rule 7:   Payments to a divorced spouse (or two "exes" or even more!) *do not* reduce the benefits paid to the worker or his or her current spouse. You all can claim your full benefits based on the same account. The worker doesn't even have to know about it.

TIME TO DECIDE: WHAT DO YOU WANT FROM SOCIAL SECURITY THE MOST?

By now you know that Social Security isn't one-size-fits-all. You have choices, some of which will yield more retirement money than others. Which path you take will depend on your personal goals. Here are the three main possibilities:

1.   Do you want immediate cash as soon as you're eligible? You'll get more spending money now but potentially less over your lifetime and a smaller benefit for a dependent, surviving spouse.

2.   Do you want to achieve the largest possible, personal monthly benefit? Put off your retirement claim until age 70. If you're

married and you're the spouse with the higher PIA, claiming at 70[8] leaves the largest possible benefit to a dependent spouse. It might also maximize your income as a couple but not necessarily.

3. Do you want the maximum benefits that you can expect as a couple over your probable lifetimes? In some cases, one of you should begin retirement benefits at 62 or 66, even though, for the early retiree, that means a smaller check (see page 64).

You might consider more than one of these goals when making your Social Security plan. Get the numbers from Social Security to see how they each work out. The following sections make some suggestions for singles, couples, widows and widowers, the divorced, and families.

GETTING THE MOST FROM SOCIAL SECURITY WHEN YOU'RE SINGLE

For single people with no dependents, the Social Security claiming game depends entirely on your finances, your interests, and your health.

Begin benefits at 70 or shortly before if you're in good health and can afford to put off taking the money. Every year you delay retirement after your full retirement age, your benefit grows by a guaranteed 8 percent of your primary insurance amount plus the inflation rate—far better than you'd get from any commercial annuity. While

---

8 Throughout this chapter, I'm using 70 as the delayed retirement age. But, of course, you don't have to wait until then. It might be optimal to claim at 68 or 69.

you're waiting, you can fill the gap with earnings or withdrawals from a retirement account. At 70, your Social Security benefit tops out except for annual COLAs, so there's no point waiting any longer.

Begin benefits at 66 or 67 (if that's your full retirement age) to avoid taking a discount on your primary benefit. Another plus if you're still working: The earnings test won't apply. You can collect your whole paycheck and your full Social Security benefit, too.

Begin benefits shortly before your full retirement age if health concerns arise or you need the money. You'll get less than your full benefit but more than if you retired at 62. Still, the general advice applies. Don't claim early unless you have a very good reason for taking that route. You'll be short-changing yourself if you live a longer-than-average life.

Begin benefits at 62 if you're in poor health and believe that you'll die well before your average life expectancy (at 62, that's 83 for men and 86 for women; for the class of people with traditional pensions, it's age 85 for men and 88 for women). This choice should be based entirely on your personal medical condition. Don't say "My mom died at 71, so I probably will, too." You cannot know. You might still be dancing at 92 and wishing you had a little more money to spend.

Choose 62, too, if that's truly the only way you can pay your bills. Your benefit will be cut by 25 to 30 percent compared with what you'd get at full retirement age. But if you need the money, well, you need the money.

But do you *really, really* need the money? It's not unusual for single people who work for middling wages (women, in particular) to file at 62 even though they're getting by on the salaries they earn. They're delighted to pull in a few hundred extra dollars a month and don't care that it's reduced by the earnings test. The money lost to the earnings test will come back, if you live long enough. But your monthly benefit check will be permanently reduced. Better to wait.

Finally, you'll choose 62 if your priority is to have more money now, period. Maybe you want to quit your job and write a novel or canoe the lakes of the Canadian northwest. Who am I to argue with that?

Special note for an older, single parent with a young child: Children can get benefits on a retired parent's Social Security record until they're 18 (or 19, if they're still in high school) if the parent puts in a retirement claim. You might want to claim early to provide the child with as many years of benefits as possible. Benefits are available for a natural child, adopted child, or stepchild. But note: If you're still working and the earnings test causes some of your benefits to be withheld, your children's benefits would be withheld, too.

GETTING THE MOST FROM SOCIAL SECURITY WHEN YOU'RE MARRIED

Some married couples draw all their benefits from a single earnings record, usually the husband's. That happens when the wife didn't stay in the workforce long enough to acquire a Social Security record of her own or has only a small one. Other couples have two substantial Social Security accounts to play around with—one for each partner. Either way, with proper timing you can add tens (or hundreds!) of thousands of dollars to your combined Social Security haul.

The Rules for Those Born on January 2, 1954, or Later[9]

Your best choices will depend on your ages, the life expectancies you assume, and how large a retirement account each of you has.

---

9 My apologies for all this 1954 stuff. Congress created the complication. We have to live with it, like it or not!

I'll start with the case of a wife with no Social Security account of her own (or only a small one). She'll be eligible for reduced spousal benefits starting at age 62 or full spousal benefits at 66 (or 67). She can't get them, however, until her husband starts collecting on his own retirement account.

When should the husband claim? If he waits until 70 to start collecting benefits, he will get a much larger check for life. During those years of waiting, however, no spousal benefit can be paid to his wife. That's money lost.

By contrast, if the husband files early (prior to full retirement age), his spouse can claim early benefits, too. But her check, too, will be reduced. Filing early also reduces the survivor's benefit available to the wife if he dies first.

In short, you're balancing extra spousal benefits during your early retirement years against a higher income during your later years (and higher survivor's benefits for a dependent spouse). If your goal is to maximize your income as a one-earner couple, William Reichenstein, a professor emeritus at Baylor University in Waco, Texas, and head of research at SocialSecuritySolutions.com, suggests the following:

- If you're both the same age, your best bet is usually for the breadwinner—here, the husband—to file at full retirement age (66 or 67) and for the dependent wife to do the same. At that point, she'll get the full spousal benefit with no discount.
- If the husband is slightly older than the wife, he should file when she reaches full retirement age. For example, if he's two years older, he'd claim benefits at 68 when she reached a full retirement age at 66. Again, she'd get the full spousal benefit with no discount.
- If the husband is four or more years older, he should wait until 70, even if he has a shorter life expectancy. By claiming

late, he will leave the highest possible survivor's benefit for his younger spouse. She would file for spousal benefits at her full retirement age—66 to 67.

- If the husband is a few years younger than his wife, he should consider claiming retirement benefits when she reaches full retirement age. By claiming early, he'll receive a smaller check, but she'll receive full spousal benefits as soon as possible. The tradeoff: She'll get a lower survivor's benefit if he dies first.
- If the husband reaches full retirement age and is still at work, he should claim his retirement benefits right away. The earnings test no longer applies, so his benefits won't be docked. To get the largest check, the wife should start her spousal benefits at full retirement age.
- If the wife is the breadwinner, use these rules in reverse.

The rules are obviously very general and don't meet everybody's needs. Many of you will take benefits early because you need the money—clever strategies don't apply. But Reichenstein points you in a good direction if you can afford the wait. For more precision, I strongly recommend that you use one of the Social Security claiming services listed on pages 78 to 80. They look at your benefits and expected retirement date and show you what you and your spouse would get at different claiming ages. They're just as valuable for couples who will be claiming early as for those who will claim late.

Everything changes if you're a two-earner couple, each with a comfortable earnings record. Neither of you will get spousal benefits. Instead, you'll receive a retirement benefit—higher than the spousal allowance—based on your personal account. When to file will depend entirely on whether or for how long you'll want to wait in order to let your future benefits increase. For example, the husband might quit working but put off his retirement claim because, as a couple, they can live on the current earnings of the wife. Conversely, you might start benefits early because you've been eased out of your job.

If you both live long enough, you'll maximize your income, as a couple, by putting off claiming until age 70. But often that's not the best strategy. Try running the numbers using various life expectancies. It might be smarter for the lower-earning spouse to file for reduced retirement benefits at 62 while only the higher earner waits until 70.

But again, I recommend the claiming services on pages 78 to 80. You'll see real numbers rather than having to guess.

What if your spouse is many years younger than you are—say, by more than 10 years? Ask Social Security for your primary insurance amounts (PIA—see page 43). In general, if the younger spouse has the higher PIA, you should make your claiming decisions as if you were two single people. If the older spouse has the higher PIA, he or she should claim at 70 while the younger claims at 62. Those fabulous claiming services will tell all.

If You Were Born on January 1, 1954, or Earlier

You can still take advantage of a loophole that's now closed to everyone else. You, and you alone, can collect spousal benefits *and* your own retirement benefit, too. Ideal candidates for this double-dip opportunity are two-earner couples where each has a substantial Social Security account. You can proceed in one of two ways:

- The lower-earning spouse—say, the wife—claims reduced retirement benefits either at 62 or when her husband reaches full retirement age, whichever is later. When the husband reaches full retirement age (between 66 and 67), he puts in a "restricted application" for spousal benefits on the wife's account. He collects those benefits until he turns 70. He then switches to his own retirement account, which has been growing at the rate of 8 percentage points a year.

- Alternatively, the older of the couple—say, the husband—files for retirement benefits when the wife reaches full retirement age. That allows the wife to collect spousal benefits on the husband's account. When the wife reaches 70, she switches to her own higher retirement benefit.

If the wife is the older of the couple, or the higher earner, just use these strategies in reverse.

Warning: You must make it absolutely clear to Social Security that you're filing for spousal benefits *only* and that you're qualified to do so. Ask for a "restricted application"—meaning that it's restricted to spousal benefits. You can claim it only if three things are true: (1) You are eligible for both a spousal benefit and your own retirement benefit. (2) You are claiming at your full retirement age. (3) You were born on January 1, 1954, or earlier. This benefit is no longer available to people born on January 2, 1954, or later.

Restricted applications are still right and proper for people of the right age!! Don't let Social Security tell you they can't be done! Frustrating but true—some Social Security reps have never heard of a "restricted application" for spousal benefits. While writing this chapter, I exchanged half a dozen emails with a friend, aged 66, whose local office kept insisting, wrongly, that she'd have to take her personal retirement benefit because that was higher than her benefit as a spouse. If this happens to you, tell the rep to go to "deemed filing" on his or her computer, which gives the rules. On your home computer, go to ssa.gov/planners, enter "deemed filing for spouse" into the Search box, call up the FAQs, and print out the rules yourself. You can apply for this benefit in person, by phone, or online. By phone, call Social Security at 800-772-1213. Even if the rep doesn't know what you're talking about, you can ask for a technical expert or supervisor. Online, search for the restricted application and go to the section called "When to Start Retirement Benefits." Find the question "If eligible for both retirement and spouse's benefit, delay receipt of retirement benefit: Yes or No." Answer "Yes." In the Comment field at the end of the online application, you might state that you're restricting the application to spousal benefits only.

If you file a restricted claim for spousal benefits and Social Security accidentally pays you your own retirement benefit instead, you have one year to fix the mistake. See "The do-over," page 77.

Some further comments:

- Restricted applications work even for spouses who are years apart in age. Older spouses claim benefits whenever it suits the couple's financial plan. Younger spouses claim the restricted spousal benefit at their full retirement age, then switch to their own, higher retirement benefit as late as 70.

- The dollar value of this claiming strategy changes if the older spouse earned less money and has a smaller retirement benefit than the younger spouse. Spousal benefits for the younger and higher-earning spouse won't be as good. Still, it's money in the bank—worth using while the younger spouse waits until 70 to collect his or her own retirement benefit.

- Wipe out of your mind the loophole called "file and suspend." It no longer exists. I mention it only to save those with long memories from hunting for it fruitlessly. Also, don't mention it to a Social Security rep when you're applying for a restricted spousal benefit. It might confuse the rep and cause your application to derail.

Beware another mistake that some Social Security reps are making! They're wrongly applying the deemed filing rules to survivor's benefits. Deemed filing covers only your spousal and retirement benefits. It does not affect your survivor's benefit. You are absolutely entitled to file for retirement benefits first and survivor's benefits later or vice versa (see below).

Are married women with paychecks being rooked? Some working wives strongly resent the spousal benefit. As they see it, the taxes they contributed to Social Security, as workers, are "lost." They'd get spousal benefits whether they had a paying job or not.

In fact, you *always* get whatever personal benefit you earned. If it's smaller than the spousal benefit, your personal benefit will be topped up to the spousal level. So your taxes aren't lost. You are simply participating in a system that gives a minimum benefit to low-earning spouses (usually women) who might otherwise be superpoor in their old age. You're fortunate if you have a solid Social Security account of your own. In the vast majority of cases, the benefit you earn by working will be higher than the benefit you could claim as a spouse. So no, you're not being rooked.

GETTING THE MOST FROM SOCIAL SECURITY AS A WIDOW OR WIDOWER

Widows and widowers who are past full retirement age and have been receiving spousal benefits should be switched to the higher survivor's benefit automatically. So will widows on spousal benefits who are not eligible for retirement benefits, even if they're under full retirement age. You'll get at least 100 percent of what your late spouse was receiving (see page 55). Your first payment generally includes the $255 lump-sum death benefit (be sure to check).

Widows and widowers who are under full retirement age and are drawing from their own, personal earnings records will not be switched to survivor's benefits automatically. That's because you have choices. Social Security will wait to see what you want to do. You might keep on drawing your personal retirement benefit and apply for survivor's benefits when you're a little older and the amount has increased. Or you could take survivor's benefits immediately, at a reduced rate based on your current age. Make an appointment with Social Security right away, to see which is best.

Widows and widowers who have earned their own retirement benefits but haven't drawn on them yet have an even better choice. You're owed a survivor's benefit *and* your own retirement benefit, too. You can't take them both at once, but you can take them serially, one after the other, in a way that maximizes your lifetime income. Which benefit should come first? That depends on how the numbers work out. For example, say that you're a widow, 60, and expect to live to your mid-70s, at least. To make a good decision, you'll need to compare your future retirement benefit at 70 with the survivor's benefit you'd get at your full survivor's retirement age. Social Security will provide the information. Here's how to play it:

If your future retirement benefit will be the higher of the two, start your survivor's benefits right away (you can do it at 60), even though you're taking a discount. Switch to your retirement benefit at 70, when it has grown to the maximum amount.

If the survivor's benefit will be the higher of the two, start your retirement benefits as soon as you turn 62 (or asap, for widows who are older than that). Switch to the survivor's benefit when you reach the right age—say, 66. You'll get at least 100 percent of whatever your late husband was receiving. There are no extra credits for waiting longer.

If your deceased spouse took retirement benefits early, however, you might do better by claiming survivor's benefits before you reach full retirement age. The numbers will tell.

Notify Social Security as soon as your mate dies (the funeral home can do it for you). All payments made for the month of the death (or later) have to be returned. Social Security pays a month "late." For example, a payment received in May was for the month of April. If your spouse died in April, the check or direct deposit received in May is an overpayment. Don't spend the money! The government will want it back. If you're paid by check, return it. If you get direct deposits, notify the bank of the death. The bank will return the overpayment, debiting it from the deceased's account. If you've emptied the account, Social Security will come after you directly.[10]

Younger widows and widowers might be able to get survivor's benefits, too. The limits that Social Security puts on earnings could reduce your payment to little or nothing (see page 44). But apply, even if you'll receive only a small amount. Every extra dollar helps. You qualify if you're caring for the deceased worker's child who's under 16 or disabled (the disability had to have started before the child was 22). You can also file for children's benefits if they're under 18 (or 19 and still in high school).

Don't drag your heels when applying for survivor's benefits! Widows who have passed their full retirement age can get up to six months' payments retroactively, but no more. Certain younger widows can't start benefits until they apply. It could get expensive if you wait too long.

GETTING THE MOST FROM SOCIAL SECURITY WHEN YOU'RE DIVORCED

The strategy for a divorced man or woman depends on two things: the size of your own Social Security earnings record, compared with

---

10 Note that the payment your spouse received in the month of the death is for the prior month, hence is good. Sometimes banks return this check, too. Social Security checks its records to see if the beneficiary is clear. If so, you'll get it back. Or, you can claim it by filing Form SSA-1724.

that of your ex's, and how old you are when you make your claim. Here are your options:

If you have no retirement benefit of your own, you'll have to depend entirely on what you'll receive as an ex-spouse. If you file as early as 62, your check will be reduced by 30 to 35 percent. If you wait until your full retirement age, 66 or 67, you'll get the full spousal benefit—half of your ex's primary insurance amount. If your ex is still working, his or her primary benefit is probably going up. So waiting to file will give you a higher future income, too.

If you have a small retirement benefit of your own, you might do better by claiming as a spouse on your ex's account. Social Security will look at both benefits and give you the larger of the two. (Technically, you get your own benefit, which is then topped up—"supplemented"—to equal the spousal benefit.)

If you're still working, try to put off your claim until your full retirement age. At 66 (or 67), you can collect a full divorced-spouse benefit plus all your earnings, too. If you claim earlier, you might run into the earnings limit, which docks your check (although, eventually, you'll get that money back—see page 45).

If you have a substantial earnings record based on your own years of work, you can live on your personal Social Security benefit and forget your ex. But that's not always the best idea. If you were born on January 1, 1954, or earlier, you're allowed to raise your total take by filing for spousal benefits at full retirement age or later (see page 64). At 70, you can switch to your personal benefit, which will have been enhanced by the annual 8 percent delayed retirement credit. Note that you can't use this strategy if you file earlier than full retirement age. Younger claimants can take only their own retirement benefits if they're higher than what they'd get as a spouse. And because you filed early, those benefits will be reduced. (Unfortunately, the special, double-dip benefit is not available to ex-spouses born on January 2, 1954, or later.)

If your ex dies and you haven't remarried, you're eligible for survivor's benefits. You get 100 percent of what your ex was getting if you've reached full retirement age when you make your claim. If you take the benefit earlier, it will be reduced.

But what if you also have a retirement benefit based on your personal earnings? You can't take both benefits at the same time but you can take them serially, one after the other. For details, see page 67.

If you have remarried, you cannot claim on your ex's account, unless he has died and your remarriage occurred after age 60. If your new spouse dies, however, you have a choice between spousal benefits on your (living) ex's account or survivor's benefits on the account of the spouse who died. Compare them to see which pays more. If you divorce for the second time and each marriage lasted at least 10 years, you can take benefits on the account of either ex-spouse, whichever is higher.

If your ex files for retirement benefits and then voluntarily suspends them, you will not be affected. Your spousal benefits will continue to be paid.

GETTING THE MOST FROM SOCIAL SECURITY AS A FAMILY

Your spouse, ex-spouse, children, and perhaps even your parents can get Social Security benefits on your record if you file for retirement benefits, die, or become disabled. Here are the rules:

Benefits for young, unmarried children. Children get their own Social Security benefits if they're under 18 (or 19 and attending high school). This rule casts a wide net. It covers natural and adopted children, stepchildren, children with a person the worker wasn't married to, and children in the care of an ex-spouse. It can even cover dependent grandchildren in certain circumstances. Benefits for children with serious disabilities continue after age 18 as long as the disability struck before they turned 22.

Mother's or father's benefits for a spouse of any age. These benefits go to a surviving spouse who is taking care of the deceased worker's child who is under 16 or disabled (the disability had to start before age 22). It can be a natural child, adopted child, or stepchild. The spouse must not be remarried. Spouses working for wages higher than the earnings limit will have their checks reduced. Ex-spouses qualify only if they aren't remarried and are caring for the worker's natural child, adopted child, or stepchild who qualifies for benefits on the record of the deceased. An unmarried partner won't be covered (well, maybe in a common-law state if you meet the state's complex rules, but it's a long shot).

Survivor's benefits for a worker's dependent parents. This rule helps aging parents if the worker who died had been paying more than half of the parent's support. The parent has to be at least 62 and not receiving a higher benefit based on his or her own Social Security earnings record.

The family maximum. Social Security sets a limit on how many dollars can be paid in family benefits on the worker's record. If the family goes over that limit, perhaps because there are several young children, spouse and dependent benefits are proportionately reduced.

Ways of Handling Family Benefits If You Have a Choice

Retirement timing. Normally, your family gains the most if you stay at work. But maybe you have plenty of savings for your older age and want to maximize the amounts that Social Security pays your young children—say, from a second marriage. By starting retirement benefits, your spouse and each child can make a claim on your account, subject to the family maximum. You might be especially concerned about the children if they're living with the other parent and you want to give them a financial boost.

Collecting a mother's or father's benefit on your deceased spouse's or ex-spouse's account. If you have young children, go ahead and file, even if you're working and your wages are somewhat higher than the Social Security earnings limit. Every dollar you net today from your mother's or father's benefit is extra money in the bank. Claiming as a young parent will not reduce your future benefits if you apply for traditional spousal or survivor's benefits at an older age.

Collecting children's benefits. File immediately after the worker dies, retires, or becomes disabled. Children's benefits can be paid retroactively but only for up to 6 months (12 months if the worker is disabled).

RETIREMENT AND DISABILITY BENEFITS

Social Security benefits go to people who qualify for coverage and are totally disabled (note that the bar for "total disability" is set high). You receive an amount, equal to your full retirement benefit, based on your personal earnings record (not on the record of your spouse). When you reach full retirement age, currently 66 to 67, your disability benefits turn into retirement benefits. The amount doesn't change, you simply get your money from a different program.

Once you're on Social Security disability, you might qualify for spousal benefits based on the earnings record of your current spouse or your ex. Check with Social Security to see what your options are at various ages. Often, the amounts are small, but better than nothing. In most cases, however, your own disability benefit will be the better deal. If you reach 66 and don't really need your retirement benefits, perhaps because you have a lot of savings or a high-earning spouse, you can ask to have the payments suspended. That allows your future retirement benefit to grow by a guaranteed 8 percentage points a year (plus inflation adjustments) until you reach 70. When you finally claim your check, it will be as much as 32 percent higher, just because you waited.

If you retire at, say, 62 due to poor health and have not applied for disability benefits, perhaps you should. At 62, your retirement check will have been reduced. But if Social Security finds that you're totally disabled, and your disability started prior to the date you retired, your check will be increased to your full retirement amount. What's more, Social Security will refund the money you lost during the months that your benefit was reduced.

Social Security's disability insurance program runs by a fiendish number of rules that are beyond the scope of this book. For information, go to ssa.gov/disability. Once you're on the program, your spouse, ex-spouse, and children might qualify for benefits, too.

IF YOU FILE FOR BENEFITS LATE

If you file for retirement, spousal, ex-spousal, or survivor's benefits after your full retirement age, you can get paid for some of the months you missed. Social Security will backdate your application to the month you reached full retirement age or six months ago, whichever is smaller. You receive the money in a taxable lump sum. There is no backdating, however, if you file before your full retirement age.

Lump sums are almost always a bad idea for retirement benefits. By taking them, you will effectively have started Social Security up to six months earlier. You'll lose some delayed-retirement credits, which reduces your basic, lifetime check. But by all means, take the lump sum if you've filed late for spousal or survivor's benefits. Those benefits do not increase when you've passed full retirement age, so you've nothing to lose.

CAN YOU DO BETTER BY TAKING SOCIAL SECURITY EARLY AND INVESTING THE MONEY?

Almost certainly not. It's tough to beat the guaranteed returns that Social Security offers to people who defer their benefit claims. Between your full retirement age (66 to 67) and 70, your future check goes up by 8 percent of your primary insurance amount each year, plus an inflation increase, guaranteed. To beat that in the market, you'd need a remarkable, steady four-year winning streak, timed exactly right.

Between ages 62 and 70, a single person would have to earn more than 7 percent a year, after investment expenses, assuming an average life span and inflation at 3 percent (meaning a 3 percent cost-of-living increase in benefits). A married couple would have to earn 9 percent or more to beat what Social Security offers for delaying their combined retirement and spousal benefits.[11] If inflation exceeded 3 percent, your market returns would have to be even higher to stay ahead of the gains that Social Security pays. In a lower-inflation

---

11 Source: economist Russell F. Settle, cofounder of SocialSecurityChoices .com.

world, you could come out ahead with lower returns but it's hardly a slam dunk. Besides, a straight investment comparison is misleading. It ignores taxes. It compares a guaranteed lifetime income with one that might or might not work out.

For a more accurate comparison, I called William Reichenstein, co-creator of SocialSecuritySolutions.com. I asked him to track the effect on your lifetime income if you take Social Security at 62 and—instead of using the monthly payment to raise your current income—you invest half of it in stocks and half in bonds. He assumed that you live in a world of 2 percent inflation and pay taxes in an above-average bracket (higher earners are the ones most likely to try this strategy). Then he tested several ways of paying your current bills while leaving your Social Security–funded nest egg alone to grow. For example, you might pay the bills entirely from existing income. Or you might spend an amount equal to your foregone Social Security benefit by taking it out of an IRA. At 70, you'd start drawing on your nest egg, taking the monthly amount you'd have gotten if you had waited until 70 to collect.

What happens? In every case, the nest egg ran out at around average life expectancy. But people in higher income brackets live longer, on average, than everyone else.[12] They'd have done better by forgetting their investment schemes and simply filing for retirement benefits at 70. Longevity dictates the return you get from Social Security, not market performance.

You might consider claiming at 62 and investing the benefits if you (and your spouse) will never need the money. That way, your heirs will inherit the account. But if you're expecting the market to pay you more than Social Security over a long lifetime, forget it.

––––––––––

12 See the National Academies of Science, Engineering, and Medicine, *The Growing Gap in Life Expectancy by Income: Implications for Federal Programs and Policy Responses* (Washington, DC: National Academies Press, 2015).

OOPS, I CLAIMED BENEFITS EARLY AND REGRET IT—CAN I CHANGE MY MIND?

Yes, you can reconsider—and should. When you took early payments, you settled for less. There are two ways of building up your benefits again.

The do-over. If you change your mind within 12 months of starting retirement benefits, you can go back and start again. Tell Social Security that you want to withdraw your claim. You'll have to pay back the money you've already received as well as all payments made on your earnings record, including spousal and children's benefits. After that, it will be as if you never made the claim at all. You can begin your retirement benefits at a future date as if for the first time.

You might want a do-over if you retired and began benefits at 62, then went back to work. Or if you took spousal benefits early and realize that you don't need the income now. Or if you inherited money. Or if you've just read this chapter and discovered how much larger your check can be if you claim at a later age. Social Security lets you change your mind only once, so be very sure of your decision. If you paid income taxes on the benefits you received and then gave back, you'll want to file an amended tax return.

The voluntary suspension. You're too late for a do-over if 12 months have passed. But if you have reached your full retirement age (66 to 67), you can tell Social Security that you want to suspend the benefits that you're currently receiving. That stops your monthly payments and no money has to be returned. From this point on, the benefit you'll claim in the future starts to grow again. Between your full retirement age and 70 you're eligible for delayed retirement credits, worth 8 percentage points a year.

Warning: When you voluntarily suspend retirement benefits, you're also stopping payments to anyone else with claims on your account. That means no spousal benefits and nothing for any qualified children. Their claims can't be paid until you start your own benefits up again. Exception: Payments to ex-spouses will be continued; they're not contingent on whether you're receiving checks.

TOO MANY CHOICES! WHERE CAN I GET HELP?

Believe me, I understand. Merely researching all these possibilities drove me crazy for weeks.

The suggestions I've given should steer you in the right direction. But to illustrate, I mostly used fixed claiming ages (62, 66, and 70). It might be more advantageous for you to take benefits at 64 or 68. Your estimated PIA might be lower (or higher) when you actually put in your claim. For married couples, options vary depending on the spouses' relative ages and earnings. There are also tons of small, technical exceptions to the general rules. To get the very best advice on when to claim Social Security benefits, you need a customized report. Several websites offer them.

You might start with something simple and free. That would be AARP's Social Security Calculator, which you can find online. It estimates your retirement benefits based on the primary insurance amount shown in your Social Security record or—less accurately— your most recent salary plus an assumed, annual 2.5 percent raise. Unfortunately, this calculator lacks flexibility. It assumes that all married people want to maximize their individual monthly checks when your actual goal might be to maximize your lifetime benefits as a couple.

Social Security has two free calculators for estimating retirement benefits. The Quick Calculator is based on earnings information that you provide and is far too quick for accuracy. The Retirement Estimator accesses your actual Social Security earnings record. It shows the general effect of delaying a retirement claim for people who are not yet receiving benefits. It's better than the Quick Calculator but still what I'd call a general guess—not good enough if your goal is to find a specific strategy that maximizes your benefits. I'd advise that you check the following three services before making your retirement claiming decisions.

SocialSecurityChoices.com charges $39.99 for a personal report. It gives you an optimal claiming strategy based on three projected lifetimes: short, normal, and long. It also shows how much money you give up over your lifetime by claiming early. Married couples can look up any claiming age for each spouse to see what the dollar values are. Phone or email consultations about your report and filing issues are included free.

SocialSecuritySolutions.com offers four levels of service at different prices: $19.95 for a report showing your optimum claiming strategy based on the life expectancy you choose plus a strategy for longer and shorter life spans; $49.95 for an advanced report that lets you change assumptions, such as when you'll start retirement or spousal benefits; $124.95 for the advanced report plus access to an expert who will answer questions; and $249.95 if you want the company to help you file.

To get a customized report from the two sites above, you have to supply your estimated primary insurance amount (see page 43) and, if you're married, the estimated primary insurance amount for your spouse. To get these numbers, call Social Security at 800-772-1213 or find them online by creating a personal MySocialSecurity account at Social Security's website, ssa.gov.

One more site, called MaximizeMySocialSecurity.com, charges $40 for a report showing the best time to claim your benefits, plus $250 if you want an hour of one-on-one advice. It handles claiming strategies for children and the disabled as well as those planning to retire.

Maximize takes a different approach to the calculations. It adjusts Social Security's estimate of your primary insurance amount to account for likely inflation and wage growth in the future. This creates higher PIAs for people in their 40s and 50s and, often, lower ones for those in their 60s. It also requires people still working to enter their projected earnings plus all of their past, covered earnings, year by year. For past earnings, create a personal MySocialSecurity account online at Social Security's website (see page 46). From there, you can transfer your earnings record, automatically, into Maximize. People subject to the Windfall Elimination Provision (see page 82) have to enter their records, too. Like the other programs, Maximize lets you change your assumptions to test various retirement strategies. Founder and economist Laurence Kotlikoff recommends that you plan on living to 100, just to play it safe.

These programs won't all agree with one another because of the different calculation methods they use. I recommend that you work with at least two sites and compare results. The cost is small compared with the increased benefits you can potentially obtain. And you'll feel better knowing that you've had some expert advice. If you're several years away from retirement, plan on getting another report when you're at the brink. Things might have changed.

A special note for divorced spouses: You won't be able to get your ex's earnings record. But Social Security will tell you what your spousal benefit might be if you claim at various ages, so you can use programs other than MaximizeMySocialSecurity.com to help you plan. Unfortunately, you can't get information on your spousal benefit by phone. You have to go to a Social Security office with your divorce papers to prove that you're entitled to the information. The same is true if you're filing for survivor's benefits.

FRAUD ALERT!

If you're eligible for Social Security benefits but haven't signed up yet, scamsters are targeting you. They're finding ways of pretending to be you and collecting your checks. Their theft won't show up on your MySocialSecurity account. You'll discover it only when you get a 1099 in the mail, showing the amount of taxable benefits you've supposedly received this year. This can't be fixed by mail or phone. You'll probably have to make several visits to the Social Security office to report (and prove) the fraud and then to get a new 1099 issued. Without that new 1099, the IRS will ding you for not paying taxes on the money it assumes that you received.

HOW SOCIAL SECURITY REPRESENTATIVES CAN HELP (OR NOT!)

Social Security representatives—in the office and on the phone—are a mixed bag. I have found them unfailingly polite. Many are very well informed. But many are not, and that's a problem for people trying to plan their future.

I strongly suggest that you speak with at least two representatives before making any decisions. If you've been to a local office, go back home and call Social Security's consumer line. If you've spoken with one rep by phone, call back and speak with another. If you get contradictory information, tell the second rep what the first one said and try to sort it out. You can ask for a supervisor at any time. You might even want to call a third time. Sometimes you get a wrong answer because you haven't supplied enough information, so always prepare your questions carefully. If you're under full retirement age, ask what the effect of filing early has on your various benefits. Take special care if reps give you advice; they're not supposed to and can get it wrong. They're also not supposed to calculate your "break even" when you're trying to decide whether to put off taking benefits. Social Security used to have a break-even calculator on its site but concluded that it was misleading and took it down. Questions involving filing for restricted spousal benefits are especially hairy. Ditto for widows, widowers, and the divorced who are trying to work out optimum claiming strategies. Even basic questions might be answered incorrectly. When I called with a personal question, for example, the rep kept insisting that my husband's full retirement age was 65 (that's a blast from the past). I asked her to check, and she came back with the right answer—66.

I don't mean to beat up on Social Security reps. They work hard and might answer dozens of questions a day. But as you've seen from this chapter, answers can be pretty complex. Reps need a lot of experience before they can be sure of their footing.

I should add that many financial planners and other advisers are almost entirely in the dark. They haven't paid much attention to claiming strategies for Social Security and might know little about the rules. Some of them subscribe to computer programs designed to help you optimize your Social Security benefits. If they don't, or give you only generic answers, I suggest that you use one of the online services I list on pages 78 to 80 and take the results to your adviser.

Ultimately, the size of your Social Security benefit lies in your hands. A Social Security rep will *never* call up and say, "Hey, if you switch benefits you could be collecting $500 more." Or "Hey, why are you applying for retirement at 65 when you and your spouse have so many more options at 66?"

Your life, your retirement, your choice.

SOME SOCIAL SECURITY BENEFITS ARE LOPPED

Some people covered by Social Security will not get the full dollar benefit. Mostly, this means workers who also have a government pension from a job not covered by Social Security. Here are the two lopping rules:

The Windfall Elimination Provision (WEP). This affects workers with two-stage careers. You earned a pension from a government agency or foreign employer that didn't withhold Social Security taxes and you also worked 40 quarters in private-sector Social Security jobs. Counting only your private-sector earnings, you look like a low-income worker with a short career. If true, that would entitle you to higher retirement benefits than other workers get, relative to your earnings. But in fact, you were never a low-income worker. You simply spent 10 years in the private sector before or after a government career. Paying you a "low-income" bonus wouldn't be fair. Social Security applies a complex formula that reduces your benefit relative to what you'd have received if you hadn't earned a government pension. The cut equals 50 percent of your government pension, or more. Note that the WEP does not affect survivor's benefits. Your dependents could get a full Social Security payment unless the following rule applies.

The Government Pension Offset (GPO). This affects workers with government pensions whose spouses worked in a job that's covered by Social Security. You can file for spousal or survivor's benefits on your spouse's Social Security account, but your payment will be reduced by two-thirds of the amount of your government pension. If your pension is large enough, this could eliminate your benefit completely. Why is this fair? Workers in the private sector usually cannot receive their own retirement benefit and a spousal or survivor's benefit at the same time. The GPO ensures that the same rule applies to government workers.

There are various exemptions from these deductions, mostly based on when you entered the workforce. For details, search ssa.gov for the WEP and GPO Fact Sheets.

DON'T FORGET MEDICARE!

Medicare starts at 65, even for people who wait until 66 or later to claim their Social Security benefits. Be sure you apply three months before your 65th birthday. Which plans to apply for depend on whether you're also in an employee or retiree group plan. Chapter 4 tells you how to decide.

GET TAX SMART ABOUT YOUR SOCIAL SECURITY INCOME

You get a big tax break on your Social Security income. For most beneficiaries, it's tax free. For the rest, half of your benefit isn't included when you are figuring how much tax on the benefits you'll have to pay.

Thanks to this special treatment, a dollar of Social Security income is worth more after tax than a dollar of income withdrawn from an individual retirement account because each IRA dollar is taxed in full.

At first blush, you might think it makes sense to take your Social Security benefits early to help pay your bills while letting your tax-deferred IRA grow. In fact, the opposite might be true. If your IRA is substantial, it's often better to draw on it for the first few years and let your tax-favored Social Security benefits grow.

The level of Social Security tax on your benefits depends on something called your "combined income." That's the modified adjusted gross income reported on your income tax return (including taxable withdrawals from retirement accounts) plus any income from tax-exempt bonds, plus half—just half—of your Social Security benefit. The other half of your benefit isn't included in the combined income calculation at all.

- Benefits are tax free for singles with combined incomes under $25,000 and married couples filing jointly with combined incomes under $32,000.
- Up to half of Social Security benefits are taxable for singles with combined incomes between $25,000 and $34,000, and couples between $32,000 and $44,000.
- Up to 85 percent of Social Security benefits are taxable for singles with combined incomes higher than $34,000 and couples higher than $44,000.

But remember, half of your Social Security benefits weren't counted when figuring how much "combined income" you're reporting. The tax break on Social Security income is better than most people think.

WILL SOCIAL SECURITY GO BANKRUPT?

No.

If you're grabbing your Social Security check at 62 because you think the system will fail, your political mind has taken over your rational, financial mind. We all see the doomster stories: If no changes are made to the program, benefits will drop by 20 percent around 2034—14 years from now. Okay, you'd be poorer but the program wouldn't fail. At that level, current payroll taxes can fund Social Security for at least the next 75 years.

And what if there were such cuts? Would it then pay to claim benefits early? Again, no I asked SocialSecuritySolutions.com and MaximizeMySocialSecurity.com to run the numbers. Financially, it would still be better to wait until 70 to claim.

But benefits won't drop. If such draconian cuts were made to the purchasing power of the 61 million people on Social Security, the economy would collapse. Workers would lose jobs, reducing the cash flow into Social Security's coffers, leading to another round of cuts and, inevitably, social turmoil. It ain't gonna happen.

There might be tweaks that reduce the future growth in benefits. But cuts rarely touch current retirees or those close to retirement. Instead, they affect the younger generations, and younger people won't want to let the program go. Social Security keeps millions of older and disabled people out of poverty and saves millions of adult children from having to support Mom and Dad. Politicians value their jobs. No president, no Senate, no Congress will let those voters down.

4

Getting the Most from Your Health Insurance—Before and After 65

Peace of mind is knowing that you can see a doctor when you're sick.

Employee coverage. Individual policies. Subsidized policies from the state and federal health insurance exchanges. Medicare, and, in the majority of states, expanded Medicaid. Equal insurance rights for same-sex married couples. In this book's first edition, I wrote that, most likely, you won't fall through the cracks in the medical system anymore—good news for people in their 50s and early 60s who retired early or work for companies or nonprofits that don't provide health insurance. That good news, however, depends on the continued existence of the Affordable Care Act (ACA—Obamacare), which provides that you cannot be refused an individual health insurance policy based on preexisting medical conditions. The ACA also ended the cruel lifetime caps on insurance payouts for people with serious diseases and lowered the premiums paid by people between 50 and 64, relative to the amounts that younger people pay. You got access to important preventive services free. It reduced expenses for seniors who take expensive drugs by capping their out-of-pocket costs when they reach the "donut hole" in Medicare drug plans.

At this writing, however, the ACA has been weakened by the Trump administration and Congressional Republicans who oppose the law. There's no longer a federal penalty for failing to carry coverage, which has taken some young and healthy people out of the insurance pool. New, lower-cost short-term policies that don't cover costly illnesses or preexisting conditions have also attracted healthy buyers (often, to their regret). As a result of these and many other damaging changes, premiums for the benchmark policies on the ACA Marketplace were an average of 16 percent higher in 2019 than would otherwise have been the case, according to the Kaiser Family Foundation. Higher premiums don't affect those with modest incomes, who will receive subsidies as long as the ACA lasts. But those of you without subsidies might be finding that you can't afford individual health insurance anymore.

Going forward, it's possible that all or part of the ACA will be thrown out. A court in Texas found the law unconstitutional, a position the Trump administration backs. At this writing, the case has been heard by an appeals court that appeared sympathetic to at least part of the Texas opinion. Ultimately, the Supreme Court will decide.

If the ACA is upheld, everything in this chapter is fine! If the law falls, however, our health-insurance system will be in chaos. The ACA governs many more parts of the medical world than you realize. For example, it includes rules for Medicare eligibility and payments to health providers, which would require new legislation to put back in place. I've included a section on some of the barriers to coverage that you'd find if we lose the ACA's consumer protection rules. Loss of those rules would affect employees in big-company group plans, too.

There's another possible outcome: The top court might decide that the "mandate"—that is, the requirement to carry health insurance—is unconstitutional while letting the rest of the law stand. In that case, everything in this chapter is, again, fine! The mandate has been a nothingburger ever since Congress removed the penalty for not being insured. Most of those who don't want a policy or can't afford one have already dropped out. Removing the mandate might lead a few more people to go bare, but otherwise the ACA would remain the same. Insurance companies would remain in the private market because, in most counties, enough people want to buy.

The mandate still applies to big-company group plans. They have to offer health insurance to their employees. But group coverage isn't cheap for most middle-class people. How much it drains your budget depends on your age, situation, and coverage choice. You have fewer decisions to make if you pass directly from a comprehensive employee plan to Medicare. It becomes more complicated if you're younger than Medicare age and will have to spend a few years in the world of individual insurance. To get the most for your money you have to know the rules.

A QUICK HEALTH INSURANCE PRIMER

Tourists (like us) in Insuranceville need to learn a few words so that we can speak with the natives. Here's the essential phrase book. With it, you'll be able to compare different policies' coverage and costs.

The *premium* is the amount you pay for the policy each month.

The *annual deductible* is the sum you have to pay out of pocket before the insurance company starts picking up bills. For example, if your deductible is $2,000, your first $2,000 in covered medical expenses are entirely yours to pay each year. The insurance starts paying as soon as your bills exceed that amount.

Your *copayment* is the fixed amount you pay for each doctor visit. For example, it might be $15 for internists and $30 for specialists. Normally, it does not count toward the deductible. You pay it even when the deductible has been met.

Coinsurance is the percentage you're required to pay toward certain bills after you've met the deductible. For example, you might owe 20 percent of the cost of a hospital visit or 50 percent of a doctor's bill.

Your *maximum out of pocket* is the most you're required to pay for the policy's covered medical services each year, no matter how sick you are. Once you've spent that amount—in deductibles, copays, and coinsurance—your policy should pick up 100 percent of your covered bills. The following year, the deductible and other kinds of cost sharing start all over again. (Your monthly premium payments aren't counted toward the maximum. Neither is the extra cost of using health providers out of your plan's network.)

Your *provider network* is the list of doctors, hospitals, imaging facilities, labs, and other professionals who participate in the plan and agree to accept its reimbursement rates. If you see a provider outside the network you will pay all or part of the bill, depending on the plan you have.

There are three general types of individual or employer plans: health maintenance organizations (HMOs), point of service plans (POSs), and preferred provider organizations (PPOs).

HMOs won't pay for doctors outside the network. Their premiums are generally lower because of their tight cost control. Usually, they require that you choose a primary doctor and get referrals from that doctor before you see a specialist. Sometimes you're allowed to see network specialists at will, although you'll probably need preauthorization for expensive specialty care. These plans might also be called exclusive provider organizations (EPOs).

POS plans require you to pick a primary doctor within the network. That doctor can refer you to outside specialists, with the plan paying a smaller percentage of those bills.

PPOs, whose premiums are generally higher, let you see any provider in the network at will. Some networks are narrow, some offer more choice. Many plans let you choose outside docs but cover their bills at a reduced rate and only for an amount the PPO considers "reasonable." All types of plans cover emergency services by doctors, clinics, and hospitals outside the network at in-network rates.

You run into *balance billing* if you belong to a PPO and take advantage of your option to see a doctor who doesn't participate in the plan. The PPO will pay a portion of the bill. But out-of-network doctors typically charge you more than network doctors do. You'll have to pay the balance, which can be much higher than you expect. For example, say that your PPO sets $100 as a reasonable charge for a routine visit to the doctor. It covers 80 percent of the bill from a network doctor and 60 percent of the bill from a doctor outside the network. In network, your plan pays $80 and you pay $20. Out of network, the plan pays $60, so you expect to pay $40. But an out-of-network doctor is free to charge much more than the "reasonable" rate—say, $200. You'd wind up owing $140. The moral: Stick with network doctors, labs, and imaging facilities, if you can.

Most balance-billing horror stories arise from emergencies, when you're rushed to the nearest hospital and it's out of network for your plan (or its doctors are). The ACA requires your PPO or HMO to cover such services at in-network rates.[1] The law, however, does not stop the ambulance service, doctors, or hospitals from billing at a higher rate and charging you for the difference. Even at an in-network hospital, you might collect large, surprise bills from a radiologist or anesthesiologist who's not on your plan. A few states have passed consumer-protection rules to limit or end the practice of surprise or balance billing by doctors and hospitals, but most patients on private plans still face that risk. You cannot be balance-billed, however, if you're on Medicare and see a "participating" medical professional.

---

1 The law applies only to plans sold by insurance companies, not to large employers who self-fund their plans. But the latter generally follow the ACA rules.

The few professionals who are "nonparticipating" can bill no more than 15 percent over Medicare's approved rate.

Separate fees are being charged everywhere. This isn't a term of art, just a new way that doctors and hospitals are squeezing more money from patients. If your child breaks an arm and it's set at the emergency room, you might be charged extra for the sling. An ophthalmologist checking your eyes for glasses might add a separate "refraction fee" for testing your visual acuity. The hospital might escort you to a room to fill out forms, then charge a "room fee." Even though these are in-network providers, insurance typically won't pay. At every turn, the medical industry is fighting to keep its revenues up. The latest? Hospitals billing for certain services by the minute.

HOW TO BECOME A MEDICAL CONSUMER

Even people with health insurance are paying more out of pocket for their own medical bills—maybe thousands of dollars a year. You might have a high-deductible policy. If you're covered by Medicare, you might not have medical supplement coverage. If you have no insurance, hospitals hit you for the highest retail cost. The medical-industrial complex cheerfully claims that raising your personal costs is a moral and social good. (Ha!) It makes you shop around for less-expensive care, which (somehow) will bring general prices down. Then, of course, they make it almost impossible for you to shop. Here's what you can do:

- *ClearHealthCosts.com*. This splendid site researches and crowd-collects costs of specific medical procedures in several cities and fills in with Medicare benchmarks for other areas. You can check on what you might pay locally for a specific need, such as a lower-back MRI (prices vary widely within a single city). You can also contribute the prices you paid for various services to the general knowledge base. You'll find readers' stories of how they were fleeced (so that you can avoid that trap) and defleeced (with a workaround that might help you, too). Be sure to read founder Jeanne Pinder's "Find Out What Stuff Costs: 10 Easy Questions" (find it through the Search box).

- *Discount drug services.* GoodRx.com sells coupons that entitle you to lower costs for certain prescription drugs (be sure that your pharmacy is in the program). BlinkHealth.com sells low-cost drugs, mainly generics, that you can pick up at a local pharmacy. And there's Canada.

- *You, the cash-paying customer.* Surprisingly, the cash cost of drugs and services might be lower than the copay on your insurance plan. For example, chains such as Walmart, Target, and Costco might charge $4 for a 30-day supply of common generics and $10 for a 90-day supply (to find them, enter "$4 prescription" into your search engine). At imaging centers, you might get a discount if you offer to pay cash. One writer on ClearHealthCosts.com reports that a center charged her insurer about $5,000 for an MRI. Her 50 percent copay came to $2,500. The cash price would have been $930.

- *Your doctor.* Some docs provide cost lists and will negotiate prices for certain cases. Others will respond, belligerently, "Why do you want to know?" *Tell* them why you want to know! Those are your dollars that go out through copays. Some docs, too, might charge less for cash.

- *Hospital price lists.* Since last year, hospitals have had to post the costs of their products and services online. But I dare you to make sense of them or even find them on hospital websites (these are all "retail" costs that are charged to the uninsured, not the discounted prices that insurance plans negotiate). You have to know the exact technical and code name of the service you want, including Tylenol and bandages. It's all baloney.

- *Sources that check complex medical bills.* Odds are there's a mistake and—I promise—it won't be in your favor. Overbilling hurts more than ever, now that you're shouldering a higher percentage of the cost. Don't settle for the opaque bills that hospitals send out. Ask for an itemized statement. Medical providers use codes to identify each treatment, making it hard for you and me to know what's going on. Services such as the Alliance of Claims Assistance Professionals or Medical Billing Advocates of America can help you find someone to check the bills and solve any problems. They cost a minimum of around $50 to $75 an hour, rising to $100 or more. So, they're best used when you have the multiple bills that accompany a major illness. For hassles with hospitals and insurance companies, also try the Alliance of Professional Health Advocates or the National Association of Healthcare Advocacy.

EMPLOYEE INSURANCE: COSTING MORE EVERY YEAR

The trends in employee coverage are not in your favor (no surprise there). Deductibles and copays are rising, and your choice gets more limited year by year. Employers are experimenting with different ways of holding down their costs (although not necessarily your costs). If you haven't yet seen any of the new, alternative plans, you almost certainly will soon.

For now, PPOs are the plans most widely offered by corporations. They charge the highest premiums and give you the widest consumer choice. HMOs usually cost the least. POS plans fall into the mid-price range.

As a supplement to your insurance, your company might offer a *flexible-spending* plan. You could deposit up to $2,700 in 2019 by means of payroll deductions and use the money, tax free, to pay for qualified medical expenses. You can spend up to the limit even if you haven't yet put all the money in. Flex plans require you to submit proof that each expense meets the test. If there's still money left in the plan at the end of the year, you normally lose it. Some employers, however, let you carry over $500 or less to the following year. Alternatively, some let you use last year's money to cover expenses incurred during the first two and a half months of the current year.

High-deductible plans are the most popular of the new, cost-shifting alternatives. At many companies, it's your only choice. Premiums are relatively low but you might have to pay a ton out of pocket if you (or a family member) have an accident or become seriously ill.

As with other plans, you pay all the medical bills yourself up to a specific annual deductible. That includes prescription drugs except those considered necessary for preventive care, which have to be provided free. For 2019, the minimum deductible was $1,350 for individual plans and $2,700 for families. Once you've met the deductible, you enter a cost-sharing zone. You pay a percentage of each bill until you reach a maximum out-of-pocket amount. The 2019 maximum, including copays and coinsurance but not annual premiums, came to $6,750 for singles and $13,500 for families (a huge amount, which rises annually with inflation). Above the maximum, the insurance company pays all the remaining costs that year as long as you're using network providers. The following year, the deductibles, cost sharing, and maximums apply again.

High-deductible plans offered by employers usually come with a *health savings account* (HSA). This account lets you put money away through payroll deductions, tax free, to pay the portion of the medical bills that you're responsible for. If there's cash left in the plan at year-end, it rolls forward to another year. Most large employers contribute something to their workers' HSAs, but smaller ones generally do not. The maximum contribution allowed for 2019 was $3,500 for individuals and $7,000 for families (these amounts rise annually with inflation), plus an extra $1,000 for people 55 and older.

Warning: You can't bring your HSA with you when you change jobs unless your new employer's plan has been set up to receive it, which usually is not the case. Nor can you roll it into an IRA. So spend the money as you go along, don't let it build up. When you leave the company or retire, the plan stays in place. Your old employer has to administer it, paying the qualified bills that you submit. So run it down as fast as you can, lest you forget it. Small HSAs with little or no activity will be eaten up in fees.

If you're buying a high-deductible health insurance plan as an individual, you can add an HSA yourself. Look for one with a no-fee checking account, if you'll use the HSA mainly as an ATM for current medical bills. Look for low fees and low minimum investments, if you'll use it mainly as an investment for paying medical bills in the future, tax free.

With all plans, you pay network health providers the fees negotiated by the insurance company. That's true even for the bills that fall within the plan's deductible, which you're paying out of pocket. Out-of-network providers will charge you their regular, higher fees.

At some large companies, employees can go online to compare costs among the various in-network providers. But who goes hopping from doctor to doctor to find a lower price on each medical service? Price-shopping is largely a fiction in the health care world and everyone knows it. Most likely, you'll probably choose to save money by delaying medical care. That might be okay but might also endanger your health.

GETTING YOUR MONEY'S WORTH FROM AN EMPLOYER PLAN

You'll be offered high-deductible plans with low premiums and low-deductible plans with high premiums. Light users of medical care should choose high deductibles (a no-brainer). But surprisingly, people who might be heavier users should consider high deductibles, too. Emotionally, we hate deductibles and paying out of pocket, says behavioral economist (and Nobel Prize winner) Richard Thaler. We're happier buying low-deductible plans. But the money you save in premiums by choosing a high-deductible plan might exceed the amount you'd pay for a low-deductible plan, even including out-of-pocket expenses, he says. This will be especially true if your employer contributes to a health savings account on your behalf (see page 94). You can use that HSA to help cover the deductibles. If you or a family member comes down with a costly or chronic illness that will cost you your plan's full out-of-pocket maximums every year, however, do the math again. If it makes sense to switch to a lower-deductible plan, you can do it during your company's annual open enrollment period, usually in the autumn.

Some other tips:

- Use the doctors in your network. It's the fastest, easiest way to save money. If that means changing doctors, so be it. Medical care is increasingly data driven rather than based on docs' knowing your history over time, so any good doctor will usually do. Like it or not, that's modern medical life.

- Reevaluate your coverage every year, during your company's open enrollment period (usually in the autumn). If premiums are rising, look at the lower-cost options.

- Use your company's flexible spending plan to get tax-free dollars for medical bills. Deposit roughly the amount of money you spend out of pocket in an ordinary year and be sure to spend it all by year-end (qualified last-minute purchases include sunscreen, a thermometer, eyeglasses, and various personal-care items.)

- If you buy an individual high-deductible plan, be sure to add a health savings account and deposit as much as you can afford. You can use that money tax free to pay for qualified out-of-pocket medical expenses. If you're healthy and don't draw much from this account, it can grow to a substantial amount over many years. At 65, you can even use it to pay your Medicare premiums. If yours is a company high-deductible plan and the company contributes to the HSA, use your own money to top it up to the maximum. Remember, however, that the HSA will probably stay with the company when you leave the job, so be prepared to submit your bills from wherever you are.

- Don't skimp on preventive services. Under the Affordable Care Act (if it lasts), most such services have to be provided free, even under high-deductible plans. They include colonoscopies, mammograms, cancer screening, and immunizations, among many others. Certain prescription drugs are also on the "preventive" list. *One warning:* You're allowed an annual "wellness" visit but not a free physical exam. "Wellness" means discussing your general health, checking the basics such as weight and blood pressure, and asking whether you're getting the tests you need. Often, you see a physician's assistant. If your doctor takes a blood test or treats an ailment, the visit isn't considered preventive anymore and you have to pay. When you make the date, be sure to ask for a "wellness visit." For the list of free services, go to HealthCare.gov and type "Preventive Care" into the Search box.

- To cut your costs for maintenance drugs, use your plan's mail-order services. If you buy through certain drug stores, you might pay nothing for certain popular generic drugs. Discuss price with your network doctors. Ask them to use only labs and other services that the network approves. Even in-network, some labs are less expensive than others. Use any tools your employer offers that help you compare costs. If your docs' prices are high, tell them about it; maybe you'll get a discount. Also, try for a discount if you're paying out of pocket. Stay out of your hospital's expensive emergency room if at all possible. Look for local, stand-alone urgent care centers that are on your plan if your health issue isn't life threatening. Okay for a broken finger; not okay for chest pains.

- Walk-in clinics at chain stores such as CVS, Publix, Target, Walgreens, and Walmart are good for minor ailments and flu shots. They're staffed by nurses and accept most major health insurance policies.

- Learn how to take care of your illnesses yourself and follow your doctor's directions to the letter. Of the people readmitted to the hospital soon after being discharged, a large percentage didn't follow their doctor's orders.

- Know the rules on emergency coverage. Under the ACA, plans have to cover you at in-network rates if you're taken to an out-of-network hospital. Before you take a vacation, find out your plan's procedure for getting permission to see an out-of-town doctor at in-network rates.

- Fight balance billing and other surprise bills. When you go to a hospital for surgery, the hospital might assign an assistant surgeon or other specialist who is not on your health plan. Result: You get a bill that far exceeds the amount that your health plan will pay (see page 90). To me, this practice amounts to theft—docs stripping you of money when you're anesthetized and can't protest. A nasty business. Totally unfair. If you get surprise bills, contact your health plan. Sometimes it will offer the providers more than its standard payment. Talk to the providers—see if they will settle for less. Contact your state insurance department to see if you're protected by law. I can't promise that any of these things will work, but they might. Almost nothing works with ambulance services, which are notorious for sending high bills that are out of network.

- Private health insurance normally doesn't cover you when you travel abroad. Instead, consider a short-term medical travel policy. It should pay most of the cost of emergency care, after deductibles and copays, as well as medical evacuation. Travel policies exclude normal treatment for preexisting conditions but will protect you if the condition suddenly becomes acute.

- If you lose your job and with it your health insurance, sign up immediately for COBRA insurance. Your company will send you a letter explaining how to do it. COBRA keeps you on your company's plan, at your expense, while you shop the ACA Marketplace for something cheaper. Never leave a gap in your coverage. Just a few unlucky days without health insurance could cost you your life savings.

- Lose weight. Quit smoking. Drink less. Eat right. Wear seat belts. Exercise. There is no doctor bill so cheap as the one that you don't incur in the first place.

Employee Benefits for Nontraditional Individuals and Couples

The constitutional right to marry, established by the Supreme Court in 2015, is a godsend for same-sex spouses who were previously barred from employee health plans. But the battle for equal treatment continues. As of this writing, here's the state of play:

- *Married same-sex couples:* Many employee health plans already extended benefits to same-sex spouses, even before the Supreme Court ruled. Now, the majority of them do. The right-to-marriage decision doesn't specifically require private companies to open up their health plans to same-sex spouses. But if the holdouts don't, they'll be vulnerable to lawsuits based on sex discrimination.

- *Unmarried same-sex couples in registered domestic partnerships or civil unions:* About one-third of civilian workers have access to employee health benefits if they register in their states as domestic partners, according to the federal government's National Compensation Survey. In general, companies offered this option only because gay couples couldn't marry. Now that they can, a number of employee plans are dropping partnership benefits and covering only spouses. Effectively, they're forcing their employees to the altar, whether they want to marry or not. More enlightened companies are keeping their benefits for domestic partners, on the ground that it's none of their business how employees choose to structure their intimate relationships. With any luck, that's the future.

- *Unmarried opposite-sex couples in registered domestic partnerships or civil unions:* About one-quarter of civilian workers have access to benefits for a committed partner of the opposite sex. They, too, risk losing health benefits if their employer decides to cover only married couples. But employers who set up this benefit for couples of the opposite sex are probably more committed to accepting nontraditional relationships, hence are less likely to drop them.

- *Transgender employees:* They have the same right to marry and the same right to enter into a domestic partnership as anyone else. They qualify as a spouse or partner under whatever health plan their company offers. But some health plans refuse to cover transition costs, such as hormones and surgery. This form of discrimination is currently being litigated.

- *Couples who switch to individual insurance from an employer plan:* Same-sex spouses must be accepted on individual policies, under the Affordable Care Act. Many ACA plans also accept domestic partnerships, regardless of sex.

THE STATE OF THE AFFORDABLE CARE ACT: THE SAFETY NET THAT REWROTE YOUR CHOICES IN MIDLIFE

What's the future of the Affordable Care Act (Obamacare)? It has grown popular. Polling supports it. Millions of people have health insurance who, otherwise, might have been left out of the system.

In the past three years, however, several of its financial pillars have been knocked away by opponents of the law. Premium increases slowed and, in some states, dropped in 2019 but they've settled at a much higher level than you'd have paid if the ACA had been left alone to develop.

Citing these high prices, the Trump administration has authorized lower-cost, lower-coverage policies, meant to attract young and healthy people as well as those priced out of the ACA. That will leave a higher proportion of older, sicker people in the ACA pool, driving up premiums even more and further damaging the plan. The new, cheap policies lack the consumer protections and breadth of coverage provided by the ACA. For example, they might exclude people with preexisting medical conditions, cap the lifetime payouts for expensive diseases such as cancer, or charge sharply higher prices based on sex or age.

Providing health insurance to people with preexisting conditions and at the normal policy price has been the ACA's most important innovation. It changes lives for healthy people as well as those with black spots on their record. To explain what I mean, let me tell you a story.

Back when I had a corporate editing job, the *Washington Post* asked me to turn in my gray flannel pantsuit and start an independent column on personal finance. I didn't worry about the financial risk of working for myself (my corporate job didn't pay me much anyway), but I was terrified at the thought of losing the group health insurance that my family depended on. After much back and forth, the *Post* agreed to put me on its own group plan even though I wouldn't be an employee. So I gambled and took the offer. Writing that column changed my life.

With a functioning ACA, you're not nailed to a job anymore to ensure yourself access to decent health insurance. Insurance companies have to take you. What's more, they have to offer you comprehensive coverage, not skinny policies that give you only the illusion of protection. They can't put a lifetime dollar limit on your coverage or the coverage of a specific disease. If you're in your early 60s, they're not allowed to charge you any more than three times what people in their 20s pay[2]; if you're in your 50s, you can be charged no more than twice as much (in the old days, those in their 60s paid four to six times more, the Kaiser Family Foundation says). If your income lies in the low or middle range, you can get subsidies to help pay the premiums (see page 107).

These guarantees let you rewrite the second chapter of your life. For example, you can retire early, knowing that you can get health insurance even if your employer doesn't have a retiree plan. You can leave a big company and work for (or start) a small business that doesn't offer benefits. You might join a small nonprofit or quit your job and become a volunteer. If one spouse retires early, the other one doesn't have to keep working just to hold on to the family's coverage. If you go on Medicare, you know there's coverage for a younger spouse. You can create a midlife budget without worrying that a single illness will blow it up. Your insurance can't hit a ceiling and run out. If you're laid off, you don't have to pray that you'll qualify for private insurance or, if not, that your body (and life) will hold up until you reach Medicare age.

That is, if the ACA survives. It's up to the Supreme Court.

While we wait for the decision, the ACA keeps chugging along, enrolling people who need health care. Many insurance companies have actually improved and expanded their offerings. The business has become profitable, due to the big increases in premiums in recent years. If your income is modest enough to qualify for subsidies, the policies have generally remained affordable. You might face high out-of-pocket costs in the form of deductibles and coinsurance, but you'll be protected from catastrophic bills.

---

2   In a few states, everyone pays the same.

The story is different for those who don't get subsidies. The fiscal attacks on the ACA since 2018 have blown up premium costs for people who have to pay entirely out of pocket. The hardest hit are older, middle-class adults, especially in rural areas. Coverage for a couple might cost half of a $50,000 income, which clearly knocks them out of the regular marketplace. They might still be able to buy decent coverage if they qualify for an ACA "catastrophic policy" (see page 109). The new, skimpy short-term policies are no substitute for the real thing. If you have employee group insurance and can't afford any Marketplace plan, consider working to Medicare age 65 instead of retiring early. For you, sadly, job lock is back.

A few states are stepping in to shore up the ACA for their own residents. They're arranging for reinsurance to help hold down premiums. They're forbidding the sale of short-term plans or the types of group plans that have, too often, been used as vehicles for fraud. Three states even require their citizens to carry health insurance on penalty of fines (the national requirement was effectively wiped out when Congress removed the fine).[3]

Conversely, other states are happy to cut away at the ACA. They're clearing a path for skimpy policies and other limited-benefit plans. They're applying for waivers, to divert public subsidies to non-complying plans outside the Marketplace. They're allowing the sale of "health benefit plans," which they claim is not insurance, hence not subject to state and federal regulations. (That's a big risk!) They back efforts to eliminate the ACA, its subsidies, and its consumer protections entirely. In short, the future of your insurance depends entirely on court opinions and politics. There are many ways to dismantle the law, if the anti-ACA trend prevails. Conversely, the ACA can be made even more effective if the forces favoring it prevail. For now, it remains the law of the land. So take advantage of it.

---

3   If the Supreme Count outlaws the federal mandate, that will probably wipe out state mandates, too.

Navigating the Individual Health-Care Marketplace

You can buy an individual policy in one of two ways. The first way is to use the ACA Marketplace online. There, competing health insurance companies post the policies they have for sale, along with their coverage details. You can choose a policy yourself, call a health insurance agent, or look for a "help" button on your state's Marketplace site. "Help" might connect you with a local, independent "navigator" who will answer questions and guide your choice (not all places have them). You *must* purchase through the online Marketplace to qualify for government-subsidized premiums. Alternatively, you can skip the Marketplace and go directly to a health insurance agent. That's generally where people go if they earn too much to qualify for subsidies. The ACA requires policies to provide comprehensive coverage, with consumer protections, no matter how you purchase them. But beware: Some agents will try to sell you cheaper short-term policies that leave you exposed to frightening costs. Make it clear that you want ACA insurance.

To find an individual policy, go to HealthCare.gov during an open enrollment period (November 1 to December 15) and put "See Plans and Prices" into the Search box. You'll be asked a couple of questions and then directed to your state's Marketplace (also known as an "exchange"). There, each plan shows you what it covers, what it costs, and—if you hunt around a bit—which health providers are in its network. It's generally easy to sign up. The ACA mandates four types of plans for individuals—Bronze, Silver, Gold, and Platinum. They all cover the same essential health benefits. But they vary in the way they price specific medical services, the drugs they cover, the doctors and hospitals in their networks, the premium cost, and the amounts you pay out of pocket. The premiums on Marketplace plans vary from state to state and even from county to county within your state.

Bronze plans generally carry the lowest premiums. They also

charge you the highest annual deductibles (typically, $5,000 to $6,000 for individuals) plus other out-of-pocket costs. Nevertheless, it's the plan to buy if you rarely see the inside of a doctor's office. If your health takes a turn for the worse, you'll have to pay the Bronze policy's maximum out-of-pocket in the current year. At the end of the year, you can switch to a plan that pays more of your costs, if that makes financial sense.

As you go up the "metals" ladder, plans charge higher premiums, reduce your deductibles and out-of-pocket costs, and pay more of your medical expenses. The annual deductibles on Silver plans commonly run in the $3,000 to $4,000 range (but can be higher). You might choose a Silver if you see doctors often but, to your knowledge, have nothing major coming up (even so, the higher-deductible Bronze plan might still be the cheapest, counting all costs—see page 110). The second-cheapest Silver plan is the benchmark policy used to calculate any subsidy that you might be owed.[4] Be sure to check what's offered by all the insurance companies on your local Marketplace. One company's Gold plan might cost less than another company's Silver plan. If your income is especially low, a "modified" Silver plan is usually the best buy of all.

Gold plans cost more and pay even more of each bill. In many (not all) plans, the annual deductible is between $1,000 and $2,000. You'd go Gold if you have a chronic illness that requires lots of drugs and doctor visits, so you use up your out-of-pocket maximum every year.

Platinum, the plan with the highest premium, requires you to pay the least in deductibles and other cost sharing. Many companies don't offer Platinum. It's usually not cost-effective. You pay a lot in premiums to avoid paying the smaller doctor bills yourself.

---

4 If your income is modest (below 250 percent of the federal poverty level), definitely select this Silver plan. It will qualify you for cost-sharing reductions on your medical bills—see page 109.

All of the Marketplace plans will cost less, maybe quite a bit less, if you qualify for tax credits to help pay the premiums.

The Joy of Subsidies If You're Eligible

Depending on the size of your income, you might be entitled to a subsidy. It's paid in the form of an income tax credit that reduces the cost of your Marketplace health insurance premiums.[5] You're eligible if your income ranges between 100 percent and 400 percent of the federal poverty level, based on your family size. The subsidy shrinks as your income goes up and eventually phases out. In 2019, individuals got the credit with incomes between $12,140 and as much as $48,650. The range for two-person households was $16,460 to $65,840. Larger families have higher maximums. These income limits rise with inflation every year. If you qualify for a tax subsidy, there's a ceiling on what you can be charged in premiums. People at the poverty level pay no more than 2.08 percent of their modified adjusted gross income. At the upper end, people at three to four times the poverty level pay no more than 9.86 percent of their income. Your ceiling payment plus the subsidy buys the second-cheapest Silver plan in your area. No subsidy is given if your income falls between 300 and 400 percent of the federal poverty level and the second-cheapest Silver plan costs less than 9.86 percent of your income.

If you do get a subsidy, you can apply it to a higher-priced Silver plan or to a Gold or Platinum plan, but you'll have to pay the additional premium cost yourself. You can also apply your subsidy to a Bronze plan, to reduce its up-front cost. To see if you're eligible for help, go to the Health Insurance Marketplace Calculator at the Kaiser Family Foundation (KFF.org).

---

5   Guidelines issued by the Trump administration would allow states to use public subsidies for limited-benefit plans that don't meet the consumer protection requirements of Marketplace plans.

The Premium Subsidy Is Run Through the Income Tax System, and Here's How It Works

When you apply for a policy on the ACA Marketplace, you're asked to estimate your income for the year. The website calculates the subsidy based on your estimate. That money can be paid directly to the insurance plan you choose. The plan will bill you monthly for the remaining premium amount.

When you file your tax return (along with a special form), the IRS will look at your actual income compared with your estimate. If your income turns out to be higher than you expected, you'll have to pay some or all of the subsidy back. If your income turns out to be lower, you're entitled to a higher subsidy than you received. The IRS will pay you the extra money in the form of a refund or a reduced tax payment. (Obsessives can report changes in their expected income during the year and their subsidy will be adjusted automatically, up or down.)

You'll pay the lowest possible insurance premium, up-front, if you assign the entire subsidy to the insurance plan right away. That simplifies your accounting, too. However, you risk a financial squeeze if you have to pay some of the money back. You might consider asking that only half or three-quarters of the subsidy be paid to the insurance company. You can claim any remaining subsidy in cash when you file your return.

Assets such as home equity and the money in retirement plans aren't counted when figuring the subsidy—only the modified adjusted gross income that you report on your tax return. *Warning: You could lose your subsidy in a year that your income jumps!* For example, you might earn a capital gain by selling stocks, bonds, or mutual funds. You might sell some real estate or take money out of an individual retirement account. That additional income could make you too "rich" for a tax credit that year. If the gains don't repeat in the following year, your income will decline and you'll find yourself back in tax-credit territory. (Inheritances don't count as income, although earnings from the inheritance do.)

If your income is too high for subsidies, you can still buy on the ACA Marketplace. Or call a health insurance agent to see if you can find better coverage somewhere else.

Special alert for people whose regular income is nearing the upper limit for tax subsidies. It will cost you a fortune if it rises above the line! As long as you qualify for the tax credit, the ACA caps your premium payments at 9.86 percent of income. But if your income rises even one dollar above the line, you're not protected anymore. You'll have to pay the policy's full market price, which could be thousands of dollars more than you're paying now.

Sooooo—if you think you might pop above the line, try a little jujitsu with your cash flow. You might take a smaller amount out of your individual retirement account, reduce your freelance work, send bills for consulting jobs at the end of the year so you'll be paid in January instead of December, pay tax-deductible bills in December, take investment losses to offset your gains, or cut down on the number of days you work in your business. If you own your own business, consider reducing your income by making the maximum contribution to a simplified employee pension (see page 188; contributing to an individual retirement account won't work). You might also put off taking Social Security until you're at least 66 or even 70 (that's a good idea anyway—see Chapter 3).

To find out how much more it will cost you if you exceed the income limit, go again to the Health Insurance Marketplace Calculator at KFF.org and enter different levels of income. You'll see immediately how your premiums and credits will rise and fall. Losing the protection of the income ceiling hammers older people, in particular, because in most states they can be charged so much more than the young.

If you can't afford a normal Marketplace policy, there's an escape hatch. It's called a "catastrophic policy." You can buy it if the cheapest policy on the ACA Marketplace costs more than 8.3 percent of your income. You still have to pay the maximum out of pocket that the law requires and are not entitled to tax credits. But premiums are relatively low, and you're covered for serious accidents or illness. You get preventive care plus three primary-care visits to the doctor at no extra cost. These policies can also be sold to anyone under 30, regardless of income.

Buyers with low incomes get an even bigger break. If your income falls between the poverty level and 250 percent of the poverty level, you're eligible for reduced cost sharing through a "modified" Silver plan. Cost-sharing subsidies can reduce your annual deductible to as little as $100 to $500. They reduce copays and coinsurance, too. You might have to hunt for these plans but be sure to do so if you think you're eligible.

Getting Your Money's Worth from an ACA Policy

- If you're a heavy user of medical care, add up the competing policies' annual premiums and maximum out-of-pocket costs. That's the amount you'll probably pay each year, so investigate the cheapest policy first. *Important note:* The "maximum out of pocket" refers only to bills you receive from providers in your plan's network. If you're treated by out-of-network providers, even inadvertently, your annual costs will rise above the so-called maximum.
- If you're a light user of medical care, add the premium and the annual deductible. That's your minimum probable cost. A Bronze plan will usually do.
- If you're middling users of care, compare what you're paying

in medical costs with the higher cost of a Silver plan. You might find that Bronze is still the most cost effective.

- On the Marketplace website, each plan posts a standardized summary of its costs and coverage so that you can make comparisons. Their designs vary widely, so take the time to read all the disclosures. It's boring and often confusing, but there's money to be made. For example, some plans might charge you no more than a copay for routine doctor visits even if you haven't yet met your deductible. That would help light users of medical care. The plans also charge different levels of coinsurance for different services. Coinsurance can be a killer if your bills are high.

- Check each plan's medical network to see which doctors and hospitals participate. Somewhere on the summary of benefits there's a link to its list. You want to see your area's top hospitals there. You also want access to specialty hospitals and academic medical centers of excellence for serious diseases. Ideally, you also want to find your own favorite doctors. If not, however, there are many good doctors. Picking new ones is often worth it when it means saving money on premiums and cost sharing. Double-check with the doctors, including the ones you're seeing now. The lists on the website aren't always accurate, or the doctors listed might not be taking new patients.

- If you take prescription drugs, check each plan's summary for the level of cost sharing. Some plans don't pay until you've met the deductible and then charge you 20 or 30 percent of the price. If you use a lot of drugs, that's going to be expensive. Other plans handle prescription drugs separately from the deductible. You might pay $10 per prescription for generic drugs, $35 for preferred brand-name drugs, $70 for nonpreferred drugs, and a percentage payment for specialty drugs. The summary gives you a link to the plan's formulary, which lists the drugs it currently covers. All the plans cover routine drugs or a reasonable substitute but vary in their choice of expensive drugs. Your doctor can appeal in special cases.

- If you're a snowbird with houses in two states, you have to buy the policy in your primary state of residence. Be sure that it uses a national provider network that will cover you all year. You can't change plans every time you migrate.
- Don't smoke. Smokers are charged up to 50 percent more.
- If you're working and your company health plan doesn't offer benefits to your spouse, he or she can buy a policy on the Marketplace and receive tax credits, if eligible. If your company does offer spousal benefits but you can't afford them, your spouse can still buy on the Marketplace, however, tax credits aren't allowed. That's a huge flaw in the program. It especially hurts lower-income workers who can't afford their employer's family policy. If an ACA-improvement law is ever passed, a fix for this should be at the top of the list.
- If you're working and have a comprehensive employee plan, you can't drop it and use tax subsidies to buy something cheaper on the Marketplace. ACA policies are for people who don't have access to other forms of good and subsidized coverage. Two exceptions: You can buy an ACA plan with subsidies if your employee plan is so poor that it doesn't offer you much or if your company charges you more than 9.5 percent of your income for individual coverage.
- If you're 65 and eligible for a company retiree plan that covers a younger spouse, your buying decision depends in part on how the plan blends with Medicare. It might pay for you to go on Medicare while your spouse gets an ACA policy. Or it might pay to keep the retiree plan. For more on this, see page 125.
- If you're in a retiree plan and under 65, you can switch to a Marketplace policy if the tax credits or coverage make it a

better deal. You have to wait for the open enrollment period to make the change.

- All individual policies have to cover the same essential medical services that the Marketplace plans do (except for short-term insurance). Tax credits, however, are available only if you buy through the Marketplace rather than from an insurance company directly.

- To claim tax credits, you have to file a tax return with Form 8962. The credits are refundable if you don't earn enough money to owe taxes in the year the credits were received. That means that the government will send you a check for what the subsidy was worth.

- You get no premium subsidy, even if you're within the income range, if the size of your expected subsidy equals the cost of the Silver benchmark plan in your area.

- If you don't qualify for subsidies, you can still buy on the Marketplace. You might also use its plans as price and coverage benchmarks for judging any health insurance plan offered by a health insurance agent.

- You can buy a plan or change plans during the open enrollment period, which, in most states, runs from November 1 to December 15. These dates apply both to Marketplace plans and the plans you buy directly through insurance agents. If you wind up with no plan because you missed the deadline, you'll be uninsured for the year. You can buy or change a plan at any time, however, if there's a change in your status. That would include divorcing, losing job-based coverage, or moving out of your current coverage area.

- If you move to a new area, coordinating coverage can be tricky. Apply for a new plan in advance so that it will take effect as soon as you arrive. If you wait until moving day or later, the new plan might not cover you for two to six weeks. During that time, you would still be on your old policy's books. It will insure you for emergency room treatment at in-network rates, but higher out-of-network rates will apply to doctor and hospital bills in your new location. Talk to your current insurer about the best way to make the change-over. Ideally, your new policy will start on the day the old one stops.

- Shop for a plan every year, don't just renew the plan you have. Prices, premiums, and services are changing all the time. The odds are high that a switch will save you money.

- Married same-sex couples can obtain family policies under federal rules. At this writing, the situation is mixed for those in registered civil unions or domestic partnerships. Some insurance companies provide you with family policies, others don't. The Plan Finder at Finder.HealthCare.gov has a same-sex filter that directs you to plans that will cover your life partner.

- Some health insurance plans include dental coverage. More often, it's available on the Marketplace as a separate purchase.

- You can get help! The ACA provides for local "assisters" or "navigators" who will help you in person or by phone. At HealthCare.gov, scroll down to "Find Local Help." It will direct you to the names of participating navigator organizations or your state's Marketplace site (where there should be another "help" button). You might also see the names of local health insurance agents who are certified to sell Marketplace coverage. Unfortunately, the Trump administration slashed the budget for navigators, making it harder for consumers to get questions answered and find appropriate policies. Some places now have no local navigators at all. For online answers to dozens of detailed questions about the ACA and who's eligible for subsidies, go to the excellent site run by the Kaiser Family Foundation at KFF.org. Search for "Frequently Asked

Questions About Health Reform." You can also get answers at HealthCare.gov by clicking on "Glossary" at the bottom of the page or entering a keyword into "Search."

If You Can't Afford a Comprehensive Medical Insurance Policy (Or Don't Want One Because You're Immortal)

Those opposed to the ACA continue to chip away at its financial foundations. A highly effective tactic has been the creation of lower-cost, limited-benefit policies that pull younger and healthier people out of the general insurance pool. Two such:

Short-term health insurance plans. Coverage lasts for up to one year. Some allow up to two annual renewals, but you have to pass a health test every time. The lowest-premium policies come with high deductibles and out-of-pocket costs, including coinsurance that might require you to pay half of your doctor and hospital bills. For low deductibles and less coinsurance, you'll pay more. They're cheaper than a Marketplace plan, but if you buy one of these skimpy policies I'd advise you not to get sick.

Short-term plans are cheap because they limit benefits. For example, they don't accept people with preexisting conditions or might impose a waiting period before covering the illness you have. There are caps on how much the policy will pay, no free preventive care, no drug coverage, perhaps no hospitalization, and a long list of exclusions. (Read it! The telemarketer will never tell you about it!) Older people pay much more for a policy than the young, and women generally pay more than men. They're called "major medical" policies, which helps unscrupulous salespeople and telemarketers to convince you that the coverage is comprehensive. If you develop an illness (even a small one) or have a serious accident, you can be dropped at the renewal date. After that, you'll be without coverage until the next open enrollment period for ACA plans. Even while covered, you might struggle to get claims paid. The insurer might investigate you, trying to prove that you had an undisclosed preexisting condition. In the meantime, none of your medical bills will be paid.

A three- or six-month plan might—*might*—be useful if you're between jobs or anxiously waiting to reach Medicare age. But they can't be depended upon. The ACA got rid of junk insurance. Now it's back.

Association Health Plans. AHPs are the group health insurance plans typically offered by trade and professional organizations to their members and small business groups. The administration has written new regulations to open them to wider industry groups, residents of a particular geographical area, and the self-employed. At this writing, a court has struck down the regulations, calling them an illegal end run around the ACA. It's uncertain whether they'll ever be offered to the self-employed. Stay tuned.

In short, health insurance is becoming both more and less expensive, more and less available, and trickier all the time. The Marketplace and its alternatives are politically driven, with forces forming on both sides. But look at it this way: At 65, you fall into the arms of Medicare, which takes care of you for the rest of your life. Whew.

THE FUNDAMENTALS OF MEDICARE

Medicare offers something for almost everyone at 65. You qualify for premium-free Part A if you've met the work requirements for Social Security (40 quarters of coverage) or your spouse or registered domestic partner qualifies and you're on his or her account. You also have to be a citizen or permanent resident. To be sure that you don't miss out on any reimbursements, start the sign-up process three months before your 65th birthday.

Medicare comes in four parts. Which parts to take and when depends on whether you have other health insurance, such as an employee or retiree group plan, and what kind of coverage is available to a spouse under 65. This guide should help you decide. But first, a quick zip through Medicare's details.

Part A covers hospitalizations, short stays in a skilled nursing facility, hospice, and a limited amount of home care (but not long-term custodial care). It doesn't cost you anything in premiums—you've already paid for it in payroll taxes. You do pay deductibles and other forms of cost sharing. At 65, sign up for Part A even if you're still working and have an employee group plan (or are covered by a spouse's group plan). For you, Part A will serve as a backup. Any qualified bills not covered by your private plan are automatically submitted to Medicare, which pays them up to the Medicare-approved amounts. One exception: Employees should not sign up for Part A if they're enrolled in a high-deductible plan that includes a tax-favored health savings account (see page 94). You can't contribute to an HSA if you're enrolled in Medicare.

Part B, also known as Original Medicare, covers your doctor bills, lab tests, outpatient care, medical equipment, emergency services, certain preventive services, and many other medical needs, such as drugs administered in your doctor's office. You can see any doctor you want as long as he or she accepts Medicare, as most do. You pay a premium that rises with inflation every year. You also pay a deductible and, normally, 20 percent of any covered service. You owe no percentage payments, however, for lab tests and preventive services. Prescription drugs aren't included in Part B. There's no cap on out-of-pocket costs.

Part C, also known as Medicare Advantage, is the name applied to Medicare plans run by private insurance companies. These plans provide the same services that are covered under Parts A and B. In fact, you have to sign up for A and B before you can enroll in a Part C plan. Advantage plans usually include prescription drugs plus some extra benefits such as free gyms, exercise classes, and vision care. In return, you generally have to stick with the doctors and hospitals in your insurer's network. There might be an option to go out of network. If you use it, however, you'll pay a higher percentage of the cost. Premiums and copays vary greatly among Advantage plans. Some cost less than you'd pay for Original Medicare plus a Medicare supplemental policy and a prescription drug plan. Others cost more, depending on the services you use. Some advertise zero premiums but charge high copays, which could run into real money if you (or your spouse) are hit with something serious. By law, there's a cap on your out-of-pocket medical costs ($6,700 in 2019), as long as you stick with network providers. Many Advantage plans cap these costs at $3,500 or less. But note: The caps don't apply to the cost of prescription drugs. For help in deciding whether to pick an Advantage plan or Original Medicare, turn to the Center for Medicare Advocacy at MedicareAdvocacy.org. Click on Topics, then scroll down at the far right to find Medicare Advantage.

Part D is for prescription drugs. These insurance plans are all privately run. Each insurer covers a slightly different list of drugs, so check for the ones you use before signing up. They also charge different premiums and apply widely different copays, deductibles, and coinsurance. You pay the least out of pocket for generic drugs. Copays rise for preferred brand names and rise again for brand names that are "nonpreferred." For expensive specialty drugs, you'll pay maybe 25 or 30 percent of the cost, which could be huge. The plan might not cover your specialty drug at all unless your doctor appeals. Buy Part D even if you currently take no or few drugs, choosing the cheapest one in your area. It's insurance against the risk that you'll suddenly need medications that could cost $2,000 or $3,000 a month or more (and saves you from paying higher lifetime premiums when you eventually sign up—see page 121). If you're in a Part C plan, it should include prescription drugs. Even with Medicare's help, however, the out-of-pocket cost of prescription drugs can be huge if you need an expensive drug for a chronic condition

Medicare supplemental insurance plans, known as Medigap plans,
are also sold by private insurance companies. They pick up many of
the bills that Original Medicare excludes, including copays and the
20 percent coinsurance that you have to pay for most doctors' bills.
There are 10 standard plans[6] identified by letters. All the plans under
a particular letter—say, all the A plans—offer the same mix of benefits no matter which insurance company you buy from. That makes
it easy to compare costs. The A plans cover the fewest gaps in Medicare, the G plans are quite rich. Starting this year, none of the plans
are allowed to cover the Part B deductible—$185 in 2019. That wipes
out Plans C and F, for anyone newly eligible for Medicare in 2020.
But if you were eligible in a prior year, you can still buy them and
your Part B deductible will be covered. The same is true for people
who own C or F already.

You cannot be turned down for Medigap if you apply within six
months after turning 65 or enrolling in Part B. After that, insurance
companies in most states are allowed to reject you or charge you
extra for preexisting conditions, making it dicey to switch plans.[7] You
don't need Medigap if you enroll in Part C, which usually includes
some form of supplemental coverage. But if you decide to switch
from Part C to Original Medicare, Medigap might not be available
(an exception is made if you move out of the C plan's coverage area).
Some people skip Medigap entirely on the risky bet that the gaps in
Medicare won't cost them much.

---

6   Massachusetts, Minnesota, and Wisconsin have their own standard
    plans.
7   Three states require Medigap plans to sell you policies, at any time,
    regardless of your health: Connecticut, Massachusetts, and New York.
    Some other states have limited protections for preexisting conditions.

Where to Get Information on the Plans

It's on the Web.

- For details on Parts A and B, go to Medicare.gov and click on "What Medicare Covers." Online, you can find and download the booklet "Medicare & You." If you're on Medicare already you'll be mailed this booklet every fall. Or call for it at 800-633-4227.

- For information on all the Part C and D plans in your area, go to Medicare.gov and click on "Find health & drug plans." Each insurance company puts up a standardized page of coverage and costs.

- Part C Medicare Advantage plans vary widely in the amounts they charge for premiums and copays. Run cost comparisons before signing up. Once you're in an Advantage plan, inertia will probably keep you there. While you're at it, run through the list of doctors, hospitals, and other providers each plan says it works with, looking, in particular, for specialty hospitals, academic centers, and national cancer centers that handle rare or complicated cases. They might be excluded. Unfortunately, the lists aren't easy to find on the website, not always accurate, and often hard to read, but they're all you have. Ask your own favorite doctors whether they are in the plan.

- Run cost comparisons for your Part D drug plan, too. There is almost certainly a plan in your area that costs less than the one you're using now. As an experiment, go to Medicare's plan finder and follow the prompts. You'll get to a page where you can enter all the drugs (with dosages) that you take regularly. You can also enter local pharmacies. Once the plan finder has this information, it will show you the drug plan or plans that you can buy at the lowest cost, counting the deductibles and copays for your particular drugs as well as your monthly premiums. Save all this information and shop again next year during the annual enrollment period. Again, you will probably find something cheaper because plans change their formularies and copays. Make a switch every year if that's what the numbers tell you. Those who don't switch are probably throwing money away.

- For tons of Medicare information, search Topics at MedicareAdvocacy.org. The Medicare Rights Center offers a hotline for answering questions (800-333-4114; medicarerights .org).
- For information on the standard Medigap plans, go to Medicare.gov, click on "Supplements & Other Insurance," and scroll down to "Find a Medigap Policy." If you enter your zip code, the website will give you the range of premiums being charged in your area. Another click shows you what each lettered plan covers, and another click, the names of the companies selling the plans. To sift for the lowest-cost policy, you have to click on each company's website and hope to get a free price quote (or else, call). The time you spend is worth it. Right now, I'm looking at standard A policies for my zip code. I could pay anywhere from $137 to $336 for exactly the same benefits. Hmmm, which should I choose?
- If you're not on the Web, you can use health insurance agents to help you find Part C and D plans.
- Be sure to open all the mail from your individual insurance company when you're nearing 65! Many plans will enroll you automatically in their own, sponsored Advantage plans, which may or may not work with your doctors. Even if you've applied for Original Medicare, you won't get it if you've already been switched into an Advantage plan. You have to specifically opt out of the Advantage plan within 60 or 90 days of getting the enrollment notice to avoid being forced to take it.

Don't Miss the Enrollment Dates! That Will Cost You More

First timers should be enrolled in Medicare Parts A and B by the month they turn 65. To remind you, Medicare will send you a letter three months before the deadline. It will contain a user name and password, directing you to MyMedicare.gov. You can sign up online, by phone, or by personal visit to a Medicare office. There's a three-month grace period for sign-ups after 65 but if you start late, your coverage will be delayed. The same deadline applies to the Part D drug plans.

If you miss the grace period for Parts B and D, you can sign up during the next general enrollment period, from January 1 to March 31 for coverage starting July 1. But it costs you money. There's a 10 percent increase in your Part B lifetime premiums for every 12 months that you delay and a smaller penalty for delaying Part D. What's more, you'll have no medical or drug insurance during the time you weren't enrolled.

Once you've enrolled in Part B, you can choose to take these services through a Part C Medicare Advantage plan. If your Part C plan covers prescription drugs, you don't need Part D.

If you qualify for Medicare, you're entitled to Part A automatically. There are no late penalties for missing the sign-up deadline. Your Medicare card will come in the mail if you signed up for Social Security retirement benefits prior to age 65. If you haven't started Social Security benefits yet, you'll have to get in touch with Medicare yourself. You'll need the card to show the doctor and hospital you're insured and for which services.

If you don't have enough working credits to qualify for Medicare automatically and don't qualify on the record of your spouse, you can buy into Parts A and B. In this case, you do have to sign up by 65. Otherwise, late penalties apply. Also, buy into Part D. If you skip this part because you're not currently taking prescription drugs, you'll pay a lifetime penalty when you finally do sign up.

If you're already enrolled in Medicare, you can change plans once a year during the open enrollment period that runs from October 15 to December 7. Your new plan will start covering you on January 1. People in Medicare Advantage plans have an additional sign-up period, running from January 1 to March 31. It's a chance to change your mind if you find that you didn't like the plan you chose last fall. You're allowed to switch to another Advantage plan or drop your plan in favor of Original Medicare plus Part D and perhaps Medigap (if you qualify).

If you are still working at 65, at a large or mid-size company, your employee group health plan covers your bills for hospitalization, medical care, and prescription drugs. Nevertheless, sign up for Medicare Part A. It doesn't cost you anything and might get you double coverage for some hospital expenses (see page 123). You can skip the B and D plans for now; they cost money and your company already pays these bills. When you retire and lose your employee coverage, you can move to a Medicare B or D plan at no extra cost, regardless of your age. Be sure to sign up within eight months of leaving your job. Otherwise, penalties apply.

If you're 65 and working for a smaller company, your employee group plan will probably turn into a modest Medicare supplement plan. You'll have to enroll, right away, in Medicare Parts A, B, and D to get full benefits and avoid late sign-up penalties. Your employer should tell you what your options are.

Normally, you have to pay a higher premium if you sign up for Parts B and D after 65. There's no penalty, however, when you're coming directly from an employer- or union-sponsored plan. The plan will give you a letter proving that you had what's called "creditable coverage," meaning coverage for employed workers that meets the rules for comprehensive health insurance. You'll have to take (or mail) it to a Medicare office, and sometimes the approval process can take months. So start your application right away. Hundreds of thousands of people are paying higher Part B premiums because they didn't understand the deadlines or found that their private or retiree coverage wasn't considered "creditable." COBRA (see page 99) isn't "creditable coverage" for part B. It might be for Part D, but why wait and take the risk?

How to Get Double Insurance Coverage If You Work Past 65

If you're 65 or older, working for a large or mid-size company, and have an employee group health plan, you're potentially doubly insured. You can have Medicare and your group plan, too.

Sorry, you can't get both plans to pay the same bills (dream on). But if you sign up for Medicare Part A, it can pick up some of the costs that your employer plan excluded. Here's how that works:

All your medical bills go to your employee group plan first, which pays them up to the limit of the policy. The group plan is your "primary payer." Any costs that your plan fails to cover are forwarded automatically to Medicare, which becomes your "secondary payer." Medicare pays any qualified bills after applying its own coverage rules, deductibles, and coinsurance.

Double insurance works in reverse if you work for a very small company (fewer than 20 employees). In that case, Medicare is your primary payer. That's where your hospital bills go first. Your group plan, if there is one, becomes the secondary payer for any qualified costs that Medicare excluded. The plans for a few mid-size companies follow this pattern, too.

There are different rules for matching Medicare with other types of health insurance, such as multi-employer plans, veterans' plans, and plans for government employees. Ask your plan sponsor about it.

When you first sign up for Medicare, you'll be asked whether you have any other health coverage as a worker, retiree, spouse, or domestic partner. It's important to list which is primary and which is secondary. Your employer plan, hospital, doctors, and Medicare all need that information so that your bills will go to the right place and in the right order. For information on which plan is the primary payer ask the director of your company's plan. You can also go to Medicare.gov and enter "which insurance pays first" in the Search box, or call Medicare's Benefits Coordination & Recovery Center at 855-798-2627.

So far, I've been talking about double coverage only for Medicare Part A, which comes at no extra cost. Doctor and lab bills, however, fall under Part B. If you want Medicare as your primary or secondary payer for those services, you have to pay the Part B premiums. Usually, that's not worth the cost, as long as you're in an employee plan.

Your Money Saver's Guide to Getting the Most Out of Medicare

- *If you have no other health plan,* sign up for Medicare Parts A and B at 65. Original Medicare lets you choose your doctors, hospitals, and other providers. Add Part D for drugs and, perhaps, a Medigap plan. A Part C Medicare Advantage plan usually includes both prescription drugs and Medigap coverage, and might cost you less. To get an Advantage plan's full benefit, stay within its network of providers.

- *If you're still working and covered by an employee group plan,* sign up for Part A at 65 but consider delaying enrollment in Parts B and D. Your private plan should cover most of your medical and prescription drug bills. When you leave the group plan, you're allowed to sign up for the rest of Medicare at no extra cost.

- *If you're working but don't like your employee group plan,* you can drop out and take Medicare instead. Note, however, that Original Medicare has no ceiling on out-of-pocket spending while employer plans do.

- *If you're still working at 65 and contributing to a health savings account,* you can't have the HSA and Medicare, too. You might find it cheaper to avoid Medicare for now and stick with your employee plan—especially if the employer also contributes to the account. Money in your HSA accumulates tax free if used for medical expenses. Warning: If you sign up for any Social Security benefits, you'll be enrolled automatically in Medicare Part A. In that case, you'll be allowed to keep and use the HSA money you already have but you won't be able to add any more to the account. You can continue to contribute, however, if your spouse goes on Medicare and you don't.

- *If you're covered by a retiree group plan,* find out how it meshes with Medicare. There's no standard approach. Some of the larger plans pay full benefits, so you'd keep it and sign up only for Medicare Part A. Others, especially smaller plans, function mainly as Medigap insurance for retirees 65 and up. They'll pay only the bills that aren't eligible for Medicare reimbursement, so you'd sign up promptly for Parts A, B, and D. Alternatively, consider a Medicare Advantage plan, if it's cheaper than all your other premiums combined and you're willing to use the network providers. But note: Once you leave the private retiree plan, you can't get it back.

- *If you're 65 and covered as a spouse on a worker's group plan,* sign up for Medicare Part A. Whether to buy Parts B and D depends on the premium the worker pays to keep you in the company plan. Sometimes it's cheaper for the worker to switch to individual coverage in the company plan while you sign up for Medicare. To meet Medicare requirements, you and your spouse have to have been married for at least one year.

- *If you're younger than 65, covered under your spouse's employee plan, and your spouse retires,* you cannot go on Medicare yet.

To get those benefits, you have to be 65 yourself. While you're waiting, you generally have three choices: (1) If there's a company retiree plan that pays full benefits and your spouse keeps it, you should be covered, too. (2) If there's no retiree plan and your spouse goes on Medicare, you can buy a private individual policy. Shop the ACA Marketplace or call a health insurance agent. (3) You can take the COBRA option offered by the employee plan. It lets you extend your group health benefits for up to 18 months (sometimes, 36 months), at your expense. Consider using COBRA if you're within a few months of reaching 65. Otherwise, you'll probably find a cheaper plan in the individual market.

- *If you're older than your spouse and haven't worked long enough to qualify for Medicare*, you can enroll at 65, provided that your spouse is at least 62 and Medicare qualified.

- *If you're a same-sex couple and married*, you qualify for spousal benefits under employee plans. You also qualify for Medicare as a spouse if you haven't worked the 40 quarters needed to claim benefits on your own.

- *If you're in a legal civil union or domestic partnership*, some employee plans offer you the same benefits as a spouse. Medicare also provides benefits if you've been legally partnered for at least a year.

- *If you signed up for a Part C Medicare Advantage plan and the plan drops your doctor or eliminates a local group of specialists*, you can probably keep them by switching to Part B (Original Medicare) during the annual open enrollment period (October 15 to December 7). Buy a Part D drug plan and, perhaps, a Medigap plan at the same time if your health is good enough for you to qualify. Alternatively, think carefully about how important those particular doctors are. The Advantage plan will have many good doctors, too, and might cost you less. If you need a super specialist who isn't in your plan's network, see if the specialist is in another local Advantage plan that you can switch to during the open enrollment period.

- *If you're in a Medicare Advantage plan and the plan denies coverage for drugs or medical services that your doctor authorizes, appeal, appeal, appeal!* The Centers for Medicare and Medicaid Services, which oversees these privately run Advantage plans, has found many of them denying legitimate claims, delaying appropriate treatments, and wrongly limiting medical services and prescription medications. Fines have been paid by some of the industry's biggest names. This is an ongoing problem with Medicare Advantage, so beware. Exercise your right to appeal the plan's decisions. If the problems persist, switch to another plan or to Original Medicare during the next open enrollment season.

- *If a hospital keeps you overnight on "observation" status but doesn't admit you,* it's potentially putting your Medicare coverage for skilled nursing home care at risk. Medicare helps pay for skilled care only if you first spend three days as a hospital inpatient. If one of those days was listed as observational, you won't qualify. Any time that skilled care appears to be in your future, you or your representative should insist that the hospital formally admit you. Note that Medicare does not pay for long-term custodial care.

- *If you're a snowbird with homes in two states,* register for Medicare in your official state of residence. You'll need a plan that covers you in both places. That probably means choosing Original Medicare plus a Part D drug plan rather than a Medicare Advantage plan.

- *If you're planning to move and are in a Medicare Advantage plan,* switch to Original Medicare shortly before you go (you don't have to wait for an open enrollment period). Your current Advantage plan won't cover providers at your new address or will cover them only at out-of-network rates. Original Medicare keeps you covered everywhere. You can even buy a Medigap plan, regardless of health, because you moved out of your C plan's coverage area. Once you've made the move, you can decide whether to switch to one of the local Advantage plans.

- *If you haven't worked long enough to qualify for Medicare,* and don't qualify as a spouse or divorced spouse, you can buy Parts A and B (they come together). The premiums are high, but aid is available for people with low incomes. Sign up at 65 to avoid paying late penalties. Alternatively, look for a policy on the ACA Marketplace, which is open to older people who can't get Medicare. You might receive premium subsidies if your income is modest. (People eligible for premium-free Medicare Part A can't shop on the Marketplace.) Also, buy Part D.

- *If you're receiving Social Security disability payments,* you can get Medicare earlier than 65. The rules are complicated. Call to find out where you stand.

- *If you're in a Part D drug plan,* shop for a new plan at every open enrollment time. These plans raise and lower their prices for drugs all the time. You might save a lot of money by switching to a new plan. Warning: Premiums are fixed for the year, but drug prices can rise and formularies can change at any time during the year.

- *If you're shopping for Medigap,* consider buying the best plan you can afford right now. It might be impossible to upgrade at a later date if your health goes bad.

- *Make use of every free preventive service you're offered.* You can find the full list at Medicare.gov. Look for "Your Guide to Medicare's Preventive Services."

- *You say you don't care how much your doctor charges?* Some doctors with wealthy patients opt out of Medicare. You have to pay the full bill yourself. Most likely, these doctors will use anesthesiologists and other professionals who also opted out. Are these better doctors? Neither you nor I have any idea. I do know that millions of people get great care from docs who take Medicare, as all of mine do.

How to Pay Your Medicare Premiums

Part A costs nothing if you qualify for coverage. Premiums for parts B, C, and D can be deducted automatically from your Social Security retirement check, if you're receiving it, or from your monthly annuity if you're a civil service retiree.

If you've put off taking retirement benefits, you can have the premiums taken automatically from your checking or savings account. Alternatively, Medicare will send you a quarterly bill, payable by check or credit card. Be sure to pay on time! If you don't, you'll risk losing medical coverage temporarily.

MEDICAID AND YOU

Single or married, those without long-term care insurance (LTC) have to depend on their savings and, perhaps, help from their families if they need care. But there's also a safety net called Medicaid, a program run by the states with joint state and federal funding. It covers nursing home expenses for people who run out of money. A few states provide modest payments for home care, too.

Singles are generally expected to liquidate their assets, such as investment accounts and home equity, to pay their nursing home bills. If the money runs out, Medicaid steps in, so you won't be evicted from your nursing home bed. Your house and furnishings don't have to be sold, however, if one of your children lived with you and took care of you.

If you're married and only one of you is sick, Medicaid sets aside a certain amount of income and assets for the healthy spouse. State rules vary widely, but in general the spouse at home can keep his or her own income, a personal pension, the house and furnishings, a car, and a modest amount of other assets. For middle-income couples, that covers just about everything. Medicaid will then foot most or all of the nursing home bill. The at-home spouse will be expected to contribute, however, if you have more assets than the Medicaid rules allow. Also, a small handful of states expect spouses to use a certain amount of their individual retirement accounts to help pay the nursing home.

Many couples wonder whether they should plan for Medicaid. If you adjust your financial position to make yourself "poor" enough to qualify, you can get government aid and hang on to most of your assets, too. You'd have to spend, or lock up, or give away any assets that exceed your state's Medicaid allowance. And it all has to be done five years in advance of applying for aid. Trusts and annuities come into play. So does long-term gift planning. You'll definitely need a lawyer with Medicaid-law expertise. To find one, search the site of the National Academy of Elder Law Attorneys (naela.org).

The chief driving force behind Medicaid planning is the desire to leave more assets in the hands of a healthy spouse at home. Secondarily, children hope to inherit their parents' money rather than seeing it spent on custodial care.

But do you want to divest yourself of property—and lose control—on a guess that you might need a nursing home someday? Trusts cost money to maintain. And what about ethics? It's one thing to worry about a spouse's standard of living, but should children's inheritances be protected at the taxpayer's expense? Especially when, financially, Medicaid is in dire straits? I'm in the "no" camp. That's why one buys long-term care insurance.

SHOULD YOU BUY LONG-TERM CARE INSURANCE?

Long-term care insurance helps pay the bills—at home or in a nursing home—if you become unable to care for yourself. Married couples in particular should consider it. The policy protects the standard of living of the healthy spouse if the other spouse falls permanently ill. A year of care can cost $90,000 or more.

But can you afford a policy? The answer is probably yes if your company offers it as a group health perk. Group LTC plans usually take all comers if you sign up during the hiring process. If you wait more than 30 days, you'll be accepted only if you pass a health exam. Spouses always have to pass an exam if the plan offers them coverage, too. You can probably take the policy with you when you leave the job at no increase in price, but check.

Policies are much more expensive outside of the workplace—so much so that they're principally bought by people with upper-middle incomes and above-average assets. Individual policies always require a health evaluation. The older you get, the higher the risk that you or your spouse won't pass. Couples can buy a shared policy that costs less than two separate policies. Policies for women are usually far more expensive than policies for men of the same age.

Premiums depend on your age when you enter the plan. The older you are when you sign up, the higher your cost will be. In theory, your premiums are supposed to stay level for life. In practice, most insurers raise them from time to time, sometimes by 10 to 30 percent—and sometimes much more. As a rule of thumb, you shouldn't spend more than 5 percent of your retirement income on LTC premiums. You can lower your annual expense by choosing a policy that covers you for three years rather than five years or more. (The majority of nursing home stays don't exceed three years.) Inflation adjustments can be cut, especially in your older age. You might set the waiting period at six months or more before the policy clicks in. To cut costs even further, you might insure only 50 or 75 percent of the expected cost of care, intending to make up the difference from personal savings.

Be sure to give yourself lapse protection. Loss of memory is a leading reason for needing nursing home care and one of the things you might forget is to pay your LTC insurance bill. Two solutions: Arrange to have the premiums paid automatically from your checking account or ask the insurance company to notify someone if your policy is being canceled for nonpayment or both. You're allowed a grace period for reinstatement.

There are two other options for LTC coverage: Move to a continuing care retirement community that includes nursing home benefits as part of the entrance fee (see page 315). Or buy hybrid life insurance that offers both death benefits and payments for long-term care in a single package (see page 370).

If you're single, you might skip long-term care insurance and put your money toward extra savings, instead. If you own a home, you can always sell it and use the proceeds toward the nursing home bill. On the other hand, you might want a policy for its home-care coverage. That takes the burden off children who might otherwise have to pay.

Special note to late-marrying couples: Long-term care might become a mare's nest when an older couple marries and they each have children with a former spouse. Their respective children expect to inherit from their parents. If one of you enters a nursing home, the spouse at home might have some financial responsibility—and, trust me, that spouse's kids won't like it. You're spending *their* inheritance on a second spouse. You can't get rid of this obligation by writing a prenuptial agreement. So . . . yet another reason for LTC insurance.

Special safety note: Buy from the highest-rated insurer that will offer you a policy. Two LTC companies liquidated in 2017 and a handful of others are reported to be weaker than you'd like. If a company fails, however, the state guaranty association picks up the tab so your claims will still be paid.

DON'T SKIMP

Health insurance is one of the most important items in your budget. Without it, a medical emergency might leave you with a six-figure bill and, these days, many hospitals sue to collect. The older you get, the higher your medical costs are likely to be. Under 65, your access to coverage is protected, even if you have a preexisting condition, provided that the ACA remains in force. From 65 up, Medicare takes a load off your mind. Still, rising coinsurance costs give all of us an incentive to shop around. We're not used to asking doctors about prices, but we're going to learn.

5

Pensions Are for Stre-e-e-etching

A new look at the comfort of a guaranteed income for life.

Traditional pensions—a monthly check for life—don't get much respect in the private sector. Not many companies offer them today. Employees with access to pensions tend to take their money in a lump sum, if given the choice, rather than sign up for a fixed and regular income. Those who do take fixed incomes, however, get a lot of comfort from their choice.

In government, by contrast, traditional pensions are generally beloved. Federal pensions rise with inflation every year and are super safe (U.S. senators and representatives are in this plan!). Almost all state and local government pensions are safe as well. True, a few of these plans have clipped benefits a bit—by raising the amount you're required to contribute, paring annual inflation increases, changing the way pension benefits are calculated, or cutting future payments to new hires. But current and near retirees from state and local government jobs can generally count on getting the checks they've been promised or are receiving now. Only in the very worst municipal bankruptcy case would pensions for current retirees be reduced.[1]

Whatever your plan, you have some critical choices to make when you retire. Your decisions will deeply affect your security in your older age.

CHOOSING YOUR PENSION BENEFITS: WHAT SUITS YOU BEST?

Most private pension plans and some government plans offer you two ways of taking benefits.

1.   You can sign up for guaranteed monthly payments for life. The checks will keep coming even if you pass 100 or 115. If you're married, you can also cover the lifetime of your spouse. Your main enemy is inflation. If the pension is paid in fixed dollar amounts, it will lose purchasing power every year. On the other hand, you'll generally spend less as you age and won't have to worry that the money might run out.
2.   You can take the value of your pension in the form of a lump sum, roll it into an individual retirement account, invest it as you please, and withdraw a preplanned amount from your IRA every year. Your enemy is investment risk. In a poorly managed IRA, the money might run out before you do. On the other hand, if you manage these investments well, you'll achieve a reliable income, keep up with inflation, and even leave something for your heirs. (Chapter 8 shows you how to do this.)

Which approach you choose will depend a lot on your temperament as well as your age and financial circumstances. What will

---

1   At this writing, there are only three cases. But others could follow.

make you the happiest? What will make you feel safe? Here's a guide
to making this important decision.

Consider taking the regular monthly pension if:

- *you have no appetite for investing.* If you took the lump sum
  and managed it yourself, you'd keep the money in bond funds
  and bank accounts with little or no diversification into stocks.
  Low-interest investments will not yield anywhere close to the
  same income for life that you'd get from a pension. If you
  put your money into the hands of an investment adviser, it
  might turn out well but, then again, it might not. It all depends on the adviser you choose. If you don't know much
  about the markets, you won't be able to tell whether you're
  getting the right investments for someone of your age and
  circumstances.
- *you want a guaranteed monthly income and have at least a
  modest amount of other savings.* Between your pension and
  Social Security, you can cover your regular bills. Social Security also provides inflation protection. Your savings give you
  flexibility and money for emergencies.
- *your pension is adjusted for inflation every year.* Nothing is
  safer than a guaranteed lifetime income that rises with the
  cost of living. This kind of pension is a gift that keeps on giving.
- *you're of traditional retirement age—say, 65 or older.* Fixed
  pensions aren't for people retiring at 60 or younger. There's
  too much uncertainty ahead.
- *you're female.* Pension amounts are figured on a gender-
  neutral basis. Lump sums are not. Because women, on average, live longer than men, lifetime benefits will generally give
  you more for your money,
- *you want to protect your spouse.* A pension can guarantee
  a monthly income for your spouse for life. By contrast, an

income based on market investments might run down, especially if your spouse survives you and doesn't know much about money management. Even if your own health is poor, which might tempt you to take the lump sum, consider your spouse's health before making your decision. Pensions help protect a widow or widower who is long lived.

- *your spouse has a 401(k) or similar plan at work.* Your spouse's plan could be the money that you invest for growth while your own plan provides a fixed income for life.
- *you're in good health and your family is long lived.* If you (or your spouse) live well into your 90s, the chances are good that the pension will pay you more, over your lifetime, than outside investments will. That is, unless you're very lucky with your investments.
- *you're a spender who will blow through a lump sum pretty fast.* A fixed pension protects you from yourself.
- *you want some quick money*—maybe to repay debts or to buy an RV for retirement travel—but otherwise would prefer a steady income. If your company allows it, consider taking a small portion of your pension in cash and the rest in monthly checks for the rest of your life. If the company doesn't offer this option, however, find the RV money somewhere else.
- *you've compared the fixed pension with what you could get from an insurance company's simple, immediate-pay fixed annuity, which also pays an income for life* (see page 152). Some companies subsidize their pensions by keeping costs low. That makes them a best buy. Others will buy you an insurance company annuity, in which case you might do better by taking the lump sum and buying the annuity yourself. To find out which is better, go to ImmediateAnnuities.com. Enter the dollar amount of the proposed lump sum into the site's calculator. You'll see instantly how much monthly income various types of annuities would pay, including annuities that also

cover your spouse. If your pension pays more than you could get from a top-rated insurance company,[2] stick with the pension. Make the same comparison if you're already getting a pension and the company offers to buy you out with a lump sum. Lump-sum offers usually aren't very good.

- *you want a regular lifetime income and an adviser tells you that you can get more per month by cashing in your pension and buying a variable annuity.* You can't. Variable annuities charge higher fees (including a fat commission for the "adviser") and their returns aren't guaranteed. If you add a guaranteed lifetime payout to the annuity, they charge even more (see page 160). Keep your pension. You'll be tens of thousands of dollars ahead. The same is true if you buy a fixed annuity with a lifetime payout (see page 173).

Consider taking the lump sum if:

- *you're a terrific investor or your money is in the hands of a good investment adviser.* You're reasonably certain that you can get more from the lump sum than the pension would pay. You also have a clear-cut spending plan that controls the amount you'll withdraw from your savings every month. You're *sure* you won't blow through the money in your early retirement years. For help in shaping a withdrawal plan, see Chapter 8.
- *you want financial flexibility.* When you invest a lump sum, you can vary your withdrawals—say, by taking more before you apply for Social Security and less afterward.
- *you have other sources of income that can support you for the next few years*—say, a spouse's earnings or other savings and investments. You'll roll your lump sum into an individual retirement account (a tax-free transaction), diversify your

---

2   For the top ratings, see page 151.

investments, and let the money accumulate. You don't have to touch it until you reach 70, when mandatory IRA withdrawals start.

- *you have little or no savings.* You'll live on your Social Security benefit. The lump sum will provide you with cash to cover health shocks or other emergencies. (Reserve it for these purposes.)

- *you're rich enough not to need a pension.* You can roll the lump sum into an IRA and leave the money to your kids. Consider switching part or all of the money to a Roth IRA. You'd pay taxes on the lump sum, but your kids could enjoy the future earnings tax free. (For more on IRAs, see Chapter 7.)

- *you live with a dependent partner, not a spouse.* Pension plans accept same-sex spouses as income beneficiaries but many don't accept those in domestic partnerships or civil unions. Rolling a lump sum into an individual retirement account can benefit you both. You might choose the traditional pension, however, if your partner has sufficient assets of his or her own for self-support.

- *your health is so poor that you don't expect to live to your full life expectancy.* You can tap a lump sum for larger payments than you'd get from a pension because the money doesn't have to cover a long life span. (If you're married, however, consider your spouse's life span before making this decision. What will he or she have to live on after you die?)

- *the lump sum would buy you an insurance company annuity that pays more than your pension will.* Unlikely, but check (see page 152).

- *you doubt that the company you work for is financially sound.* Most private pensions are insured by the Pension Benefit Guaranty Corporation. If your plan fails, the PBGC will pick up the payments but not necessarily in full (see page 143). Prudence suggests that you take the lump sum.

- *your spouse agrees.* The pension laws are written to protect dependent spouses, usually women. You cannot take a lump sum from a private sector plan unless your spouse consents, in a notarized statement filed with the plan. Memo to spouses: Don't give consent lightly. Once the money leaves the pension plan and goes into an individual retirement account, the IRA holder could name anyone as beneficiary. Spouses lose their legal protection except in cases of divorce. (Some public sector plans can leave out a spouse without consent—see facing page.)

ARE YOU MARRIED? PROTECT YOUR SPOUSE!

There are two ways of taking a pension: a larger monthly payment that lasts for your lifetime and then stops (a *single-life pension*) or smaller payments that last for the lifetimes of you and your spouse (a *joint-and-survivor pension*). By federal law, the default choice for federal and private pensions is joint-and-survivor. If you die, your spouse (including a same-sex spouse) is entitled to a benefit worth at least 50 percent of the amount you received, for life. Many companies give you the option of leaving your spouse 75 percent of your pension amount or even 100 percent. (Some plans contain "pop-ups" that raise your payment if your spouse dies first.)

Couples should take great care when making this decision. The most common pension regret that I hear from married retirees is that they took the single-life option (with the spouse's consent) and wish they hadn't. You might be attracted to the larger monthly payment because money is tight. But if it's tight now, what will happen to the survivor if the pension holder dies and that source of income ends? What if the death occurs in an accident two weeks after retirement? If your spouse depends on your income, it's better for the two of you to reduce spending now, as a couple, than to live higher on the hog and risk leaving the survivor broke. In some plans, taking a single-life pension will also cut your spouse out of retiree health benefits if you die first.

The single-life choice might work fine if your spouse has a sufficient pension or assets of his or her own, or if your spouse is so ill that he or she is likely to die before you do. Otherwise, don't disinherit your spouse. Take the full 100 percent joint-and-survivor payments if they're offered. At the very least, take the version that leaves your spouse with 50 percent of what you received as a couple and ensure that there are plenty of other assets for his or her support. Remember that, at your death, a spouse will lose one of the two Social Security checks you collect as married retirees. You don't (or shouldn't!) want your spouse to lose your pension income, too. Think of duty as well as love.

Spouse Alert #1! Many state and local government pension plans do not cover spouses automatically. The retiree will receive a single-life pension unless he or she specifically chooses joint-and-survivor. As a spouse, you might not even be aware that a choice is possible. Your beloved retiree might choose the single-life check thoughtlessly—to provide a larger income, not specifically to cut you out. But the result is the same. Surprise, honey: when I die, you're broke!

Spouse Alert #2! If you'll need the pension, be sure to preserve your right to receive it. Private plans that provide lifetime payments generally have to offer you a "preretirement survivor's annuity." It's a form of life insurance. The annuity guarantees that if your spouse dies before his or her pension starts, you'll get at least half of what the lifetime monthly benefit would have been if he or she had retired early. You pay for this insurance in the form of a small reduction in the future pension check if your spouse lives.

As a spouse, you can waive this right to a preretirement annuity. If you do and the worker lives to retire, you'll have a slightly larger pension income, as a couple. If your spouse dies before retirement, however, your future pension vanishes. A surviving spouse gets *nothing*.

I once got a sad letter from a widow. She had waived her preretirement benefit thinking that it covered only the years before her husband retired—and indeed, the company's form letter was none too clear on this point. When he died unexpectedly, she was horrified to learn that she had lost his postretirement pension, too. So read this offer carefully and get all your questions answered. Don't waive the preretirement benefit if you'll need your spouse's pension to live on. If you've already waived it and change your mind, it can be reinstated provided that your spouse is still alive.

Spouse Alert #3! Be sure you have copies of any beneficiary forms the plan requires, especially for state and local plans that aren't covered by federal law. Your spouse might have provided that you get a portion of his pension if he dies but the pension plan might lose the form (it happens). If you don't have a copy, your pension might not be paid, even though it's clear that you should get the money.

SAY NO, LOUDLY, TO PENSION MAX

A financial adviser or insurance agent might present you with what sounds like a fabulous idea—"pension maximization," or "pension max" for short. At retirement, you take the larger, single-life monthly payments and use some of the money to buy an insurance policy on your life. If you die first, your spouse can use the insurance proceeds to buy a lifetime annuity supposedly equal to what the pension paid. If your spouse dies first, you'll live on the higher payments for the rest of your life. Ta-da!

As you've probably guessed, there's a worm in this apple. Several worms, as a matter of fact. To begin, the fancy, computerized, pension max presentations are often misleading. After paying for the insurance policy, you might have less to live on—after tax—than if you had taken the joint-and-survivor annuity (most of these presentations don't show after-tax results). To make the plan appear to work, the insurance agent might lowball the size of the policy you need or the size of the premium you'll have to pay. If you die, your spouse might not be able to buy an annuity that replaces your pension in full. What's more, the market will have changed, perhaps raising the annuity's cost. If your spouse skips the annuity and invests the life insurance proceeds in mutual funds, there's no guarantee that he or she will manage it well or that it will last for life.

This scheme might work if your spouse is seriously ill and you expect to outlive him or her. But if you're so sure, why buy the insurance at all? It also will work if you both live a long time so that, by the time you die, the proceeds of the insurance should readily cover the annuity your survivor needs. But what if you die sooner than you both expected? Or what if you reach a point, in older age, where you can't afford the insurance premiums anymore?

My bottom line: If you're of traditional retirement age and want your surviving spouse to have a known income for life, do *not* gamble on pension max. Take the 100 percent joint-and-survivor deal.

HOW SAFE IS YOUR PENSION IF THE PLAN FAILS? IT DEPENDS

Most private pensions are backstopped by the Pension Benefit Guaranty Corporation. It's supported by fees from the employers that provide the plans (details at PBGC.gov; click on "Workers & Retirees"). Part or all of your pension will be paid from the guaranty fund if your plan fails (or your company dumps the plan in a reorganization proceeding). Some nonprofits also belong to the PBGC (ask your employer about it). At present, the fund that insures plans run by a single employer are in good health, meaning that retirees in failed plans will receive whatever benefits the PBGC offers.

A minority of private, single-employer companies transfer workers' pensions to an insurance company. At that point, you'd lose PBGC protection. If the insurance company failed, your annuity would be backed by your state's insurance guaranty association. State protection is more limited than the coverage that the PBGC provides (find your state's details at nolhga.com), but it would be surprising for a major insurer to go broke.

Multi-employer plans are another story. They cover workers in industries such as construction, trucking, and mining and are arranged through collective bargaining. Many different employers contribute to a single plan and the majority of plans are sound. But a large minority have failed or currently foresee insolvency. The PBGC maintains a separate fund for multi-employer plans. At this writing, the fund is forecast to run out of money by 2025 unless employers or the government shore it up. Entire pensions are at risk. Even if an underfunded plan hasn't failed yet, its benefits could be cut. (Congress has been at work on a bailout for multi-employer plans but can't reach agreement on what, if anything, to do.)

Many nonprofits create what's known as "church plans" and do not belong to the PBGC. These could include such employers as religious institutions, schools, and hospitals, including very large ones. If your church plan fails, part or all of your pension vanishes.

There's no backup insurance for federal, state, and local pension plans other than law and politics. So far, that combination has proved pretty powerful. Many states with underfunded plans have reduced or eliminated cost-of-living increases for future retirees and sometimes for current retirees, too. But cuts to basic benefits have been rare.

And, of course, there's no backup for lump sums invested in stocks and bonds.

KEEP TRACK OF YOUR PENSION!

When companies are bought or merged, pension records sometimes go astray. The same can be true when pensions are transferred to insurance companies, especially payments owed to people who quit a job, mid-career, to go and work for someone else. If your former company doesn't exist when you're ready to retire, pensions can be hard to track. Store every letter or email you get on the status of your pension plan in a file or box. That way, you'll know where to start looking when payments are due. Keep the plan up to date with your current address. Employers are supposed to hunt for missing retirees who are owed benefits but sometimes they don't hunt very hard. If your plan failed, check the PBGC. It maintains a list of people in failed plans who are owed money and haven't been found.

DO YOU ENVY PEOPLE WITH PENSIONS?

Younger people aren't much interested in traditional pension plans. They want retirement accounts where they can invest their savings for (of course!) stupendous growth. But perspectives change as the years go by. If you won't receive a pension and the thought of a guaranteed income lights you up, you can buy a pension in the form of a lifetime annuity—as you'll see in the chapter coming up.

6

Should You Buy Yourself a Pension?

*Lifetime annuities, the Rodney Dangerfield of investments,
don't get no respect—except from me.*

When you retire, peace of mind means fresh money landing in your
bank account every month. That's how you lived when you had paychecks coming in. Losing that paycheck is startling no matter how
much money you've saved. The wife of a major multimillionaire told
me a couple of years ago that she worried about how they'd pay their
bills when her husband retired and his professional income stopped.
(Maybe she was a bigger spender than I'd thought.)

Most of us don't have major millions to rely on, so creating a
reliable lifetime income becomes a challenge. There's Social Security—guaranteed and inflation indexed but probably not enough to
live on. You can make regular withdrawals from your savings and
investments (see Chapter 8), with the potential for capital gains but
at the risk of running out.

There are also lifetime pensions—an object of envy for people
who don't have them. Corporate pensions are nice even though their

fixed payments gradually lose value to inflation. Government pensions that rise with the inflation rate are even better.

The funny thing is that you can buy yourself a pension in the form of a commercial, immediate-pay annuity. It gives you an income for life, guaranteed by the insurance company. Yet buying one is probably the last thing on your list.

Why do retirees turn their backs on lifetime annuities? And can I change your mind? Annuities aren't for everyone, but for the right person they are the answer to a prayer. Annuities are created by insurance companies and sold through insurance agents, banks, brokerage firms, and financial advisers. They come in many different types.

Some are complex annuities that combine investment products with a lifetime income. These I generally do not—repeat, *do not*—recommend. Instead, consider the simple, low-cost annuities that are designed purely as personal pensions.

Simple annuities are easy to understand. You put up a sum of money in return for a monthly lifetime income. The size of your payment depends on your age and the current level of interest rates.[1] At this writing, for example, a 65-year-old man might put up $100,000 in return for $570 a month for the rest of his life, depending on his state of residence. The older you are when you buy the annuity, the higher the payment. A 70-year-old man might get $650 a month. Payments to women are lower than payments to men of the same age because, on average, they live longer. The monthly income from their investments has to be stretched over a longer period.

The insurance industry calls this group of simple products single premium immediate annuities (SPIAs). They can cover your own life or the life of yourself and a spouse or partner. You might choose to annuitize part of your savings and invest the rest.

---

1   All prices in this chapter are based on the level of interest rates in mid-2019. At higher interest rates, monthly payments would be higher, too.

ANNUITIES AND THE "SUCKER FACTOR"

What bothers people about annuities is what I call the "sucker factor." If you put up $100,000 and die next year, you'll feel (from the grave) that you were a sucker. That's because the remaining money stays with the insurance company, in its reserves. It's used to help pay the annuity holders who lived longer than you did.

But it's this very sucker factor that makes immediate-pay annuities so attractive. Because some people will indeed die early, the insurer can afford to pay everyone more per month than they could prudently draw out of their personal investments. That's true whether you die early or late.

For example, take that 65-year-old man who has $100,000 in savings. An immediate annuity would pay him $570 a month. What if he skips the annuity and invests the same sum in stock and bond mutual funds? A prudent withdrawal rate would be 4 percent plus an increase for inflation in every future year. That means he starts with only $333 a month—$237 less than the annuity would pay. His investments should last for 30 years or more, but he'll probably never catch up with the monthly income he could have had from the annuity.

Now let's say that our man dies after just a few years. So what? The annuity served its purpose. It raised his standard of living, paid him more than he'd have gotten from his investment plan, and insured him in case he lived "too long." Among the people most likely to live longer than average are those with a good education, good health habits, and some retirement savings salted away, which probably describes you. Of course, maybe you think you'll be short-lived, in which case annuities wouldn't be worth it. But can you be sure? Unless you're ill, why would you bet on dying sooner rather than later?

If the sucker factor still drives you nuts, there's a way to make yourself feel a little better. You can buy an annuity with payments

"certain" to last for 10 or 15 years, even if you die earlier. That ensures that you (or, rather, your heirs) will get at least some of your
money back. For example, say that you buy a lifetime annuity with
10 years certain and die after seven years. For the following three
years, your monthly check will be paid to your beneficiary. You could
also buy a cash refund option that guarantees a return of all the
money you put in.

Every benefit has a price, of course. In return for the cash refund
or the certainty of 10 or 15 annual payments, you have to accept a
lower monthly check. Even so, that check will be larger than the
amount you could prudently have taken from a mutual fund account
invested in stocks and bonds. That's especially true if you keep most
of your savings in bonds or certificates of deposit.

Another common rap against immediate annuities is that you
lose control of your money. True, but only that portion of your
money. You shouldn't even consider annuitizing all the savings you
have. Retirees need ready cash to cover health shocks and other
emergencies, as well as gifts and pleasure spending. You should also
keep some funds invested in stocks, whose long-term growth will
provide a cushion for your older age (see Chapter 9). Ideally, you'd
buy an annuity that, together with your Social Security, covered all
(or most) of your basic bills. The rest of your money would remain
under your control.

Finally, there's the legacy question. You can't pass the lifetime
value of an immediate-pay annuity to your heirs. But realistically,
what are your plans for the money you've saved? Will you use it
chiefly for your own support with the remainder going to the kids?
Fine. The money you put into the annuity gives you a higher guaranteed income while you live. The rest of your money can be invested
more aggressively to provide a fund for the family you'll leave behind.

You are *not* a candidate for annuities if you're living on Social
Security (and perhaps a fixed pension) with only a small amount
of ready savings. Those savings should be kept on hand for surprise

expenses. You also wouldn't annuitize if your health is poor or if you're so rich you can't run out of money.

However, if you're living on interest, dividends, and Social Security and feel pinched, your life might improve if you took some money out of bonds or certificates of deposit and used it to buy an immediate-pay annuity instead. You haven't reduced your capital, you've simply shifted that capital into a higher-paying, guaranteed investment. Suddenly, you'll have more cash in your pocket. You can take a cruise, make gifts to your grandchildren, or go out to dinner without feeling that you've overspent.

You're an Ideal Candidate for an Immediate-Pay Annuity If:

- you're in good health, have a reasonable amount of savings but don't feel safe financially.
- you're temperamentally unable to invest a large portion of your assets in stocks so you keep most of your money in bonds or certificates of deposit.
- you like receiving a regular income.
- you want investments that pay without your having to work at it.
- having a sufficient retirement income takes priority over leaving a large legacy.

When you're shopping for any annuity, by the way, check the insurance company's safety-and-soundness ratings. Tip-top scores aren't essential. Insurance companies rarely go out of business. Even if they get into trouble, they'd normally sell their book of annuities to another company. If the annuity you're looking at meets your goals and the company is well diversified among many lines of business (*not* just annuities), it's fine to accept a rating that's a couple of notches down the scale. Top-rated companies generally pay you a little less income per month than lower-rated companies do.

But don't go too far down the quality ladder. Insurance expert Joseph Belth, who blogs at josephmbelth.com, proposes the following cutoffs:

- *For "extremely conservative" investors who still want the highest scores:* AAA or AA+ from Fitch Ratings and Standard & Poor's; A++ from AM Best; and Aaa or Aa1 from Moody's.
- *For "conservative" investors:* no lower than AA from Fitch or Standard & Poor's; A+ or A from AM Best; and Aa2 or Aa3 from Moody's.
- *If you choose to take the next step down:* You're at A+ from Fitch and Standard & Poor's; A- from AM Best; and Baa1 from Moody's.

Unfortunately, you can't count on keeping the insurance company that you chose so carefully. It might decide to exit the annuity business and sell its customers to an insurer with lower credit ratings and perhaps higher internal policy costs. You're not necessarily stuck. You can roll over your annuity into a better one or one with a stronger company, tax free. Still, it's a pain.

A NOTE ABOUT SALES COMMISSIONS

The size of the sales commission on annuities isn't disclosed. It's a hidden cost, built into the contract. *Never* work with a salesperson who claims that you pay no commission because he or she is being paid by the insurance company. That's a lie. The sales commissions and other expenses are effectively deducted from the monthly payment you receive. An agent who will lie about this will lie about anything. Some annuities are indeed issued with zero commissions, but you can't buy them directly. They're designed to be sold by fee-based financial advisers. The adviser decides how large a fee to add, to cover his or her services. It might be more, or less, than you'd pay for the same annuity sold on commission. You won't know. But at least the fee will be disclosed.

WHAT KIND OF INCOME DO YOU WANT FOR LIFE?

Annuities, as a pension substitute, pay lifetime incomes in various ways. Here are the two best choices for people who want to be sure that their money never runs out. They're low cost, too.

Immediate-pay fixed annuities.[2] These annuities couldn't be simpler. You put up some money and in return get a fixed monthly income for life, starting right away. It's just like having a regular paycheck. Immediate-pay fixed annuities cost the least of all the types of annuities available and usually pay you the most per month. As a sample strategy, you might put half your savings into one of these annuities and half in stock-owning mutual funds. At first, you'd spend the annuity income and barely touch the stocks, leaving them alone to grow. As the years passed and your annuity payments lost purchasing power, you'd start dipping into your growth investments to help support your lifestyle. You can buy an inflation rider to raise your annuity's value in future years, but at the cost of a considerable drop in your guaranteed annual income.

Immediate-pay fixed annuities are also easy to shop for. Just go to ImmediateAnnuities.com and enter the lump sum you want to commit. You'll get a list, showing the various types of payment methods available. You might cover only your life, or your life and that of a spouse, or your life with a payment made to a beneficiary if you die early. Click the boxes next to the lifetime payment schedules that

---

2   The insurance industry, which loves to confuse you, sells another type of annuity it calls "fixed-index" (see page 173). It's complicated, way more expensive than immediate-pay fixed annuities, and pays agents much higher commissions. It's not a true pension substitute. Beware.

interest you. You'll get a free report showing the top 10 or 12 insurance carriers for each of those categories and how much they'll pay each month. No salesperson will call. If you want help, call Immediate Annuities.com founder and insurance agent, Hersh Stern, at 800-872-6684. You can buy through Stern or use the list as a benchmark when talking to your own insurance agent or financial planner. Sales commissions run from 1 to 3 percent. In general, the higher the commission, the less you'll be offered per month.

Next, check the payouts available from the two companies that don't charge commissions: Vanguard.com[3] and TIAA.org.[4] Choose the insurer that makes the best offer, consistent with the safety-and-soundness rating you want. Depending on your age, the highest-paying insurer might give you anywhere from 4 percent to 20 percent more than the lowest payer.

If you have been saving money in a tax-deferred variable annuity (see page 158) and want to convert it to an immediate-pay annuity, find out what your current insurance company will offer you per month. Compare that quote with the payments available through the sites above and choose the best one. If you decide to switch companies, your new insurer will handle the paperwork.

Deferred-income annuities, also known as longevity insurance. You invest in this annuity now but put off receiving income for several years. The delay improves your future spending power. For example, say that a 65-year-old woman puts up $100,000. If she chooses an

---

3 For information, click on "Personal Investors," then "Investing," then "Annuities," then "Get Income in Retirement." Call 800-600-4816.

4 You're eligible if your current employer offers TIAA in its retirement plan; if you formerly worked for such an employer; or if you're a close family member of someone eligible for the plan. These annuities can be purchased only with retirement plan money including IRAs. Call 800-842-2252.

immediate-pay annuity, she'll get $543 a month, at current interest rates. But if she can wait 10 years before receiving income, she'll get $1,149 a month. That's thanks to the interest earned on her $100,000 over the past decade and the fact that she's starting at an older age. At 75, her annuity payments can be larger because they're covering a shorter life span. Deferred annuities pay more per $1,000 invested than immediate-pay annuities do. Sales commissions run 2 to 4 percent—again, with a lower commission producing a higher monthly payment.

Here are some reasons to choose a deferred-income annuity: It pays more per $1,000 invested than immediate-pay annuities do; it frees you to spend more of your ready savings in the early years of retirement, knowing that, later, a new monthly check will start coming in; if you take a post-retirement job, you can set up payments to start when you expect the job to come to an end. You might be able to buy the annuity in installments rather than putting up a lump sum, but your future monthly income won't be as high. Some deferred-income annuities provide cash in emergencies or let you change the date when you expect to start taking income. You might want a benefit paid to heirs if you die before the annuity payments begin. Buying any of these perks, however, reduces your future payout.

Warning! There might be a problem if you buy deferred-income annuities through a tax-deferred retirement saving plan, such as an IRA or 401(k). The annuity has to be valued and counted toward the size of your required minimum distributions (RMDs), which start at age 70½. If it isn't yet paying an income, you'll need enough liquid assets in your IRA to cover the amount the annuity adds to your taxable distribution. So take care not to spend those assets too fast. Alternatively, you could put the annuity into its own IRA and solve the RMD problem by turning it into a monthly income at 70½.

There's another exception to this potential RMD trap. You can transfer up to $130,000 of your IRA or employee plan assets into a qualified longevity annuity contract (QLAC). QLACs aren't counted toward your RMD until you reach a later age—all the way up to 85, if you wish. Prior to that age, you can leave the annuity alone to increase in value, with no withdrawals required. That's a good move, assuming your purpose is to provide yourself with a future guaranteed income and intend to spend the money. But it's a bad investment if you merely want to defer some taxes on your RMDs, says Michael Kitces, a principal in the wealth management firm Pinnacle Advisory Group of Columbia, Maryland. You'll have to live much longer than your life expectancy to generate more wealth from the QLAC than you'd get if you kept your IRA in traditional investments and took the expected RMDs.

Fixed-term annuities. These annuities pay a fixed income for a certain number of years and then stop. You can use them as a financial bridge. For example, at 65, you might put some savings into a five year annuity to help cover your bills while you wait until 70 to collect Social Security.

Charitable gift annuities. Charitable gifts are beyond the scope of this book. But they're certainly another way of providing yourself with a lifetime income. You give a lump sum to a charity that guarantees you a fixed monthly payment. Your gift also generates tax deductions and avoids the capital gains tax if you donate appreciated securities. At your death, the charity takes any money remaining. There are other types of gift annuities, too. Ask the nonprofits you're interested in for details.

IF A SIMPLE ANNUITY SOUNDS GOOD, WHEN SHOULD YOU BUY IT?

Annuity companies usually say, "Buy sooner rather than later." That sounds pretty good if you're keeping a lot of money in safe, low-interest bank accounts. Immediate annuities will pay you much more per month than you're earning now. You're losing potential income every year you wait.

Nevertheless, financial planners generally advise you to put off the annuity decision. The older you are when you buy, the higher the monthly payment. Even more important—by waiting, you allow for surprises in your life that might change your mind. For example, your health might take a turn for the worse, you might inherit money, or you might have to use a chunk of cash to help one of your children. The delay preserves your options.

How long should you wait? Your window for buying immediate-pay fixed annuities is age 70 to 80, most of the experts say. By then you should have a good fix on how your retirement plans are working out and how long your other investments are likely to last. Consider deferred-income annuities between ages 60 and 70 to give your future income time to grow.

DON'T GIVE IN TO TEMPTATION! PROTECT YOUR SPOUSE!

An annuity that covers two lives pays less per month than an annuity that covers only one. For example, take a 70-year-old couple with $100,000 to spend on income protection. If they choose to cover the lifetime of only the husband, they'll get $650 a month. If they cover both lives, they'll get $531. The younger the spouse, the lower the joint monthly payment.

Differences this large tempt a surprising number of couples to gamble on taking the higher check today. They'll think about the future tomorrow. The future, unfortunately, usually arrives in the form of an obit for the husband and much reduced circumstances for the wife. So please. It's cruel and unusual punishment to knowingly slash the future income of a dependent spouse, even if the spouse agrees.

There are a few circumstances when you might want to cover only a single life. For example, maybe your spouse or partner has enough assets to be self-supporting. Maybe he or she is ill and likely to die first (although you can't be sure). Maybe you have life insurance that you think will protect your spouse or partner if you're the first to die (but will it, really? Check "pension maximization" on page 142). Or maybe the spouse is so young that adding her to the annuity (in this case, it's usually a "her") would slash monthly payments by 30 to 50 percent (younger spouses definitely need life insurance protection).

If your spouse or partner is roughly your age, however, and his or her lifetime financial protection isn't guaranteed, choose a joint-and-survivor annuity that covers you both.

WHERE TO GET HELP WITH AN ANNUITY PURCHASE

You can buy the simplest annuities with a phone call: at Vanguard .com, TIAA.org (for those eligible—see footnote 4 on page 153), and ImmediateAnnuities.com. But they're generally not a do-it-yourself investment. This chapter should help you decide whether you want to consider annuities and, if so, what kind. After that, it's helpful to have an adviser—*not a salesperson*—explain these products and help you decide whether they fit your needs.

Ideally, you'd work with a fee-only financial planner (see page 28) who helps you explore your personal retirement goals. He or she should be familiar with the best ways of matching simple, immediate-pay or deferred-income annuities with your other investments to produce a livable budget. Unfortunately, many good planners ignore even low-cost annuities. That's because sales commissions are usually built into the cost structure and fee-only firms don't take commissions. But these firms are starting to pay more attention as the benefits of immediate-pay annuities become clear. A few insurers offer annuities with no commissions, especially designed for financial advisers. Up-to-date fee-only planners should research them. They also might work through Hueler Income Solutions, an online service that offers annuities at the same low prices that institutions get.

If you work with a planner, broker, adviser, or agent who takes commissions, however, you will *not* be steered toward a simple low-cost annuity. They'll have something else in mind.

THE SEXY, CONFUSING, HIGH-COMMISSION COMBO ANNUITIES THAT FINANCIAL ADVISERS LOVE TO SELL

Now we've arrived at a special class of annuities that combine investing with promises of a secure retirement income. They're sold—*insistently* sold—by financial advisers who earn sales commissions. If you even breathe the words "income investment" you'll find it hard to escape the room until you've signed up.

These wonders are called *variable annuities* or *fixed-index annuities*, paired with *living-benefit guarantees*. They're sold as a combo "safe" stock market–linked investment with a guaranteed lifetime income on the side. Their value, as retirement income, can rise with the stock market but never fall. Wow. All gain, no loss. Super-high fees but, heck, you wouldn't begrudge them to an adviser who brings you such a fantastic opportunity (would you?).

Unfortunately, it's much harder than you think to turn living-benefit annuities into stories of investment success. You buy them in the hope of earning a higher retirement income than a plain-vanilla immediate-pay or deferred-income annuity would provide. But the high fees are likely to drain that hope away. You're forced to lock up your money for 5, 7, 10 years, or more. If you need cash, you can take out only a limited amount each year. If you take too much there's a stiff penalty and you might lose your lifetime income guarantee. These are not liquid investments. Large early withdrawals will smash your investment to smithereens.

Advance warning, when you read about living-benefit annuities: They're complicated! The people who buy them rarely understand how they work. Some of the salespeople might not know much, either, except that the product pays high commissions (in the range of

3 to 6 percent, depending on the product or distributor). If up-front commissions are low, there might be an annual fee that will cost you more in the long run. *Always* look at the list of fees in the front of the prospectus, if there is one. If not, ask the salesperson how much the product costs, in sales commission and assorted annual fees. A fair adviser will tell you. An adviser who won't, or who says, "the insurance company pays," is not the sort of person you want to be mixed up with. No matter how the money is distributed to salespeople, the buyer pays.

Occasionally, living-benefit annuities become a good deal, although you can't predict those magical periods in advance. For success, you need a high interest–rate guarantee, low commissions and fees, and some strong stock markets, especially near the beginning of your contract. If your adviser suggests that you buy one of these annuities, work your way through this section before making a decision. First, I'll cover the variable annuity, then the fixed-index annuity. You might conclude that instead of a "yes," your best answer is "no."

A Sort-of-Simple Explanation[5]

The Variable Annuity with Living Benefits
This product comes in two parts—an investment fund (which can be purchased separately) plus a lifetime income guarantee, called a living-benefit rider. You buy now and plan to start benefits in 10 to 20 years. Here's how it works.

Part 1 of the contract: a variable annuity (VA). This is a pure investment. You put your annuity money into a mix of stock and bond

---

5   I've streamlined the example so that your eyes won't glaze over. Each insurance company has its own special rules and products with new products being created all the time.

mutual funds (called "subaccounts" in annuity-speak). The insurance company gives you a list to choose from. Any gains accumulate tax deferred. There's a stiff surrender charge if you cancel the annuity within a certain number of years—usually five to seven, although some run as long as 10.[6] The risk, of course, is that your investment fund will do poorly. It might not provide as much future retirement income as you had hoped. This leads me to . . .

Part 2 of the contract: a living-benefit rider, known as a guaranteed lifetime withdrawal benefit (GLWB). Insurance companies solved the investment risk by adding a second part to the variable-annuity contract—a minimum lifetime income guarantee. You can receive that income no matter how well or poorly your investments perform. If they do poorly or provide only mediocre returns, the annuity will pay the promised amount, starting in the year you choose to retire. If the market does well, you'll get more than the contract guarantees. Naturally, buyers assume that their future income will increase because they're investing at least some of their annuity money in stocks. Anyway, that's what the salesperson's presentation will show. But you have to be lucky to gain more than the promised minimum amount. The explanation lies in the size of the annual fees you pay for the rider and the way the contract works.

How Parts 1 and 2 of the contract work together: Your living-benefit annuity has two values—an *investment value* and a *benefit base* or *income base* (different companies use different names).

The *investment value* reflects the gain or loss in the mutual funds you choose for the variable annuity, minus the annuity's costs. If

---

6   You're paid a bonus for locking up your money for 10 years, but you give it back in fees. Many insurers sell VAs with short or zero surrender charges. But agents earn less for selling them, so they usually don't bring them up.

you put in $100,000 and the market increase, after costs, is 8 percent, your investment value rises to $108,000. If the net decline is 8 percent, the investment value drops to $92,000. You can always withdraw the annuity's investment value in cash (although there are usually penalties for early withdrawals plus a 10 percent tax penalty if you're under 59½).

The *benefit base* is your original investment plus a guaranteed annual percentage increase. A typical minimum increase today is 6 percent.[7] If you invest $100,000, the benefit base will rise to $106,000 in the first year, $112,360 in the second year, and so on. It keeps on rising by 6 percent, even if the stock market does poorly. After 10 years, you're going to feel pretty good. Your $100,000 is now worth $179,000 and it happened without regard for what the stock market did.

There's a hitch, of course. This is the insurance industry, not a public charity. You appear to have $179,000, in this example, but you *cannot* withdraw that money in a lump sum. An annuity's benefit base is not real cash (alas), it's just a number used to calculate a future guaranteed income. To collect on that paper gain you have to start taking annual lifetime withdrawals. You might or might not receive the full value of that apparent $179,000, depending on how long you live and what the spousal benefits are.

So far, I've been talking about the minimum annual gain in the benefit base that the annuity guarantees. In a strong stock market, your benefit base can grow to a larger amount. That's one of the things that sells consumers on the product. If the value of the mutual funds in your annuity rises by more than, say, 6 percent, *after costs*, the increase is added to your base (a "reset"). That puts your future guaranteed lifetime payments on a permanently higher level.

As an example, take the $100,000 annuity mentioned above. In

---

7 I'm using 6 percent for all my examples in this section. Be aware that different contracts provide different guarantees.

the second year, your guaranteed benefit base is supposed to rise 6 percent to $106,000 on your contract's anniversary date. Let's say, however, that the mutual funds in your annuity do much better than that, raising the net value of your investment fund to $120,000. That higher number becomes your new benefit base. Instead of $106,000, you'll have $120,000.[8] In the third year, your annual 6 percent gain will be figured on that higher base. Good news.

The story isn't nearly as pretty, however, when the stock market falls. To show the effect, let's assume that your $100,000 mutual-fund investment declines in the second year to a net value of $90,000. Your guaranteed benefit base will still rise by 6 percent of your original $100,000 investment. On paper, you now have $106,000, which is nice. But for your future income to rise above the guarantee, the value of your investments—again, after costs—have to make up the $10,000 market loss, *plus* 6 percent, *plus* something more. The longer it takes for your investment to recover, the further it will fall behind the guaranteed, annual 6 percent increases in the benefit base. You'll always have the guarantee but you might never qualify for an income higher than the guarantee. That guarantee (not any investment gain) is what GLWBs are all about.

Now the Really Bad News: *Costs*

High annual fees make it especially hard for you to earn more than the minimum guarantee. A low-cost company such as Vanguard charges 1.7 percent of your benefit base for a variable annuity with a living-benefit rider, which gives long-term holders a good chance of coming out ahead. But most commercial insurance companies charge 3.5 percent or more for the total package—the annuity, the mutual funds, the living-benefit rider, a death benefit (contained

---

8   The fee for the guarantee is generally calculated from the benefit base, so as the base rises, so does your cost.

in most contracts), and overhead. That's at least $3,500 *a year* for every $100,000 in your account. Fees rise even higher if you want payments made to a beneficiary when you die. All these crazy expenses come out of your contract's investment value. They're listed near the front of the prospectus, along with the maximum fees that the insurer can charge. Be sure to look at them! Don't buy the annuity based on the sales brochure alone. If the salesperson says that you'll get the brochure in the mail, wait for it before committing.

Fee-based advisers (see page 29) sell annuities with no sales commission. But they're probably charging you 1 or 1.25 percent a year for managing your money, in addition to the annuity's direct expenses. That might cost you just as much as buying from a commissioned salesperson. So, let's look at the real annuity math.

Say that you're paying 3.5 percent in fees and your contract's benefit base is rising by 6 percent a year. Your investment fund will have to rise by 9.5 percentage points (after costs) just to keep you even, and more than 9.5 percentage points before your future payment can rise above the minimum. That requires strong stock market returns, especially when you first buy, or a lucky "wow" year when your investment values suddenly shoot up. You might have earned a reset if you happened to buy the annuity near the bottom of the market in 2009 or 2010 or at the start of the run-up in 2017. But not in most other years.

What if the value of your investments rises but only by a modest amount? Any rise less than 9.5 percentage points, in this example, leaves your investment values behind the guaranteed increase in the benefit base. You might think that your mutual funds are doing well, but they're not doing well enough to qualify you for an income higher than the guarantee.

What if the stock market declines in value? You might land in a hole that you can't dig out of. At that point, your investments will have to rise by enough to regain your market loss *and* cover your annual expenses *and* exceed the annual increase in your benefit base before you'll get anything more than the guaranteed minimum payment.

Some annuity sellers make this investment goal even tougher to reach by requiring you to hold at least 20 to 30 percent of your investments in bonds. So you don't get the full value of a strong stock market year.

Bottom line: You have to hit a hot market to fulfill your hopes of a payment higher than the minimum guarantee. That outcome is stacked against you because of the fees. You'd wind up with little more than a very expensive deferred annuity.

How Is the Living Benefit Paid?

Let's say that you start with $100,000. Ten years later, your benefit base has risen to $179,000. And say that your contract, allows you to withdraw 5 percent a year, calculated from your base. In my example, that's $8,950 a year for the rest of your life (and your spouse's life, if the contract covers both of you). If you put off taking the income, your $179,000 benefit base will continue to increase, resulting in higher withdrawals when you do finally start. You might also get a higher percentage withdrawal for waiting past age 65 or 70. With some GLWBs, you can buy a rider that raises your payments if you enter a nursing home. In no case, however, can you take the benefit base in a lump sum. It's a theoretical amount, used for monthly payment calculations only.

There's another form of living-benefit rider called a Guaranteed Minimum Income Benefit (GMIB). It's not much sold today but is often found in contracts sold a decade or more ago. With older GMIBs, you turn your benefit base into a lifetime annuity. With newer ones, you take lifetime withdrawals, much as you do with GLWBs.

IF YOU'RE MARRIED, WILL YOUR SPOUSE GET LIFETIME BENEFITS, TOO?

Most of the living-benefit riders sold today allow your spouse to continue receiving payments from the benefit base if you die first. But you have to choose that option in advance. The premium might be higher than that for a single-life rider. Alternatively, your guaranteed withdrawal rate might drop to 4.5 percent from 5 percent.

Don't fail to take this rider if you have a dependent spouse! A salesperson might encourage you to cover your life only because it costs less and is an easier sale. But you might die five years after starting the payment stream while your spouse lives on for 25 years more. There's a death benefit, which you might assume continues the payments to the spouse. But it merely ensures that, if you start receiving income and die, your heir will receive the same amount you originally invested minus any withdrawals you took. If you have an older annuity that doesn't allow for continuing payments to a spouse, consider switching to a better one (in a tax-free exchange) or buying more life insurance so your survivor won't go broke

YOUR LIVING BENEFITS ARE ALWAYS PAID FROM YOUR OWN MONEY FIRST!

Many buyers of living-benefit annuities don't understand where the money comes from to pay the lifetime income they receive. You're told that your benefit base is increasing by, say, a guaranteed 6 percent a year. That sounds as if you're earning 6 percent on your investment. The salesperson might even encourage you to believe that. But it's not true! Not even close.

The monthly payments you receive from the insurance company, for all or most of your life, will be subtracted from your annuity's investment account—in this example, at the rate of 5 percent a year. That's your own money. It's made up of the original sum you put up, plus any interest or dividend income, adjusted by market gains and losses, and minus fees. In other words, *you're paying yourself.* And by the way, you're continuing to pay the contract's high annual fees. You start getting paid with the insurance company's money only if you live long enough for your own money to be exhausted.

That, of course, is what any lifetime annuity is for—to protect you if you outlive your resources. But strategically, you'd like to start receiving payments from the insurance company's money as soon as possible. You can make this happen by exercising a right included in the contract. You're allowed to make withdrawals from your investment account every year, up to a fixed percentage amount. In the example I've been using, you could take out 5 percent. Presumably, you'd put it into other investments, such as mutual funds that don't sock you for high fees year after year. The faster you work your investment account down to zero, the sooner the company will have to start using its own resources to make your guaranteed lifetime income payments.

For more on this game plan, see the next page.

If You Already Own a Variable Annuity with a Living Benefit, How Do You Get the Most Value from It?

Your best option for income will depend on how well the investments inside your annuity are doing. Have you had good luck or bad luck?

The good luck case: Your investments are worth as much as your guaranteed benefit base or more. You have three choices:

1. Leave the annuity alone and let the rising value of your investments increase your guaranteed future monthly payments. Presumably, the hope of a higher guaranteed lifetime income is the reason you made this investment in the first place.
2. Annuitize the money now, turning it into an income for life. To

see how much you can get per month, go to ImmediateAnnuities .com. You'll almost certainly find insurers offering better deals than you'd get if you annuitized with your current company. You can switch to the new annuity in a tax-free exchange.

3. Withdraw the money to make other investments. The withdrawals are taxed (see page 179).

The bad luck case: Your investments haven't done well enough. They've fallen way behind the value of the annuity's benefit base and will probably never catch up. Remember that your benefit base rises smoothly at, say, 6 percent a year. Meanwhile, your investment account is at the mercy of up-and-down markets and is chopped every year by fees. What's your next move? You have two choices:

- Do nothing. Your benefit base will continue to grow by 6 percent. At some point in the future, you can turn that higher amount into a monthly income for life. You will gradually be getting your own money back. You might or might not retrieve all your money by the time you die, so start early.
- Make the smart choice, which I'm guessing will apply to most of the readers of this book. Start taking your guaranteed minimum withdrawals right away (say, at 5 percent a year).[9] Take the money even if you're still working and don't need it. Every withdrawal reduces the size of your investment account. Your goal is to strip out your cash while you're still alive and invest it somewhere else, where you're not paying 3.5 percent in annual fees. Meanwhile, your benefit base will continue to increase. Once you've emptied your investment account, the insurance company will continue to pay the monthly income you were promised. You will then

---

9   If you're at least 59½. There's a 10 percent tax penalty if you take the money at an earlier age.

be enjoying your own money (which you've withdrawn and reinvested) and the insurance company's money, too. You'll finally be profiting from the protection you paid for.

What to do with withdrawals you make from your investment account will depend on your circumstances. If you own the living-benefit annuity in an individual retirement account, you can roll the money directly into your IRA and reinvest it. If you own the annuity outside an IRA, you'd simply take the money, pay the taxes, and spend or reinvest the net proceeds.

Three caveats: (1) You usually have to hold the annuity for a certain number of years or else pay an insurance-company penalty. Wait for the penalty period to expire before starting withdrawals. You do, however, have access to some of the money—maybe 10 percent a year—penalty free. Your company's customer service rep can tell you what the dollar amount would be. (2) A few contracts cancel your lifetime income if you take *any* withdrawals over the first ten years. Stay away from them. (3) Your contract might promise a higher guaranteed payment once you reach a certain age. If you're close to that age, wait until you pass it before starting withdrawals.

How Should You Manage Your Variable Annuity Account When You Also Have Money in a Financial Advisory Account?

Your financial adviser might have put half of your nonannuity money into stocks and half into bonds, or even 60 percent in bonds if you're a conservative investor. But the same allocation would be a mistake for the mutual funds in your variable annuity. Your annuity contains its own safety net, in the form of the living-benefits rider. You can—and should—put as much money into your annuity's stock investments as the company allows. If the insurance company allows only 60 percent in stocks, consider increasing your stock allocation outside the annuity, even if you invest conservatively.

Are You Still Unsure About How to Get the Most Value Out of Your Existing Living-Benefit Annuity?

No surprise there. In this section, I've passed on advice from the best annuity experts I know. Still, the living-benefit options are confusing.[10] How much are you really paying in fees? When is the best time to start withdrawing benefits? If you die first, what does your spouse or partner actually get? Should you switch to an annuity with lower costs? Are there angles to your contract that, if used, will yield a higher payment? How much can you withdraw without losing your income guarantee or reducing it sharply? If your insurance company offers to give you cash in return for surrendering a future benefit (see page 173), should you accept? Does your older, "vintage" contract have valuable benefits that you shouldn't give up? How should you evaluate a fixed-index annuity?

For answers to these and any other questions you have about your existing annuities, I recommend a service called Annuity Review, run by Mark Cortazzo at the MACRO Consulting Group in Parsippany, New Jersey (AnnuityReview.com). Cortazzo is a financial planner and annuity expert. For $299, his team will analyze up to two variable annuities with living benefits. He'll advise on the investments you've chosen, check the spouse protection (if any), and tell you how to make the most of your guaranteed withdrawals. If you're already working with an adviser, you might use this service as a second opinion.

More Things You Need to Know About Variable Annuities with Living-Benefit Riders

1. What propels the sale of these annuities isn't the guaranteed minimum income. You can get higher payments from a simple

---

10 This book's biggest understatement.

deferred-income annuity. Instead, you're hoping to exceed that minimum, thanks to the stock market's expected long-term gains. Toward that end, you should invest as much of your annuity money as possible in stock-owning mutual funds, says annuity expert Moshe Milevsky of York University in Toronto. Aggressive investors are the ones most likely to beat the minimum guarantee (always assuming that the stock market goes up, especially in the annuity's first few years). If your insurance company limits your stock holdings to 60 or 70 percent of your investment, with the rest in bonds, it's programming you to fail. Annuities invested in a moderate mix of stocks and bonds will probably never yield enough to increase your future retirement income.

2. Your insurance company usually has the right to increase the internal cost of your existing annuity, up to certain caps. That can reduce any chance you have of earning a future income higher than the guarantee. Be sure to read the fee table at the front of the prospectus. There, you'll see the maximum fee possible and the rate of cost increase that's allowed. *Never* buy without having the time to read the prospectus and the fee table first.

3. Don't add more money to the annuity if your investment value is below the benefit base. Doing so helps the insurance company, not you. The more money you have in the annuity, the less likely the company will ever be forced to use its own funds for your lifetime payments. You should be thinking about taking money out, not putting it in, says Tamiko Toland, head of annuity research for CANNEX USA, a firm that specializes in annuity pricing information.

4. Variable annuities with living-benefit riders often include a death benefit, payable to your spouse or another beneficiary. If you make withdrawals from your investment account, the death benefit usually declines by the same amount.

5. If you buy a variable annuity with a living-benefit rider and

you're married, be sure that you're buying a joint benefit that covers your spouse. If you don't, and you die first, your spouse or partner will receive what's left of the money in the investment account (if any) or perhaps a death benefit, but no lifetime income payments. Many salespeople don't point this out (or likely don't know it!), especially if you're buying the annuity with funds from your individual retirement account. The IRA might name your spouse or partner as beneficiary but that's not enough. He or she has to be on the rider, too.

6. Don't hold an annuity inside a self-directed IRA at a brokerage firm. For convenience, the broker will usually name the IRA as the annuity's beneficiary. If you die, your spouse will get the proceeds of the IRA but won't qualify for continuing annuity income. Hold variable annuities with a living benefit outside your self-directed IRA.

7. Some variable annuities let you change your mind. You can drop the living benefit rider and stop paying the fees or withdraw your cash anytime without penalty.

8. Annuities can be cash cows for insurance agents and other salespeople who choose to put their own interests ahead of yours. They'll watch to see when your annuity can be exchanged without penalty. Then they'll tell you that a better one has come along and encourage you to switch. If you do, the adviser earns a new commission, you start a new penalty period, and you might have lost some valuable benefits by giving the old investment up. On the other hand, a proposed switch to a low-cost annuity, such as those sold by Vanguard or TIAA, can make a lot of sense.

9. The mutual funds you buy inside annuities generally yield less than the same funds bought independently of annuities. That's because of the tax treatment as well as the annuities' fees. Outside the annuity, you pay the low capital gains tax on your shares' increase in value; inside it, you pay at the ordinary income rate

when your gains are withdrawn. Over all but the very longest holding periods (15 to 20 years or more), you'll net more from direct mutual fund investments than you will from buying the same funds inside a variable annuity, after taxes and fees.[11] You also pay lower investment charges and no sales commission if you buy the funds from a no-load mutual fund group.

10. *Pay attention to surrender periods!* You're locking up your money for four, seven, maybe even ten years. You'll pay a pretty penny—and lose money—if you break the contract early. Once you pass 70 (or maybe 68 or 67?), accepting long surrender periods is a terrible idea.

11. Don't buy a living-benefit rider unless you intend to use it to create a future, lifetime income. That's the only reason to spend your money on the guarantee. If you don't intend to take lifetime payments from your annuity, forget the rider. Invest elsewhere at a lower cost.

12. There's bad news even if you annuitize. You are a captive customer. The insurance company will pay you less, per dollar invested, than you could get on the open market. But you can't buy on the open market because your guaranteed benefit base works only with the annuity you already have.

Special Note to People Who Bought a Living-Benefit Rider Before the 2008 Financial Collapse

You're in luck. In the early '00s, insurance companies competed to offer ever-richer benefits without charging you as much as they really cost. Guaranteed lifetime accumulations and payments ran to 7 percent.

---

11 The break-even period is shorter if you're in the top federal and state income tax brackets or if you buy from a low-cost provider such as Vanguard or TIAA.

Lately, many insurers have been suffering seller's remorse. Those guarantees are too rich compared with what the companies can earn from interest rates today. Some of them are asking you to give up your high future benefits. In return, they'll add money to your investment account. They might also try to get you to cancel a lucrative death benefit that would go to your spouse or another beneficiary.

If you still want the lifetime income, throw the offer away. The "free" cash doesn't begin to cover the value of the big payouts you'd lose. You might take it, however, if you're seriously ill, with a shortened life span, and the annuity's income rider doesn't cover the lifetime of your spouse.

In some cases, the insurance company forces you to make a change, in order to reduce the insurer's risk. For example, you might be required to shift the investments in your annuity toward more bonds and away from stocks. If you don't, you'll lose your high lifetime income guarantee. The lower allocation to stocks makes it less likely that your guaranteed income will rise in the future. To me, that's dirty pool. You've lost a benefit you have been paying for. If you're facing this demand, shift your investments as required but don't sit on them. Instead, start taking your annual guaranteed payouts immediately (see page 167). Right now. That's the best way of getting value for your money.

The Fixed-Index Annuity with Living Benefits

This deal, too, gives you the hope of gain coupled with the promise of no loss. It's known as an "index annuity," "equity-indexed annuity," or "fixed-index annuity" (FIA). Regrettably, it is not truly fixed and not truly indexed. The various names give salespeople options when they pitch it. You want growth? They say "equity index." You want safety? They say "fixed." A fixed-index annuity has nothing to do with the simple, fixed immediate-pay annuities I wrote about on page 152. Or the multiyear guaranteed annuities on page 263. These confusions of nomenclature are what make it so dangerous for the average person to stray into what amounts to the financial industry's worst neighborhood. Like variable annuities, FIAs can be purchased purely for investment, with your gains taken at the end of a fixed term. If you also want an income for life, you can purchase a Guaranteed Lifetime Withdrawal Benefits rider (GLWB).

Three facts to know before you start: (1) FIAs appear to be linked to stocks but they're not. They're credited with an interest rate that is influenced by the market's performance but does not reflect it. In design, they're expected to yield bond-like returns or, if you're lucky, a little more, according to CANNEX, the annuity pricing firm. (2) There's no prospectus, so you don't get a fee table up front. Some states require fee disclosure in other ways, but not all of them. So *ask*! Otherwise, you won't necessarily know what you're paying for the annuity in expenses, commissions, and annual fees. All you'll see is the interest credited to your FIA after the mystery costs have been deducted. You might see the price of the living-benefits rider if you choose to buy it, but not always. (3) You might have purchased a five-, seven-, ten-, or even (no!) a fifteen-year annuity. But its terms might not be guaranteed past the first one, two, or three years. After that, you'll be offered new terms, maybe not as good. The insurer can use various means to lower your interest-crediting rate if its expenses rise. That's like betting on a horse after the race is over.

In concept, fixed-index annuities with living benefits resemble their variable cousins, discussed above. They come in two parts— an investment (which can be bought separately) plus a guaranteed living-benefit rider. The guarantee pays, even if your investment does poorly. If it does especially well, your future income might—might— exceed the guarantee. What's different about FIAs is the restricted way that the insurance company figures your investment gains. Here's how it works:

Part 1 of the contract: the investment. This is a tax-deferred investment. You sign up for a specific term, ranging from seven to fifteen years, with a penalty for early withdrawals. Your gain, if any, depends partly on how well the stock market performs over a specific period—usually, as measured by Standard & Poor's 500 stock market index, not counting dividends. (That's a loss right there. A substantial part of the S&P's long-term returns—2 to 3 percentage points a year—comes from reinvested dividends.) Some insurers use specialized, "hybrid" market indexes, hoping to reduce volatility or beat the S&P—hard to do, more complex, and more expensive.[12]

The rest of your potential investment profit depends on how much of the S&P's gain the contract gives you. Here are several possibilities: (1) You'll get a percentage of any market increase (excluding dividends), called a "participation rate." Participation rates currently range from 30 to 50 percent, depending on the length of the contract. (2) There might be a cap on how high the value of your account can rise—say, between 3 and 6 percentage points. If your FIA carries a 6 percent cap, and the stock market rises by 20 percent, you'll get only 6 points of that gain. (3) Many annuities offer a spread between the index return and the amount you're credited with. For example, say the spread is 2 percentage points. If the index rises by 1 point, you get nothing. If it rises by 5 points, you're credited with 3 points. (4) Some products carry both a participation rate and a cap. (5) The latest, hottest offering is "no caps," or 100 percent of the index's gain. Wow. But the index probably won't be the S&P, it will be something manufactured by the sponsor, and there will be caps or participation rates to contain your potential gain. The 100 percenters are easier to sell, but—trust me—the insurer and the salesperson pluck the same fees and profits as they do from any other fixed-index annuity and you get the same returns.

---

12 Hybrid indexes created by the insurers can also be used to project higher future investment returns than you're likely to get.

There are also various ways of calculating the stock market's gain, when figuring out how much to credit your account. Most common is point-to-point, meaning you get whatever gain occurred over the 12 months from the day you bought. Alternatively, you might receive an average of the period's monthly gains. Or perhaps the average gain over a two- or three-year period. The monthly average is least likely to outperform, but every method has its day in the sun, depending on what the market does. You cannot guess, let alone do the math. Some FIAs offer a first-year "signing bonus," but you pay for it in the form of a longer surrender period or lower credited investment returns.

If the stock market falls, you'll get zero interest for the year. That's the "no loss" clause. Your investment value will not decline. As you've seen, however, you pay for this protection by giving up part of any market gain—maybe a substantial part. *Warning:* The insurance company can change the amount you're allowed to earn on your account. Usually, it makes these changes once a year, on your contract's anniversary date. It might decide to lower the amount of the stock market's gain it will credit you with, or set the cap on your gain at a lower level. Such changes reduce the insurance company's risk by reducing your chance of gaining more than the company planned for. So, you're not really "in the market" or linked to stocks, you just think you are. Instead, FIAs compete with bonds—in good years, paying a little more, in bad years not. There's a minimum investment guarantee. At the very least, you might get back the money you put in (or, more likely, 87.5 percent of the money you put in) plus annual interest at 1 percent and plus or minus various, arcane market adjustments. You can withdraw up to 10 percent of your investment every year without paying a surrender charge. For larger withdrawals, the surrender charge is stiff.

One more problem: Because you don't know what you're paying for the fixed-index annuity itself, the "adviser"/salesperson can play games with you. He or she might smile and tell you that you pay no annual fees, no commissions, and no investment charges. That's absolutely not true. The costs are built into the product and come out of your investment return. Typical (hidden) commission: 6 to 8 percent for FIAs with a five- to seven-year surrender charge and higher for ten and fifteen years. You should *never* purchase the longer-term products; they're structured solely to benefit the agent (and I have my doubts about the shorter-terms, too). By one calculation (at RetirementIncomeJournal.com), agents might be taking 40 percent of a multiyear contract's potential profits.

You can renew this annuity when its term is up. The costs and options at renewal might not be as good as those you started with.

Part 2 of the contract: the guaranteed lifetime withdrawal benefit (GLWB). This works just like the GLWB I discussed on page 160. You're assigned a "benefit base" (or similar name) that rises by a fixed amount each year—say, 6 percent. If the investment value of your annuity rises significantly, your future lifetime income could exceed the payout guarantee. If not, you'll get the minimum that the contract calls for. Always remember—you are *not* earning 6 percent on your investment. When your annuity payments start, you're receiving your own money back in annual increments (say, 5 percent a year), depending on the contract. With some GLWBs, you can purchase a rider that raises payments if you enter a nursing home.

Sometimes, you'll find a fixed-index annuity with a higher lifetime income guarantee than variable or even immediate annuities pay, after the 10-year mark. That's because the insurance company is rarely called upon to pay it. Most of the people who buy the GLWB rider *never use it*! They take whatever money is in their investment account at the end of the term, and run. They never turn their benefit base into an income for life, hence wasting all the money they spent on their guarantee.

Why do so many people fail to use their lifetime benefits? Partly because they fall victim to the sucker factor and won't annuitize (see page 148). And partly because the annuity was mis-sold. The sales-person might have shown you a chart projecting high future returns that, in fact, were entirely unrealistic. Disappointed by the actual re-turns, investors bail out. Note that investment FIAs (without GLWBs) have earned their own Investor Alert at FINRA.org, the organization that oversees securities firms, so check it out.[13] Thanks to new reg-ulations, the industry has been moving toward cleaning up its act. But bad sales are still being made, especially to seniors—painful, if you're in your 70s, locked into an FIA, and need access to cash.

MORE THINGS YOU NEED TO KNOW ABOUT FIXED-INDEX ANNUITIES WITH LIVING BENEFITS RIDERS

1. Your principal probably won't rise very much. You're unlikely to get a lucky, big stock market year that resets your future lifetime income at a higher payout (if that's what you're hoping for, try a VA with a GLWB instead). Your investment fund might earn a little more (or a little less) than high-quality bonds, and less than you'd get on a straight FIA without the benefit rider

2. "Advisers" who tout FIAs with surrender periods of 10 years or more are likely being driven by sales commissions. The same insurance company probably offers lockup periods of only five years, which pay almost as much as the 10-year FIA and give you more flexibility. Not surprisingly, the commissions aren't as high.

3. If you're a single woman who wants a deferred investment and will definitely turn the guarantee into a lifetime income, you might choose an FIA over a deferred-income annuity. FIAs offer unisex pricing, which might pay you a little more money despite the high fees. There might be other, particular circumstances

---

13 FINRA's Alert calls them equity-indexed annuities.

where the lifetime guarantee on a VA or FIA looks better, at first. But again, only for people who will actually use the lifetime benefits.

4.   Fee-based financial advisers can offer FIAs with richer guarantees but there may be no difference in returns after they deduct their fees.

What Happens When You Reach 70½?

If your guaranteed living-benefit rider is inside a traditional IRA, there could be a problem. You'll have to start required minimum distributions (RMDs) at 70½, and they might be higher than the annual amounts that the GLWB or GMIB allow. GLWBs generally let you take the higher amount without breaking your lifetime income guarantee, but check. If you have an older GMIB, however, it might not offer you that option.

You can avoid having to deal with RMDs by turning the FIA into an immediate-pay lifetime annuity. Age 70½ is a little young for that, but you might have no choice. The annuity forces your hand.[14]

HOW ARE ANNUITY WITHDRAWALS TAXED?

When you're buying a pension in the form of a commercial lifetime annuity, taxes matter. Here are the rules, in brief:

•   The income from investments left inside a variable annuity accumulates tax deferred. You can change the investments from one of the annuity's mutual funds to another with no tax consequences.

---

14   You don't face a minimum withdrawal risk if you buy the annuity with funds from a Roth IRA.

- You can switch from one variable annuity to another with no tax consequences through what's called a 1035 exchange. The agent will handle the transfer for you.

- For "qualified annuities"—purchased with funds from a retirement account and rolled into an IRA (see Chapter 7): All the income you withdraw from a traditional IRA is taxed at ordinary income rates. Income from a Roth IRA can pass untaxed (see page 193).

- For "nonqualified annuities"—purchased with savings you keep outside a retirement account: Any earnings on your annuity investments are taxed as ordinary income, not as capital gains, regardless of the source. If you take a lump sum, the earnings are taxed all at once. If you annuitize, the monthly benefits you receive from an immediate-pay annuity, a deferred-income annuity, or a variable annuity, are partly tax free (because it's a return of your original investment) and partly taxable (due to the earnings on your annuity investments). The same is true if you annuitize a guaranteed minimum income benefit (GMIB—see page 164).

  If you're taking minimum annual withdrawals from a GMIB without annuitizing or from a guaranteed lifetime withdrawal benefit (GLWB), they'll be taxed entirely as income until you've received an amount equal to all the earnings on your investment. After that, the withdrawals are considered a tax-free return of your original capital. If you have a GLWB and live long enough to use up your investment earnings plus your principal, all the income becomes taxable again. That's because you're finally being paid entirely by the insurance company rather than from your own money.

- If your investments lose money and your account is smaller than the amount you originally put into the annuity, all your withdrawals are considered a tax-free return of principal.

- When you die, your estate will potentially owe income taxes on the value of any tax-deferred annuities that are left to heirs. They're also subject to estate taxes if you're in that nosebleed bracket.

- You owe income taxes on any investment gains if you give the annuity to a charity.

- You can switch money from a 401(k) or similar tax-deferred retirement plan into a qualified annuity tax free.

- Income from annuities is not counted when figuring the tax, if any, you owe on your Social Security benefits.

- Money withdrawn from a tax-deferred plan, prior to age 59½, is subject to a 10 percent tax penalty on the earnings, unless the money is withdrawn at a level of payments expected to last for your lifetime.

SUMMING UP

Should you consider an immediate-pay annuity

▶ No—if you are living on Social Security plus modest savings. You need your savings at hand for flexibility.

▶ No—if you're living on Social Security plus an inflation-adjusted pension with savings on the side. You already have enough steady income to last for life. Your inflation adjustment is your longevity insurance.

▶ No—if you have so much money that you'll never run out (sigh).

▶ No—if you have a substantial amount of investments, are tapping no more than 2 or 3 percent of the total every year, and are living comfortably on the money. You already have enough income to last for life.

▶ Maybe—if you have a substantial amount of financial assets but need to withdraw more than a prudent amount each year to pay your bills (see Chapter 8). You have little or no margin for error if you hope to make your money last for life. Annu-itizing part of your savings in, say, your early 70s raises the amount of income you can depend on. Ideally, the annuity payments plus Social Security would cover your bare mini-mum expenses, or close to it. That frees you to invest more of the rest of your money in well-diversified stock-owning mu-tual funds for growth.

▶ Yes—if you have substantial savings and are trying to live only on interest and dividends because you're afraid of touching the principal. Shifting some of your principal into an annuity will increase your standard of living and give you the lifetime income guarantee that you don't have today.

▶ Yes—if you're so afraid of stocks that you're keeping all or most of your money in certificates of deposit and bond mu-tual funds. You might put part of your bond allotment into an immediate-pay annuity, to get a higher income from the "safe" part of your portfolio. Annuities do the most for people concerned only with income and who want no market risk.

Should you consider a deferred-income annuity?

▶ No—if you fall under any of the "no" categories listed above.

▶ Yes—if you'd like to spend more of your savings in your early retirement years. A deferred-income annuity delivers a guar-anteed monthly payment, starting 10 or 15 years from now.

▶ Yes—if you plan to work past the normal retirement age and want to provide an income that replaces your paycheck when you finally leave the job.

Should you consider a variable annuity with a living-benefit rider?

▶ No—if you're forced to keep more than 20 percent of your annuity investment in bonds. You'd be paying a high price for a lifetime income that will probably never exceed the guaran-tee. Assuming that you plan to hold the annuity for 10 years or more before making withdrawals, consider a deferred-income annuity instead. Or a stock-indexed mutual fund.

▶ No—if you're in your 70s or older. Your money will be locked up for five to seven years (or more). The only product even to consider is one with no penalty for early withdrawals.

▶ Maybe—if you're satisfied with the minimum lifetime income guarantee *and* choose an annuity that lets you invest at least 80 percent of your money in stocks *and* doesn't charge more than 2.5 or 3 percent in total fees, including all the mutual fund and advisory fees, *and* you're prepared to live with getting only the minimum. You might be one of the charmed savers who do better than the guarantee by lucking into some strong bull markets during the annuity's early years or one sensational market at the right time. If not, you fully understand that the only way to get value from the guarantee is by annuitizing or taking fixed withdrawals for life and then living a very long life.

▶ Yes—if you're satisfied with the minimum lifetime income guarantee *and* are willing to bet some money on getting good enough stock markets to exceed the guarantee *and* buy a low-cost annuity that gives you a shot at winning your bet (Vanguard—1.7 percent) *and* won't be disappointed if you get only the minimum. Some fee-only advisers sell no-load annuities, but you have to factor in the advisory fee and the underlying cost of the investments.

Should you consider a fixed-index annuity with a living-benefit rider?

▶ No—if you're buying because you expect a stock-linked investment return that's higher than the guarantee. Odds are you won't get it. FIAs produce bond-like returns.

▶ Maybe—if you're looking at the rare annuity that guarantees a higher lifetime payout rate (say, 6.5 percent) than you'd get from other types of annuities *and* a fixed lifetime income is all you want from the investment *and* you won't need the money early *and* you will actually make the annual withdrawals.

► Maybe—if you're happy with the minimum income guarantee and want to preserve the ability to change your mind. The FIA lets you choose to cash out at some point in the future. You might take a loss, but that's the breaks.

► Never—if you're at a "free dinner" for seniors and a fixed annuity is on the menu. It will be high cost. The salesperson will try to talk you into putting most of your assets there. The FIA will lock up your money for 10 years or more. Forget it. Just eat the rubber chicken and go home.

Fundamentally, annuities are not an investment even if they're tricked out to look like one. They're a risk-management tool. They insure you against the risk of living beyond the amount of money you have in savings and investments. They help alleviate the fear that you might become a burden to your children. But if you're allergic to annuities and want to create a lifetime income directly from your savings and investments, flip to Chapter 8.

7

Powering Your Retirement Savings Plans

If you haven't saved pots of money, don't waste time kicking yourself. It's never too late to give your future a boost.

When retirees are asked if there's anything they'd have done differently in their lives financially, the number one answer is (drumroll . . .) save more money. Younger, we tend to behave as if the retirement fairy will magically carry us through. That's everyone's Plan A. By midlife, with faith in magic dimmed, we move to Plan B, otherwise known as "I'll work till I drop." But you can't count on keeping your health or your job from now to the horizon. You also need Plan C.

Plan C—to make up for lost time—is to "power save." If you're working, squeeze your paycheck like a sponge in order to put more money away. If you're no longer working full-time, find part-time work and save every dime.

If you're living entirely on your savings, go to Plan D. Trim your budget and manage withdrawals and taxes so that your money will last a few extra years. Check the tax-saving rules later in this chapter.

Central to all these solutions is the nation's greatest gift to savers, the tax-favored retirement plan. With these plans, the earnings on your savings build up tax deferred (sometimes tax free). They come in many types, for employees and the self-employed. With employee plans, contributions are deducted from your paycheck automatically—a splendid and reliable way to save. Cash unseen is cash unspent. Your company might even match a percentage of the money you put in, a freebie no employee should miss. Contributions to plans for the self-employed can be automated, too. Typically, your money is invested in mutual funds.

Tax-favored retirement plans are solely for people with paychecks. You have to fund them with earnings, not with unearned income such as Social Security, pension, interest, dividends, or rent. Still, the size of your unearned income matters. The higher it is, the more of an earned paycheck you might be able to put away.

Some people think it's no longer worth contributing to a plan when they're close to retirement age. Why put in money just to take it out a couple of years later? Two reasons. First, those might be your highest earning years, so the tax benefits are the greatest. Second, you *won't* be taking out all of the money right away. You might live for another 30 years or more. That's a barrelful of time for your pre-retirement contributions to grow tax deferred. So please. Take these tax breaks while you're still working and can get them.

THERE'S A TAX UMBRELLA FOR EVERYONE

Tax-favored savings plans pop up everywhere in the working world. Which ones you can use depend on your employment status. Here are your choices:

If you work for a company with a retirement plan, you can have a percentage of every paycheck put away. On average, workers in their mid-50s to mid-60s are contributing 8.4 percent of the money they earn, according to a 2018 study by Vanguard called "How America Saves." At 65 and up, they're saving 9.1 percent. Stretch savers do even better. The maximum contribution allowed in 2019 was $19,000 plus another $6,000 if you're 50 or older.[1] Realistically, that's too high an annual goal for many workers. But you can probably raise the amount that you're contributing now. Ask your employer to deposit another 2 or 3 percent of your pay into the plan. Odds are, you won't even miss the money after a couple of months have passed. Vanguard reports that women, well aware of their longevity, save a larger percentage of their pay than men on earnings of $50,000 and up.

The type of plan that you have available depends on where you work. Businesses generally offer 401(k)s.[2] Public school teachers, university employees, and employees of certain other tax-exempt institutions get 403(b)s. Certain state and local governments provide 457s. These plans differ slightly in their contribution and withdrawal rules and often in the range of investments available. But they all defer the tax on your earnings.

Some companies let you put more than the dollar limit into your 401(k). You get no tax deduction for the excess but the investment earnings build up tax deferred. When you leave the company, you can roll the money into an individual retirement account (see page 204).

If you're a middle-income employee and participate in a company plan such as a 401(k), you're allowed to fund a personal IRA on the side. You could start the IRA and tax deduct your full contribution if you're single and your modified adjusted gross income didn't exceed $64,000 in 2019. There's a partial deduction for employees with incomes up to $74,000. For marrieds filing jointly,

---

1   These numbers rise with inflation every year unless inflation is very low. Contribution limits for the year immediately ahead are usually issued by the IRS around mid-October. You can find them at IRS.gov.

2   These plans are all named after sections in the Internal Revenue Code.

the limits were $103,000 for the full deduction and up to $123,000 for the partial. If you are married to someone with a workplace plan and have no plan of your own, the income caps for tax-deductible IRA contributions are even higher.

If you work for a company and have freelance income on the side, you can start an IRA for that separate income regardless of the size of your regular paycheck. If your outside earnings are substantial, consider a simplified employee pension (SEP-IRA) or a solo 401(k) rather than a regular IRA.

If you have no employee plan, invest in an individual retirement account. The basic IRA is stingier than the 401(k) but for the average earner it works just fine. You could contribute up to $6,000 in 2019, or up to $7,000 if you were 50 or older (that's called the "catch-up" provision). If you're married and your spouse has no earnings, he or she can put away up to the same amounts in a personal spousal IRA (with money provided by you). That adds up to as much as $14,000 in savings per couple.

Note: You can't put anything more into an IRA than you actually earn. If your part-time job pays, say, $4,500, that's your maximum contribution.

If you have a 457 plan, your annual contribution limits are the same as those for an IRA, with this exception. You may be able to contribute up to twice the maximum amount in the three years before you reach the plan's normal retirement age (if the plan allows it), provided that you haven't previously used the "catch-up" provision for those 50 and up.

The savings options brighten if you're self-employed and earn a substantial income. You might start a SEP-IRA (handled like an IRA) with a maximum contribution of up to $56,000 in 2019. If you work with your spouse you can each fund an account. Any other employees have to be included in the plan, on the same terms and at your expense, if they worked for you in at least three of the past five years.

Even better, consider a solo 401(k) if you have no employees except possibly a spouse. There you could contribute as much as $56,000 in 2019, plus $6,000 if you were 50 or older, plus a second account for your spouse.

Annual contributions are not required with either of these plans. You can put in zero if your business had a bad year.

Where to find individual plans: IRAs, SEP-IRAs, and solo 401(k)s can be had from mutual fund groups, investment firms, financial advisers, banks, and insurance companies. I vote for the plans offered by no-load (no sales charge) mutual fund groups, such as Vanguard, Fidelity, and T. Rowe Price, or full-service discount brokers, such as Charles Schwab and TD Ameritrade. They'll charge you lower fees for services and investment products than if you go through advisers who earn sales commissions. The lower your costs the higher your long-term returns.

Funding an individual IRA takes discipline. There's no employer to do it for you by sluicing the money out of your paycheck and into your IRA account. The best way to protect yourself against your desire to spend is to set up your own automatic savings plan. Make the IRA contributions through your online bank account, on whatever schedule suits your paycheck. Or authorize your IRA trustee to take the monthly amounts out of your checking account.

Small business alert! The 2018 business tax cut law allows certain small businesses (qualifying as "pass-throughs") to deduct up to 20 percent of their business income. If you do so, however, you'll reduce the value of your contributions to employer-sponsored retirement plans, including SEP-IRAs and solo 401(k)s. Effectively, you'll wind up with a partial deduction for your contribution but will have to pay taxes on the full amount when you draw the money out. That could make Roths more valuable than tax-deferred plans. There are lots of angles here that only an accountant can sort out.

Spouse Alert! If your spouse dies while holding an employee 401(k) or similar plan, you inherit the money automatically. That is, unless you signed one of the plan's consent forms allowing the money to be left to someone else (think carefully, before doing so). Some solo 401(k) plans also include automatic spouse protection, but check.

No spouse protection is built into IRAs or SEP-IRAs in most states. The owner of the account can normally leave it to anyone he or she wants, inside or outside the family. To be on the safe side, ask your mate to get a copy of the IRA beneficiary form that he or she signed, to see where the money will go. Sometimes spouses are cut out of their inheritances by accident (see page 223).

Spouses have a half interest in an IRA that's a marital asset if you live in one of the community-property states.[3] The half interest retained by the worker can be left to anyone. But if your mate put someone else's name on the beneficiary form, you will have to fight for your half of the money. The plan trustee has to follow the beneficiary form unless ordered otherwise by a court. If, say, a husband left the whole IRA to his children from a previous marriage and the money was paid out, you'd have to sue the children. You can agree to have your share of the IRA go to someone else, but it has to be in writing, notarized, and filed with the plan trustee.

Nonspouse inheritor alert! If the owner of the 401(k) dies and there's no spouse or named beneficiary, the plan has rules on who gets the money. It might descend generationally. It might depend on

---

3   Alaska, Arizona, California, Idaho, Louisiana, Nevada, New Mexico, Texas, Washington State, and Wisconsin.

the will (assuming there is one). You might have to jump through hoops to prove that you're entitled to inherit.

My plea to everyone with an employee retirement plan: Fill out the darned beneficiary form! Make multiple copies. Store it all over the place so that heirs can find it (and in case the plan loses the form, which happens). Make sure you have forms from any 401(k)s you left with former employers, too. If they're lost, or blank, or wrong—well, you're dead and don't care. But your family sure will. They'll lose money you intended them to have.

RETIREMENT PLANS AND TAXES: PICK YOUR POISON

Retirement savings plans come in two versions: traditional plans and Roths. They're differently taxed. Which is the better bet depends on how you see your retirement income playing out.

Traditional Plans

Traditional IRAs, 401(k)s, and similar plans make up the bulk of retirement accounts. Contributions are deductible on your tax return. The money you put away grows tax deferred. When you start drawing it out, it's taxed at your ordinary income rate. That's the whole deal. No taxes now but definitely taxes later.

These accounts are intended, specifically, to help you retire. You'll generally pay a 10 percent penalty in addition to income taxes, if you withdraw money before you reach age 59½. The penalty is waived in certain circumstances such as disability.

You're not required to take withdrawals until age 70½.[4] After

---

4   Congress might raise this age to 72. Watch for it.

that, the tax man cometh. You have to start taking out money in an increasing percentage every year. The amounts are dictated by the IRS and depend on your age (and the age of your spouse, if he or she has been the sole beneficiary of the account for at least one year and is at least 10 years younger than you are). Generally, the minimum required withdrawal starts at a little less than 4 percent.

Your plan's trustee will tell you how much you have to take. If you're holding more than one 401(k), you have to draw the proper percentage from each one individually. If you have more than one traditional IRA, however, you can take the total required withdrawal from just one of the accounts or from any combination of them. You can do the same if you have more than one 403(b). But you have to keep the types separate. You can't count a withdrawal from a 403(b) toward the amount you have to take from your traditional IRA.

Be sure to get the numbers right. The IRS squashes people who don't make their withdrawals on time. As a fine, it takes 50 percent of the money you should have taken from your plan but didn't. To make it easier to keep track, consolidate your retirement accounts. Your 401(k), 403(b), and 457 can all be rolled into a single IRA.

Naturally, there are tiny differences among these plans. What's a tax code for if not to complicate things? Here are three: (1) If you hold a 401(k) or 403(b) and leave your job at age 55 or older, you can make penalty-free withdrawals as long as you stay in the plan. You don't have to wait until age 59½. (2) If you hold a 457 plan and have left your job, there's no early withdrawal penalty at any age. (3) If you hold a traditional IRA and are under 59½, you can take out money penalty free at any time by using a rule called 72t. You can also use it for a company plan such as a 401(k), if you've left the company.

Rule 72t is a godsend for people who need money early but perhaps for only a few years. No early withdrawal penalty is due provided that the amount you take would result in "substantially equal"[5] payments over your lifetime (or the joint lifetimes of you and the IRA's beneficiary). What's especially valuable is that you don't have to make these withdrawals permanent. You can stop or reduce them if they've been running for at least five years or when you reach 59½, whichever is longer. That lets you use IRA funds for short-term needs—for example, to pay your bills while you're looking for a new job or until Social Security starts—without depleting the entire account.

Note that you're avoiding only the 10 percent early withdrawal penalty. Any money you take out of a traditional IRA, at any time, remains taxable at your ordinary income rate. Your heirs will be taxed on withdrawals, too, but won't owe the 10 percent penalty.

Roth IRA Plans

Roths have a different story to tell. There's no tax deduction for the money you put in. All the earnings grow tax free. In fact, they can grow tax free for the rest of your life. You're never required to take money out. Heirs who inherit Roths can take advantage of its tax-free accumulations, too.

Another plus is that you can withdraw your own contribution at any time and at any age without penalty, so you always have ready

---

5   There's more than one way of calculating "substantially equal" payments and the method chosen makes a huge difference to the amount you can take each month. The IRS's free Publication 590-B, "Individual Retirement Arrangements," leads you through the numbers for one of the methods, although, if it were me, I'd throw in the towel and ask an accountant or planner. Even the IRS threw in the towel. Pub 590-B advises that you see a professional if you want to consider the two other methods.

access to your savings. If, say, you put $5,000 into a Roth today and suddenly find that you need the money, you can take it right out again, no muss, no fuss.[6] You can take out the earnings on your Roth investment tax free provided that you've passed 59½ and have held the Roth for at least five years. It takes only one small investment to start the five-year clock. From that point on, you're covered for all additions to the account as well as for any new Roths you establish.

You can find Roth versions of IRAs and solo 401(k)s. Many companies offer Roth 401(k)s to their employees. Unfortunately, they're not yet common in 403(b)s, 457s, and similar plans, which generally are slower to adapt.

Any employee can contribute to the Roth version of a company retirement plan.

There are income limits on who's allowed to start an individual Roth IRA, but they're so generous that most people qualify. In 2019, singles could contribute the full IRA amount to the Roth (see page 188) if their modified adjusted gross income didn't exceed $122,000 and a partial amount on incomes up to $137,000. For married couples filing jointly, the income limits were $193,000 for the full contribution and up to $203,000 for the partial.

If you're an employee who's contributing to the company plan and earns more than the limit, there's a backdoor way to set up an individual Roth IRA. You can start a traditional IRA, which will be nondeductible because of your high earnings level, then transfer that money immediately into a Roth. There are no income limits

---

6   You will get a 1099-R form from your IRA trustee, which might make you fear that you're being taxed. You aren't, but you have to report it properly on your tax return. The 1099-R shows code J for an early withdrawal. You show the withdrawal on your 1040, on the line that asks about IRA income. In the space next to it, that asks how much tax you owe on that money, put down zero. Fill out IRS Form 8606 for nondeductible IRAs and file it with your return.

on transfers. (Some taxes will be due, however, if you have owned a traditional IRA for a while.)

Should you take the traditional IRA or the Roth if you have a choice?

Consider the Roth for several reasons. You always have cost-free access to your own contributions if you need them. Tax-free income feels like a triumph when you retire. Withdrawals from a Roth don't count toward your "combined income" (see page 84) when you're figuring whether your Social Security checks are taxable (withdrawals from regular IRAs do count). There are no age requirements for withdrawals. You can leave the money to heirs tax free.

On the other hand, consider a traditional plan if you're in a high tax bracket and expect to be in a lower bracket when you retire. It's advantageous to take the deduction while your earnings are still high.

Should you mix it up?

If your employer offers both a traditional plan and a Roth you can, if you want, allocate part of your contribution to each. The traditional plan gives you a tax deduction now, the Roth gives you tax-free income in the future. If your employer matches the money you put up, a match using company stock will always go into a traditional plan, so you might wind up with both types, like it or not. (Note that you might have to stay with the company for three to six years to collect the entire matching amount.)

If you're offered only a traditional plan, you might put in just enough money to cover the full employer match. For the rest of your annual contribution, consider starting a Roth IRA outside the plan. Once you've put your annual maximum into the Roth, you can return to your employer plan in order to save even more.

If your employer doesn't offer a match, set aside enough of your paycheck to join the plan—perhaps 3 percent. After that, consider an independent Roth. This approach makes sense, however, only if you *will* fund the Roth! If you find that you're slacking on your contributions, forget the Roth and increase the amounts you're putting into the company plan. There's nothing like automatic payroll deductions to build up a retirement account.

If you're still on the company payroll past 70½, you can keep making contributions to your 401(k). No withdrawals are required until you leave the job. You can also contribute to Roth IRAs as long as you have earnings. The same is true for 457 and solo 401(k) plans.

With traditional IRAs, by contrast, 70½ is the witching age. Contributions stop and withdrawals start, even if you're still at work.[7] Keep making contributions as long as you have earnings.

INVESTING YOUR RETIREMENT PLAN

I'll reserve most of my comments on investment strategies for Chapter 9. Here I'll just outline the choices you're likely to have to make when managing your retirement plan.

- Employer 401(k) plans provide you with a menu of mutual funds to choose from—usually 10 or more. You're expected to diversify your contribution among the various investment types—large stocks, small stocks, international stocks, bonds, and so on. Often, employers provide online tools to help you decide what percentage of your money to keep in each type of fund. For more on this decision—called "asset allocation"—see page 246. Keep it simple. Two to four funds will usually do. Look for the lowest cost options.

---

7   Congress is considering allowing contributions to continue past 70½. Stay tuned.

- Most of the mutual funds in retirement plans are "managed funds," meaning that they're run by investment professionals. These managers try to pick the stocks and bonds that will beat the market. Good luck with that. They generally miss (see page 273). They also carry higher costs, especially those that invest primarily in funds created by their parent investment firm.

- If you're lucky, your company's menu will include "index funds." These funds, essentially run by computer, invest in the market as a whole. Years and years of studies show that the returns from index funds beat a large majority of similar funds run by professional managers. They're also lower cost. You can read more about index funds on page 269. A sound 401(k) buy would be a set of three core index funds that cover all the main markets: U.S. stocks, international stocks, and high-quality U.S. bonds.

- Another good choice is a target-date mutual fund, if your company offers them. Target-date funds contain both stocks and bonds in a mix considered appropriate for your age. As the years go by, your fund gradually shifts away from stocks and toward fixed-income investments. It's one-stop shopping. The best target-dates use index funds as their primary investment vehicle. Others use managed funds—often those tied to their parent investment firm. If you don't choose a 401(k) investment when you're first hired, you might be defaulted into a target-date fund automatically. For more on target-date funds and how to use them, see page 292. Larger plans might include collective investment trusts (CITs—you'll see "Trust" or "Tr" in the name). They cost less to run, which makes them top deals if invested in index or target-date funds.

- A few plans offer funds invested in sectors of the stock market, such as health care, real estate, or technology. Index investors don't need to buy these sectors separately. Your index fund owns them all. Why duplicate what you have already? You might also find emerging markets funds covering companies in Southeast Asia, Latin America, Eastern Europe, and Africa. Again, don't buy them separately. They're probably included in your plan's broad international fund.

- Special-sector funds on the fixed-income side might include a short-term bond fund (see page 266), a high-yield bond fund, which invests in the bonds of lower-quality companies (see page 288), and a stable-value fund, backed by insurance companies and paying a fixed rate of interest.

- For those who want professionally managed portfolios (other than target-date funds), a growing number of plans offer personally managed accounts. At a cost of perhaps 0.25 to 0.6 percentage points a year (or more!), managers will choose funds for you and change them as needed. That's on top of the underlying costs of the funds themselves. To be worth their fee, these managers should take all your financial assets into consideration, not just the money in your 401(k). In general, they're for people with a high net worth who might otherwise choose a personal financial adviser. Be warned: You might be shifted out of your target-date fund and into a managed account automatically when you reach a certain age or 401(k) balance. Don't accept the switch if it will cost you more.

- If your plan offers stock in your company, avoid buying anything more than a small amount of it—say, 5 percent of your investments or less. Both your job *and* your retirement savings shouldn't ride on just one company's success. If your company uses stock to match your contribution, you don't have to keep it. Exchange it for mutual funds. It's not disloyal. Your employer won't care.

- Your plan might also provide a brokerage house window. That lets you put part or all of your 401(k) into the hands of a stockbroker or financial adviser to be managed independently. Your "reward" will be higher costs and probably poorer results than if you had stuck with index funds or target-date funds. (That's an editorial comment.)

- A handful of plans let you put part of your money into a deferred-income annuity that eventually will provide you with an income for life. For more on deferred-income annuities, also known as longevity insurance, see page 153.

- The splendid Thrift Savings Plan (TSP) for federal government workers offers target-date funds invested only in index funds. The mix includes government bonds, corporate bonds, large-company stocks, medium and small company stocks, and international stocks. Participants can also invest in these funds separately if they want a different mix from the ones that the target-date funds supply. The Thrift Savings Plan is the simplest, finest, and lowest cost retirement plan on the planet.

- Some public school teachers and state and local employees with 403(b) and 457 plans can choose from a mix of mutual funds. Others aren't so lucky. The majority of these plans restrict your investments to tax-deferred annuities. There are fixed annuities with an interest rate that appears attractive but might drop to a below-market rate in the future. There are also variable annuities that let you put your money into stock funds, bond funds, and short-term money market instruments.

In general, these 403(b) and 457 annuities are lousy deals. They're larded with fees that chop your investment returns. There's usually a penalty if you switch your money to another type of investment before five or more years have passed. You might be drawn into these annuities because you're approached by a colleague who sells them on commission. Trust me, your colleague is doing you no favors. Before you sign up, ask your employer for a list of your investment choices. Choose mutual funds (preferably index funds) if they're available. If not, go for the lowest-cost annuity on the list and petition your employer to do better by you.[8]

- Many college and university employees are offered excellent 403(b)s. They're often invested with TIAA, a low-cost investment company that provides a sensible mix of mutual funds and inexpensive annuities. Almost without exception, the university-based economists, professors, and financial researchers I speak with are invested entirely in index funds, usually with TIAA (some have switched to Vanguard).

- Many 401(k) and 403(b) plans carry high annual and investment fees. If your plan falls into that category and there's no employee match, you might consider saving in a low-cost Roth IRA outside the plan, provided that you're within the income limits (see page 194). To find out how your plan's fees and options stand up to the competition, check the 401(k) Ratings Directory at BrightScope.com.

- If your spouse also has retirement accounts, don't invest as if you live on different planets. Assuming that you'll go off together into the sunset, your plans should complement each other. For example, say that you like the idea of holding 60 percent in stocks and 40 percent in bonds for a couple your age. That's the way you allocate your own 401(k). But, unknown to you, your spouse's plan might be 100 percent in stocks—perhaps because he or she hasn't looked at it for many years. As a couple, you're farther out on an investment limb than you'd like. On a rainy Sunday, fire up your laptops

---

8 Congress is considering legislation that would help 401(k) plans add annuities. Whether they will be better than 403(b) annuities remains to be seen. Buyers might run into complications when required minimum withdrawals from your retirement plan begin (see page 220).

(or pull out your printed plan documents), reevaluate each plan's investment options, and work out a combined asset allocation that makes sense to you both.

• If you have an independent IRA, a financial adviser might suggest that you invest all or part of it in a variable annuity. The pitch: The gains from the mutual funds in your annuity will accumulate tax deferred. But the gains in your IRA are already tax deferred. All the annuities do are add costs. You'd make this choice only if you're buying the annuity as an investment that you expect will increase substantially in value (see page 162).

USING A SELF-DIRECTED IRA

A self-directed IRA opens you to a wider range of investments than is offered by mutual fund groups. A plan at a brokerage firm, for example, lets you buy almost any of the firm's products—not only individual stocks but also the structured notes, annuities, partnerships, and other exotics on offer, usually at high cost. Awful stuff. Personally, I wouldn't touch 'em.

If you want to buy gold, you have to open an IRA with a trustee willing to handle that type of investment. Your trustee can purchase gold, silver, or platinum bullion coins and bars (but not numismatic coins). All transactions have to be entirely independent of you, your relatives, or any businesses you own. For example, you can't sell to the IRA coins you already possess. You can't hold the coins in your personal safe-deposit box; they have to be kept in an approved depository at the IRA's expense. If you violate the rules and the IRS finds out, your tax shelter will blow up. Then, the entire sum in the IRA could become taxable in the current year plus a 10 percent penalty if you're under 59½.

Self-directed IRAs can also be used for holding business interests, such as shares in a movie deal, private equity, and startups. The trustees who manage these kinds of investments often double as the agents selling the deals. They earn fees from them, which the IRA pays. Buyer beware.

IRAs are not allowed to purchase collectibles, such as gems, antiques, rare books, or art. Nor is an IRA allowed to hold life insurance.

Real Estate and the Self-Directed IRA

You can use IRA money to invest in rental real estate and other properties. But why would you want to? The rules make it costly to hold real estate in an IRA, especially when compared with buying real estate stocks.

For example, you need a trustee willing to oversee the IRA and a manager to handle the property for you. It has to be purchased with IRA funds. Mortgage lenders don't like IRA real estate, so it's probably going to be a cash transaction. All rental income goes back to the IRA, and the IRA pays all the expenses. The account will have to hold some cash in case your property doesn't throw off enough rent to cover the monthly bills. It also needs cash for unexpected expenses such as repair costs if a tenant damages the place. If you still have earnings from a job, you can provide the IRA with some ready money by making annual contributions. If you're not working, you'll have to be prepared to transfer money into your real estate IRA from another IRA if cash runs short. You normally can't get a home equity loan on the IRA's property. If you do find a mortgage, the portion of the profits financed by the loan becomes unrelated taxable business income, with the tax paid from the IRA every year. An IRA can't deduct capital losses or the property's expenses, including depreciation. Any profit is fully taxable. You can't take advantage of the low tax on capital gains.

It's essential that you and your close relatives not be connected with the property in any way. The IRA can't buy it from you, rent it to you, or let you use it rent free. You can't manage the property or put sweat equity into it—all work has to be done by outside contractors. You can't collect the rents yourself or even change a lightbulb or repair the steps. If you do, you can be nuked by the IRS. A traditional IRA would collapse; you'd owe taxes on its entire value. If you're using a Roth IRA, no taxes would be due but you'd lose the tax shelter on all future gains.

Real estate is especially risky for people with traditional IRAs who reach 70½. At that point, you have to start taking your required minimum withdrawal and real estate isn't liquid. If you don't have enough money in other IRA accounts to make the full withdrawal and can't sell the property in time, your required withdrawal might fall short. That triggers a 50 percent penalty on the amount you failed to take. The IRS doesn't accept a letter saying, "Gosh, I couldn't sell the house." You should have thought of that.

Given the complications and expenses, especially the management expense, it's much smarter to hold real estate outside an IRA. That reduces your costs, provides tax deductions, lets you put in sweat equity, and reduces your taxes when you sell. If you ignore all this excellent advice (!), buy your real estate with an IRA set up exclusively for that purpose. If for any reason you make a mistake that causes the real estate IRA to become taxable, the savings in your other IRAs will remain safe and tax deferred.

WHAT TO DO WITH YOUR EMPLOYEE PLAN WHEN YOU LEAVE YOUR JOB

When you leave a job, your number one objective, financially, is to preserve the tax umbrella over your retirement savings. There are seven ways to do this:

1. If you take a new job with an employer who also offers a 401(k), you can move your money into the new employer's plan. Your

old mutual funds will be closed out. You'll choose new ones, and the entire transfer will be tax free. This choice is a good one because it consolidates your retirement savings into a single account. The transfer can be slow and arduous because of the paperwork. But the result is worth it, so keep at it.

2. If you want, you can generally stay with the old 401(k), even after you retire, as long as you have at least $5,000 in the plan. There are pluses and minuses to this choice for retirees. *The pluses:* Your money might be managed at a lower cost than you'd pay elsewhere. You're familiar with the mutual funds. If you're between 55 and 59½, you can generally make withdrawals without penalty. You're in a safe investment world where the financial wolves can't get you. You can get a stable-value or guaranteed-income fund that pays higher rates on savings than money market funds. *The minuses:* There might be limits on how and when you can take the money out, so check the withdrawal rules. Some plans, especially smaller ones, charge higher fees than you'd pay at a no-load mutual fund. You might lose track of the old 401(k) and your heirs might never find it.[9] The office that runs the 401(k) might be less responsive to retirees than to current employees. Be sure to use the same personal email address for your old employee plans and every new one. That makes it easier for plans to keep track of you.

3. Most commonly, people leaving an employee retirement plan transfer the money, tax free, into an IRA known as a "rollover IRA." There's no dollar limit on the amount you can roll. For this new investment, you have several options:

---

9   If your former company was sold or went out of business, you might be able to find out what happened to its 401(k) plan by going to the website of the federal Employee Benefits Security Administration (dol .gov/agencies/ebsa). Under "Topics," click on "Form 5500" (an annual disclosure form for employee-benefit plans), and do a search.

You might choose the IRA offered by the investment company that already administers your plan. That's an especially attractive choice if your plan is being managed by a no-load mutual fund group such as Vanguard or Fidelity, a discount broker such as Charles Schwab, or a low-cost firm that specializes in retirement plans. You can keep the mutual funds you have or choose new ones.

Alternatively, you might roll your 401(k) money into an IRA offered by a different investment firm from the one that your company is using now. The best choices would be the low-cost providers mentioned above. Make the change, for sure, if your current 401(k) is with a firm whose advisers charge sales commissions, even if you're not using those advisers. Such firms often put high-cost mutual funds into their IRAs.

Beware, beware the friendly "advisers" who call, mail, and even visit you at your desk at work. They're usually selling terrible stuff that will make them rich while drenching your retirement dreams. Run away if they mention fixed or variable annuities, nontraded real estate investment trusts, energy partnerships, or private placements. These high-cost, high-commission investments should be off the table (see the importance of fiduciaries—page 34). Also, check the costs of the mutual funds the adviser recommends. They'll probably be a lot higher than those you're paying in your 401(k).

The rules for switching money out of 403(b) or 457 plans are the same as those for 401(k)s. It's easy if your employer allowed you to invest in mutual funds. If your plan held only annuities, however, you might be stuck for a while. There could be surrender charges for removing the money before a certain number of years have passed.

4. If you leave a job and have less than $5,000 in your employee plan, don't ignore it. If you fail to choose a rollover IRA or some other option, the company might make a forced transfer of your

money into an IRA of its own choosing—perhaps one with high fees and low returns. Over time, the balance might decline rather than increase and you risk losing track of it. If you have just a little more than $5,000 in the plan, the company might transfer your money into a low-paying IRA at a later date. Best advice is to roll over small plans into your own IRA. Don't consider staying in the employer plan unless your balances are higher.

If you have less than $1,000 in the employee plan and don't do a rollover, the employer can simply send you a check, which will trigger taxes and perhaps a 10 percent tax penalty if you're under 59½.

5. If you have multiple retirement plans, roll them together into a single IRA. Separately, they're a pain to keep track of and probably add to your costs. Traditional retirement plans can be rolled into traditional IRAs. Roth plans are rolled into Roth IRAs. You can switch a traditional IRA into a Roth but you'll have to pay taxes on the amount of money moved (see page 208).

    If you maxed out on your tax-deductible contributions to your 401(k), some plans allow you to put in money after tax, with the earnings on those contributions tax deferred. When you leave the plan, you can do one of two things: (1) Roll the tax-deferred portion into your new employer's plan or into a traditional IRA. The after-tax contributions can roll into a Roth IRA, tax free. (2) Roll the entire amount into a traditional IRA. In this case, however, when you make withdrawals, you will have to adjust for the portion of the IRA on which you have already paid the tax (such fun!). Always file Form 8606 with your tax return when making after-tax contributions, so the government (and you!) can keep track of what's taxable in your IRA and what isn't.

6. With many 401(k)s, you can ask the plan to send you installment payments for a fixed number of years. Some let you make withdrawals whenever you want. The plan might also offer a

lifetime immediate annuity from a particular insurance company (see Chapter 6). Before saying yes to an annuity, check ImmediateAnnuities.com to see if there's a different insurer that will pay you more per month. A few plans offer deferred-income annuities as one of your investment choices during your working years. When you leave the job, these contracts will remain in force.

7. Keep track of your beneficiary form! You cannot count on the company to do it for you. If the form can't be found, and you die, the money will be paid into your estate (see page 217).

8. If you want to buy individual stocks (I hope you don't—see page 279—but just in case), roll your retirement plan into a self-directed IRA with a discount or full-service brokerage firm or financial adviser.

    Note: When you move money from one plan to another, the check should go directly from your old plan to your new one without passing through your hands. The trustee of your new plan will tell you how to do it. If the check goes to you, it's counted as a taxable withdrawal. To avoid paying taxes you have to deposit it into your personal bank account, write a new check, and send it to the new plan within 60 days. Don't try it. Too much can go wrong.

Important tax-saving note for people who own company stock in their retirement plans: If the stock has risen substantially in value, you'll save taxes if you *don't* roll over this portion of your 401(k) into an IRA. Instead, ask the plan to distribute the shares directly to a brokerage account (say, at a discount brokerage firm, including the firms attached to mutual fund groups such as Charles Schwab, Fidelity, and Vanguard). If you do that, you'll owe ordinary income taxes (plus a 10 percent penalty if you're under 55) only on the value of the stock when it first went into your plan. For example, if you hold the stock at an average price of $10 and it's now worth

$30, your ordinary tax rate applies only to the $10. When you sell it, the remaining $20 will be taxed at the low capital gains rate. If you had rolled that stock into an IRA, you'd owe ordinary income taxes on the entire amount when you took the money out.

There are lots of complications to this tax-smart transaction. Talk to an accountant before making a decision.

SHOULD YOU SWITCH MONEY FROM A TRADITIONAL IRA INTO A TAX-FREE ROTH IRA?

You can roll any amount of money from a traditional IRA, 401(k), or similar plan into a tax-free Roth IRA regardless of how much income you earn. There's a cost to this transfer, however—perhaps a big one. You pay current income taxes on the money you move even though you don't withdraw any of the cash. Sometimes the tax is worth paying, sometimes not.

You might switch to the Roth if: (1) You don't expect to need the money until your later age, if ever. (2) You plan to leave most or all of the Roth to your heirs and want them to receive it tax free. (3) You expect to be in the same (or a higher) tax bracket when you retire, although you can't know for sure. (4) You're young enough so that the future growth in your investments could more than offset the cost of paying the current tax. (5). You're between jobs, so your income (and tax) will be unusually low this year. (6) You can pay the taxes out of pocket without having to take money out of your tax-sheltered retirement account.

You might not switch to the Roth if: (1) You'll have to use funds from the IRA to pay the tax. That greatly reduces the amount of money left to grow tax free. (2) You expect to drop to a lower tax bracket when you retire or move to a state with a low or no income tax. (3) The Medicare tax on the transfer (see facing page) would bump you into a higher bracket. (4) The added income from the transfer might cost you some tax breaks that you get now. (5) You're 65-plus and expect to withdraw a substantial amount of your IRA during your retirement.

In short, Roth conversions are generally great for people who don't need the money and want to pass most of it to heirs tax free. For the average person, however, the size of the current tax might overwhelm any likely benefit from future tax-free growth.

Note that there are no do-overs on Roth conversions. You will owe income taxes on the sums you convert. You might regret your choice later, if you drop into a lower tax bracket or your Roth investments lose money.

If you decide to convert, call up the firm where you keep your traditional IRA and tell it to make the change. Presto, it's now a Roth. If you want to convert only part of your savings, the firm will roll that portion into a separate Roth account. The best way to proceed is to convert just enough money each year so that the extra income you have to report doesn't push you into a higher bracket.

Check all the costs of conversion, not just the income tax cost! An unpleasant surprise lies in wait for people on Medicare who switch a large amount of traditional IRA money into a Roth. That's because the amount of your transfer is added to your taxable income for the year. If it bumps up your income by too much, you'll have to pay a higher premium for Medicare Part B (the medical plan) and Part D (the drug plan). In 2019, you owed a higher premium if you were single with a modified gross income above $85,000 or married filing jointly with an income above $170,000. If your regular income for the year is, say, $50,000 and you convert $120,000 into a Roth, you put yourself into higher-premium territory.

When figuring whether you owe this higher premium, the government looks at the most recent tax return it has available. That generally means that in 2019 your premium is based on the income you reported in 2017. If you're married filing jointly and your spouse is on Medicare, he or shc will pay the higher premium, too. Once you've completed the Roth conversion and your income drops back, your Medicare premium will return to its normal, lower level. (You can apply for relief from the premium increase if your income has declined for certain specific reasons, including losing a job or losing your spouse.)

Next there's the potential higher tax for people on Social Security. The Roth conversion might raise your reported income by enough to increase the tax you owe on your Social Security benefits (see page 84).

Finally, if the sum you convert to a Roth is large enough, it might also lift you into the select group that pays a 3.8 percent tax on unearned income. You're caught if your income for the year exceeds $200,000 for singles and $250,000 for married couples filing jointly. Unearned income includes interest, dividends, capital gains, rent, and so on.

There are plenty of calculators on the Web that purport to show you whether it's worth converting to a Roth but none of the ones I've looked at include the potentially higher Medicare and Social Security costs or the tax on unearned income. So don't make a move without talking to a tax accountant. Roth conversions aren't a game for amateurs.

WHEN YOU'RE TAKING MONEY FROM SAVINGS TO PAY YOUR BILLS, WHICH TYPE OF ACCOUNT SHOULD YOU TAP FIRST?

Retirees have many possible sources of income: Social Security, taxable savings and investment accounts, tax-deferred retirement accounts such as traditional IRAs, and Roth IRAs that grow tax free. The more tax-efficiently you use your money, the longer your nest egg will last. Here are some general rules on which accounts to tap first:

- Normally, spend taxable savings before dipping into a traditional IRA or similar account. "Taxable savings" means money that's not held in a tax-deferred or tax-free retirement account. You'll owe taxes only on the interest, dividends, or capital gains those investment have achieved. The principal is returned to you tax free.

- There are a couple of times when you should tap a traditional IRA first, before using taxable savings. For example: (1) You're in a low tax bracket and your heirs are in a high one. The IRA money is worth more if you take it now. (2) You want to shrink your IRA so that, when you reach 70½, the required withdrawals won't be as large. That might save you from paying a higher tax on your Social Security benefits when IRA withdrawals start.

- If you're in the low, 12-percent tax bracket, consider withdrawing extra money from your IRA even if you don't need it now. You'd take just enough to keep yourself in that same bracket without going over. Take it from the stock funds you own and reinvest it in stock funds in your taxable account. From this point on, you'll get the low capital gains rate on their increase in value.

- Spend taxable and tax-deferred savings if that helps you put off taking Social Security until you reach 70½ if you're single, or perhaps 66 to 70½ if you're married. At older ages, you will get the highest possible individual or family benefits for life.

- Normally, tap a traditional IRA before tapping a Roth. The longer the Roth can grow tax free the better. But tap the Roth first if you're in a particularly high tax bracket and expect your bracket to drop in future years.

- If you have both a taxable and a tax-deferred account for long-term investments, stuff the taxable account with stocks. That way, your profits will be taxed at the low rate for capital gains. All your taxable bonds, such as Treasury funds, go into the tax-deferred account. Interest income is taxed at ordinary income rates no matter where the bonds are held.

DID YOU INHERIT AN IRA? HERE'S HOW TO STRETCH ITS FABULOUS TAX SHELTER OVER YOUR ENTIRE LIFETIME

The tax breaks in an IRA don't have to end when the owner dies. If you inherit an IRA, most or all of the money you receive can continue to grow tax deferred or tax free. To get these lifetime tax breaks, however, you have to play your cards right.

You've played your cards wrong if, dazzled by the inheritance, you cash out of the IRA and pop the proceeds into your bank or investment account. Any money you remove from a traditional IRA becomes current income. You'll have to report it and pay the taxes all at once. Most likely it will push you into a higher bracket, which can eat up your inheritance fast. Generally, no taxes are due if you cash out of an inherited Roth IRA, but you lose the right to let the money grow tax free in future years.

You will probably want to take at least some of your inheritance for current use. But anything you intend to save or invest should stay cradled in its tax shelter. Here's how to handle an IRA you inherit, be it a traditional IRA or a Roth.

If you inherit an IRA from your spouse, you have four choices:

1. Treat the IRA as your own, telling the trustee to change the name on the account. You'd do this if you're happy with the cost and services of the current IRA plan. You don't have to keep the same investments. You can look over the menu of mutual funds the plan offers and make different choices.
2. Roll the money into a new IRA in your name, income tax free.

You'd do this if you're not happy with the current plan and want to switch. For example, you might want to leave the broker that your spouse used and reinvest with a no-load mutual fund group. The new firm will help with the transfer.

3. Roll the money into an IRA you hold already. You'd do this to consolidate your accounts. Traditional IRAs can be rolled into other traditional IRAs tax free. Roths can be rolled into Roths.

4. There's a special option for spouses who inherit a traditional IRA when they are under 59½. Normally, people that young cannot make withdrawals without paying a 10 percent tax penalty. But if you need money now, you can avoid the penalty by retitling the account as an "Inherited IRA." An "Inherited IRA" is a legal term of art. Instead of putting only your own name on the account, you retitle it using both your name and the name of the spouse you inherited from. For a rundown of all the rules, see page 214. *Please note:* If you make this choice you should retitle the IRA again when you reach 59½, putting it into your name alone. That gives you the option of stopping withdrawals and waiting until you're 70½ to start again. Holding the IRA in your own name also gives your beneficiaries maximum flexibility for timing their own withdrawals from what remains of the IRA, when you die.

What if you're under 59½ and you inherit a Roth IRA? Don't bother retitling it as an Inherited IRA. You can draw out your spouse's contributions at any time and at any age without penalty. That will probably be enough to satisfy your immediate need for cash. There's a penalty only if you withdraw the earnings on the contributions if you're under 59½ and your spouse held the IRA for fewer than five years.

Spouses who inherit an IRA should name new beneficiaries right away. For example, you might name your kids. Once their names are on the account, they'll be able to continue using the IRA tax shelter at your death. If you die before naming new beneficiaries, the money will usually go into your estate, where complications arise (see page 217). Always use the IRA's official beneficiary form. That's the only way of passing the tax shelter to your heirs (see page 223).

If you inherit an IRA from someone other than a spouse—for example, from your parent or life partner:

You're not allowed to roll the money into an IRA of your own. Instead, you have two choices:

1.   Take your full inheritance out of the IRA right away. That might make sense if the amount is small and you need the cash. If it's a traditional IRA, you'll pay income taxes on the money in the current year. Nonspouse beneficiaries *do not* pay penalties for withdrawals made when they're younger than 59½. If you inherit a Roth IRA and cash it in, no taxes are due.

2.   Retitle the account as an "Inherited IRA"—a legal entity that keeps the tax shelter going. That's a terrific option, especially for sizable IRAs. Once established, the Inherited IRA lets your investments continue to grow, tax free or tax deferred. Each year, you're required to withdraw at least a minimum amount based on your life expectancy. In mid-life, however, the minimums are small. At 40, you'd have to withdraw only about 1/44th of the amount. The next year, 1/43rd of the amount, and so on. Potentially, the shelter can last as long as you live.[10] When you die, your heirs can put any remaining money into an Inherited IRA

---

10 That is, unless Congress changes the law. Proposals in Congress would require nonspouse beneficiaries to withdraw Inherited IRA money over as few as five years or, perhaps, ten years. If passed, it would presumably grandfather heirs who are using the stretched-out withdrawal rules today. Even with a shorter withdrawal period, however, the Inherited IRA is worth doing.

of their own. *To reach this happy result, however, you have to get the paperwork right!* One small slip and the shelter will collapse, forcing you to take the money (and pay any taxes) all at once. Check out the rules, below.

The All-Important Rules for Creating Inherited IRAs

The retitling rules for Inherited IRAs are very specific. You have to put your name on the account *as beneficiary* and the name of the account's original owner. It's helpful to include the date the original owner died. That's true both for a traditional IRA and a Roth.

Here's an example of how the rules work if you inherit money from someone other than your spouse:

Emily Jones dies, leaving her IRA to her son, Riley. The account should be retitled "Emily Jones IRA (deceased February 2, 2019) for the benefit of Riley Jones, beneficiary." If Emily has another son, Justin, and leaves half the IRA to each of them, Riley would title his half as shown above. Justin would title his half "Emily Jones IRA (deceased February 2, 2019) for the benefit of Justin Jones, beneficiary." The wording can change a little bit, but the same essential facts must be there.

If you're inheriting from your spouse, you'd set up an Inherited IRA only if you're younger than 59½ and want to start drawing out money right away. Here's how the rules would apply to you:

Matthew Smith leaves his wife, Amanda, a traditional IRA worth $150,000. The account should be retitled, "Matthew Smith IRA (deceased January 5, 2019) for the benefit of Amanda Smith, beneficiary." That allows her to make early withdrawals without paying the 10 percent tax penalty. If Amanda's financial adviser makes a mistake, however, and retitles it just plain "Amanda Smith," it becomes her personal IRA. In that case, she won't be able to avoid the early withdrawal penalty until she passes 59½. Mistakes are not unusual, so keep an eye on this.

What if you're the second-generation beneficiary of an Inherited IRA? You, too, can keep the tax shelter going. All you have to do is retain the name of the original owner when you retitle. For example:

Riley Jones, son of Emily, dies. Emily had left him her personal IRA, which he converted into an Inherited IRA. He made six years' worth of withdrawals before his death. Riley's daughter, Rebecca (Emily's granddaughter), inherits. She's allowed to convert the account into an Inherited IRA of her own. The proper new title would be "Emily Jones IRA (deceased February 2, 2019) for the benefit of Rebecca Jones, beneficiary." Rebecca can't restart the clock by taking withdrawals based on her own life expectancy. However, she can complete the withdrawals that her father, Riley, was entitled to over his lifetime. The assets in that single IRA account could eventually be stretched over 80 tax-free years or more (assuming that Congress doesn't change the law). Note that you don't have to limit your withdrawals to the minimum required. You can take any larger amount you want, in any year. Choosing the minimum, however, preserves more of the money for your older age.

Withdrawals from Inherited IRAs have to start right away. You can't delay them until you reach 70½.

Super important! Don't make contributions to your Inherited IRA! If you do, you'll blow up the tax shelter and everything will be taxed at once. If you're eligible to make annual IRA contributions, put them into a separate account.

If you inherit money from a 401(k), 403(b), or similar employee plan:

The tax rules are the same as if you inherited an IRA. Spouses can roll the money into an IRA in their own names. Nonspouse beneficiaries, who want to preserve the tax shelter, can roll the money into an Inherited IRA. There will be complications, however, if your 403(b) is invested in an annuity. You might be hobbled by the annuity's terms, such as surrender penalties.

IF YOU'RE THE PERSON WHO STARTED THE IRA, HOW CAN YOU HELP PRESERVE THE ACCOUNT FOR YOUR HEIRS WHEN YOU DIE?

Four tips:

1. Name one or more beneficiaries for every IRA account you own, using the account's official beneficiary form. If your spouse is the beneficiary, he or she can turn the money into a personal IRA. If you name someone other than a spouse, specify percentages—for example, "one-third to each of my three children, Kai, Juno, and Dion." Name names! At your death, the children can ask the IRA trustee to split the account into three pieces so each of them can set up an Inherited IRA of his or her own. If more children are possible, you might say "to all my children, in equal amounts."

   Make sure that the beneficiary form jibes with the provisions of your will. If there's a difference between the two, the people named on the beneficiary form will get the money (see page 223).

   Don't leave the beneficiary form blank! If you do, here's what will probably happen. (1) Your IRA money will be paid into your estate and distributed according to the terms of your will. A cash distribution would be taxable all at once. (2) The estate can roll the money into an IRA for your spouse but he or she might need to get an IRS ruling approving it (cost: $10,000 and up), which takes time. (3) Nonspouse heirs might also need an IRS ruling to have their share rolled into Inherited IRAs. And they won't be able to stretch the distributions over their lifetimes. They'll have to take the money over just five years or the remaining expected lifetime of the deceased IRA holder, depending on when he or she died. (4) Money from traditional IRAs is taxed as income to the beneficiaries in the current year. Money from a Roth is not taxed, but if the beneficiaries have to remove it over, say, five years, they lose the option of letting it accumulate tax free for many years more. (5) The estate will have to do a special tax return. (6) It's all a mess, just because you didn't fill in the beneficiary form.

2.   File copies of the IRA beneficiary form with your plan trustee, your lawyer, your financial adviser, and in a place in your home where your heirs will find it. Do not expect the IRA trustee to keep track. If the form can't be found, the proceeds will be paid into your estate. It will be as if you had left the beneficiary form blank.

3.   Tell your heirs about the Inherited IRA option and what it can do for them. You might even leave a letter with a copy of your will. There's no guarantee that your beneficiaries will know about Inherited IRAs. Their financial advisers might not know, either.

4.   You can name a trust as beneficiary of your IRA, but do it only if you have a very good reason. Trusts are complicated and expensive. You'll need an experienced estate-planning attorney to avoid wrong-footing the many IRS rules. One mistake and the IRA's tax shelter could blow up.

     Trusts are worth their cost if you're leaving the IRA to young children who aren't capable of handling money. Or you want the income from the money to go to your second spouse, with the principal going to children from your former marriage when the second spouse dies. Or your beneficiaries are spendthrifts or have drug problems. For a simple inheritance, however, leave the trust out of it.

IS MY IRA SAFE?

Yes. By law, your investments are kept in a separate trust, not mixed with the assets of the investment company. If the company goes broke, your accounts are protected.

DEFEND YOURSELF FROM FINANCIAL "ADVISERS"!

I'd guess that the majority of advisers—brokers, planners, mutual fund call centers, insurance agents—know almost nothing about the rules for Inherited IRAs. They might tell you to roll the money into an IRA of your own, which you can't do if you're not the IRA owner's spouse. They might say there's nothing to do except take the money and pay the tax, which you now know is wrong. They might "help" you by putting the money directly into your own name, making it taxable immediately or costing you the tax-free gains provided by a Roth. If you make a mistake based on bad advice, tough luck. It can almost never be undone. For more details on inheriting IRAs, I recommend two books, both by retirement plan experts: *The Retirement Savings Time Bomb . . . and How to Defuse It (2020 edition)* by Ed Slott and *The $214,000 Mistake: How to Double Your Social Security & Maximize Your IRAs, Proven Strategies for Couples Ages 62–70* by James Lange. You need to know the rules yourself to be sure that your adviser does the right thing.

AFTER THAT MAGIC AGE . . .

You can't hang on to a traditional retirement plan forever. When you reach age 70½, you have to start taking required minimum distributions (RMDs) every year.[11]

The IRS sets the withdrawal rates. They're intended to empty all your plans over your lifetime or the joint lifetimes of you and your spouse if your spouse is your beneficiary and he or she is more than 10 years younger. For your official federal life expectancy, see the IRS's Uniform Lifetime Table. You can find it on the Web or in the IRS's free Publication 590-B, "Individual Retirement Arrangements"[12]—a guide to how these plans are taxed.

How do you figure your withdrawals? It's a nuisance but not terribly hard—and I say this as one who's allergic to arithmetic. The steps are:

1. What was the value of your IRA last December 31? If this is your first withdrawal, you need the December 31 value before the year you turned 70½. Count any annuities you bought with IRA funds (except qualified longevity annuities—see page 154). For the value of the annuities, you'll need your insurer's help.

2. What is your life expectancy according to the IRS's Uniform Lifetime Table? Use this table if you're unmarried or if your spouse is your beneficiary and is no more than 10 years younger

---

11 Congress is considering changes to many retirement rules—among them, raising the age for RMDs to 72 and allowing workers to continue adding to their IRAs past 70½.

12 Publication 590-A covers putting money into retirement accounts. Publication 590-B covers taking it out. These withdrawal rules apply to money held in all employer-sponsored plans and all IRA-based plans except Roth IRAs.

than you are. If your spouse is more than 10 years younger, use the Joint Life Table.

3. Divide the value of the IRA by your life expectancy. That gives you the minimum withdrawal for the current year.

4. Do this for each traditional IRA, SEP-IRA, and SIMPLE IRA that you have. Add up the results. That's the amount that must be withdrawn. You can take it from one IRA or from several as long as the total dollar amount is met.

5. Go through these same steps for every 403(b) you own. Again, you can take the annual payment from any of your 403(b)s as long as you withdraw the required total amount.

6. If you own more than one type of plan—say an IRA, a 401(k), and a 403(b)—you have to withdraw from them separately. Money taken from an IRA can't satisfy the amount you're supposed to take from your 401(k). You can get rid of all these separate calculations by consolidating your retirement accounts into a single IRA.

7. If you're holding more than one 401(k), you have to take the required minimum from each of them separately. Consider rolling multiple 401(k)s into a single IRA, for ease of management. If you can't or don't want to figure out the proper withdrawals yourself, your retirement plan will usually help. The trustee will calculate the payment and move the money to any account you name. You'll also find calculators on the Web. Or ask an accountant or qualified financial planner.

8. After you turn 70½, you can transfer up to $100,000 directly from your IRA to a qualified charity. It counts toward your required minimum withdrawal but isn't taxed to you as income. Consider this option if you take the standard deduction rather than itemizing and therefore can't deduct these gifts on your tax return.

It's critical that you take at least the minimum required amount each year. If you withdraw too little, you'll be socked with a 50 percent penalty on the sum that you should have taken but didn't (unless you can convince the IRS that you were all thumbs with the life-expectancy tables). Don't wait until the very end of the year for the withdrawal. If there's some sort of delay at the financial institution that's holding your money, you might miss the deadline.

How do you decide which investments to sell when making withdrawals from your retirement accounts? See page 252.

What if you're still working at 70½? In this case, no federal law requires you to start withdrawals from your company plan. You can continue to contribute, assuming that your plan allows it. Normally, withdrawals will begin after you retire. There's an exception for people who own more than 5 percent of the company, including owners of solo 401(k)s. They have to start withdrawals at 70½ even though they're still on the job.

Traditional IRAs work a little differently. Once you reach 70½, you can't make contributions, even though you're still earning a paycheck. You must start taking annual withdrawals. There are no such restrictions on Roth IRAs. You can continue to make contributions past 70½ and never take withdrawals if you don't want to.

What will you do with your RMD if you don't need it right away? Invest it for your own future or for the future of a younger spouse. You can't use the withdrawal to start a new IRA, even if you're still working. But there are plenty of other investment choices. Alternatively, if your spouse is still working, consider using the RMD to help pay your current bills. That might free your spouse to increase the amount he or she puts into a personal IRA or 401(k).

MAKE SURE THAT THE RIGHT PERSON GETS YOUR MONEY!

When you set up an IRA, the paperwork includes a beneficiary form. Don't fail to fill it out. The form normally dictates who gets the money left in the IRA when you die. It trumps what it says in your will or your prenuptial agreement and can even preempt a divorce agreement. It ignores what you've promised or what's fair. In most states, the person or persons named on the IRA beneficiary form inherit the money, period.

Say, for example, that you divorce and remarry. The divorce agreement stipulates that your ex has no claim on your IRA. Your will leaves the money to your second spouse. But you forget to take your ex off the IRA beneficiary form. Too bad for the new spouse. In about half the states, your ex inherits the lot. I've read of cases where the money went to a sibling or a parent instead of to a spouse or child simply because the IRA owner neglected to change a form that he or she created years ago.

There are two exceptions to this rule. The first is for community-property states, where a spouse has a half interest in a plan that's a marital asset (see page 190, footnote number 3). The second exception applies to a handful of states that remove the name of an ex-spouse after the divorce. But state law can be tricky so don't count on it. Fix the beneficiary form yourself.

To change your IRA beneficiary, ask the IRA trustee for a new form. You should name primary and secondary beneficiaries in case the primary beneficiary dies before you have time to change the form (for example, if you and your spouse die in the same accident). It's important to check the wording with the lawyer who drew up your will to be sure that you get the result you want. For example, when leaving an IRA to a child you should probably add the words "per stirpes." That lets your child's children (your grandchildren) inherit if the child dies before you do. Specify "stepchildren" if you want them to inherit, too. Once you've filled in the form, get it witnessed properly and send it back. Do this any time your life circumstances change—for example, if you marry, divorce, have a child, or a beneficiary dies. I know that paperwork is boring and you probably assume that you have plenty of time. But—not to be morbid—you have no idea how much time you have. Now is always the best time to set things right.

8

The Speed Limit on Retirement Spending: Still 4 Percent?

When to step on the gas, when to tap the brakes.

We've reached a central question in retirement planning: How much cash can you take from your nest egg every year without running the risk of eventually going broke? We're talking about your financial nest egg, also known as your "portfolio"—stocks, bonds, mutual funds, certificates of deposit, and so on. The next chapter talks about how to invest these savings for the best results. This one helps you budget by showing how much you can afford to spend. That spending rate is your speed limit. It helps ensure that your money will last as long as you do.

Spending rules are important even when you don't follow them to the letter. They save you from accidentally using up too much of your money when you first retire.

Many retirees manage their spending so well that they don't have to touch their basic savings. Their IRAs remain mostly intact until they're required to start making withdrawals at age 70½, and even then, they take only the required minimum.

The rest of us, however, will depend partly on our savings to pay our monthly bills. It's critical to know how much we can afford to take.

Here's the classic answer to the question: You can take 4 percent of your total financial savings in the first year you retire (or the first year that you start drawing on the money). In each following year, take the same dollar amount plus an increase for inflation. If your investments are well diversified, you can start with 4.5 percent.

That's been the gold standard in financial planning ever since it was developed 25 years ago. It would have carried you through the worst periods that the U.S. economy has endured, measured from the mid-1920s. If you stick to that withdrawal rate and are properly invested, your money should last at least 30 years. For any period better than "the worst," your money will last a lot longer than 30 years. You'll have more to spend in your later years and can leave a legacy as well.

The 4 percent rule is based on the historical performance of U.S. stocks and bonds. But what if the next 30 years take a different course? That's a question I've asked myself as my husband and I plan for the day when we won't have paychecks anymore. The projected Quinn budget works on a roughly 4.5 percent initial withdrawal plus inflation adjustments, but we're prepared to be flexible. We want to spend enough to be able to enjoy ourselves yet not so much that we start to worry. Leaving money for our kids is on our minds, but primarily we'd like to maintain the style of living that we worked for. Those are pretty common goals. You're probably in a similar emotional place.

There's also the question of being "properly invested." The research on the 4 percent rule (and other withdrawal rules) assumes that you're keeping half your money broadly invested in blue-chip stocks and the rest in intermediate-term government bonds.[1] That assumption might stop you cold. Many retirees wouldn't dream of holding as much as 50 percent of their savings in stocks. You should succeed with the 4 percent rule while holding just 30 percent in stocks, but it's a close call. If you don't trust stocks at all and own just bonds and certificates of deposit, your safe, initial withdrawal rate goes down to about 2.5 percent.

So, it's more than a question of whether a 4 percent withdrawal rate works. The question is whether it works for *you*. If not, what are your alternatives?

Before we go further, let me explain how the 4 percent rule came to be.

UNPACKING THE FAMOUS 4 PERCENT (OR 4.5 PERCENT) RULE

The 4 percent rule arose from research done by financial planner Bill Bengen of El Cajon, California, in 1993. His clients wanted to know how much they could safely withdraw from their nest eggs each year without the risk of running out of money. He tested various spending rates against historical investment returns, using 30-year periods that overlapped.[2] Here's what he came up with:

1. It's generally safe to spend 4 percent of your nest egg in the first year you retire. Withdraw the money at the start of the year, put it in your bank account or money market mutual fund, and use

---

1 Whenever I use the generic terms "stocks" or "bonds," I *always* mean stock or bond mutual funds or exchange-traded funds. *Never* individual stocks or bonds. See page 279 for the reasons why.

2 "Overlapping" means that every January 1 he started a new 30-year period. The first period ran from 1926 to 1956; the second from 1927 to 1957; the third from 1928 to 1958, and so on.

it to help pay your bills. In the second year, withdraw the same dollar amount plus an increase to cover the inflation rate. In the third year, do the same. Proceed this way, year after year.

As an example, assume that you start with $100,000 at a time when inflation is running at 3 percent. In year one of retirement, you'd take out $4,000 (your 4 percent). In year two, you'd increase your withdrawal to $4,120—last year's $4,000 plus $120 (that's a 3 percent increase for inflation). In year three, you'd take $4,244—last year's $4,120 plus $124 for inflation. And so on and so on. After inflation, you will have roughly the same amount of money to spend every year. In the rare case of deflation (last seen from 1930 to 1933), you'd lower your withdrawal by the deflation rate.

2. Bengen's basic studies assume that half your money is invested in Standard & Poor's 500 stock index of leading U.S. companies and the other half in an index of intermediate-term U.S. Treasury bonds (maturing in four to ten years). You can't buy these indexes directly but you can come very close to their performance by holding low-cost stock and bond index mutual funds (see pages 269 and 286).

3. Bengen found that you could hold as little as 30 percent in stocks and still succeed—just barely—with a 4 percent cash withdrawal rate (plus inflation increases) over 30 years. The rest of your money would go into intermediate-term bonds. Below 30 percent, you wouldn't make it through a worst-case economic scenario. You could also succeed—just barely—if you held 100 percent in stocks, but it would be too wild a ride for retirees. The optimum appears to be 50 percent in stocks. Those interested in building more wealth could go up to 75 percent, provided that they could live with wide swings in the value of their investment portfolio.

4. Bengen used his annual withdrawals to *rebalance* his portfolios every year. Rebalancing means that you bring your percentage

allocation to stocks and bonds back to its original starting point. For example, say that your investment plan calls for you to hold 50 percent of your money in stocks and 50 percent in bonds. Over the year, stock prices rise so that you're now 55 percent in stocks. To rebalance, you'd take most of your annual withdrawal from the stock account (and perhaps some from the bond account) to bring your allocation back to 50/50. For more on rebalancing, see page 239. The division you choose between stocks and bonds is known as an "asset allocation" and should be spread over your entire financial holdings, taxable accounts as well as retirement accounts. Bengen assumed that you'd stick with the same allocation for life.

5. All withdrawals go into a cash account that you can draw on to pay your current bills.

6. Historically, it hasn't mattered how well or badly stocks or bonds performed during a given year or handful of years (except, of course, for your emotional well-being). Eventually, one period's losses were restored by another period's larger gains. Bengen called 4 percent (plus annual additions for inflation) the SAFEMAX. That withdrawal rate would have carried retirees successfully through the 1929 stock market crash, the Great Depression of the 1930s, and the Stagflation that began in 1973. The initial pot of money always lasted for at least 30 years. In 97 percent of the 30-year periods, the money lasted for much longer than 30 years—an important point for retired people with a younger spouse. It's also useful information for retirees who want to spend more than 4 percent.

7. Bengen assumed that you are a buy-and-hold investor, making adjustments only to keep your asset allocation on track. If you try to time the market by buying and selling when you think stock prices are low or high, you're on your own. You will almost certainly earn less than the market averages, over time. No spending rule will work.

8. In 1998, Bengen updated his research to add smaller-company stocks to the investment mix. The new allocation still put 50 percent of the retirement portfolio into intermediate-term Treasury bonds. On the stock side, he put 23 percent into Standard & Poor's 500 stock index and 27 percent into an index of smaller stocks. Historically, smaller-stock indexes swing more widely in price than the S&P but they have also delivered stronger long-term growth. With this simple diversification, Bengen's SAFE-MAX rose to 4.5 percent[3] in the first year, plus annual inflation increases. The money still lasted for 30 years or more.

    The 4.5 rule worked for people holding anywhere from 45 to 65 percent in stocks. Below or above those percentages, they wouldn't have made it through every historical 30-year period. With too little in stocks, you don't get enough growth to deal with unexpected inflation. With too much in stocks, you're hit so hard when the market falls that your withdrawals eat up your nest egg before it has a chance to recover.

    Bengen let the small-stock index stand in for other types of diversification, such as international stocks and real estate investment trusts. If they were included in the mix, it's possible that his suggested safe withdrawal rate would rise a little higher.

9. Bengen made no adjustment for taxes because everyone's tax situation is different. He assumed that you held the money in a tax-deferred retirement account. So your 4 or 4.5 percent withdrawal isn't spendable income. You have to reduce it by the amount of income tax you pay. You should also reduce it by the amount you pay in investment fees.

10. The withdrawal rule is applied only to the value of your stocks, bonds, mutual funds, certificates of deposit, and similar financial investments. That's the pot of money that you're trying to

---

3   For Bengen's data, see his book *Conserving Client Portfolios During Retirement*, published by the FPA Press.

stretch over 30 years. Don't count the cash you've set aside for current bills. And don't count any nonfinancial assets, such as home equity or investment real estate. If you need to tap real estate equity, there are other ways (see Chapter 10).

11. The 4 or 4.5 percent rules assume that you want a steady, annual inflation-adjusted income that you can budget for. You don't want an income that rises or falls depending on market performance.

12. It's too early to know if the 4 or 4.5 percent rule will work for those who retired in 2000, the year when the tech-stock bubble burst. Over the following 20 years, those retirees endured a second stock market crash, when the financial system almost came apart, and years of low interest rates on bonds and bank accounts before stock prices decisively moved up. Nevertheless, the rules are working so far for investors who stayed the course.

SEVEN QUESTIONS ABOUT "SAFE" WITHDRAWAL RULES

Should the withdrawal rule be raised to 5.5 percent?

If you're flexible about your spending, you can start cash withdrawals at 5.5 percent of your nest egg plus an annual inflation increase. This rule is based on research by financial planner Jonathan Guyton of Cornerstone Wealth Advisors in Edina, Minnesota (cornerstonewealthadvisors.com). Bengen settled on 4 or 4.5 percent because it carried retirees successfully through the three worst 30-year periods for investment growth that the U.S. economy has ever known (those starting in 1929, 1937, and 1973). But all the other periods showed decent and sometimes outstanding growth. So why plan for the worst? Guyton asks. The odds strongly favor something better. Starting at 5.5 percent provides you with a higher income, a more comfortable life, and, he says, a 99 percent probability that your money will last for 30 years or more. His only caveat: You have to be willing and able to cut your spending a bit if the markets turn bad for several years. For example, you might stop taking inflation increases until stocks recover or lower your annual draw by 10 percent. When you reach your mid-70s, spending might fall of its own accord.

The 5.5 percent rule nicely coincides with what your gut would tell you anyway: Relax when things are going well; tighten up when they're not. If the markets do splendidly when you first retire, reconsider your position and think about spending more. If they do poorly, temporarily reduce the amounts you take from your investment accounts.

Should the withdrawal rule be lowered to 3 percent?

Historically, the 4 percent rule has carried retirees through previous periods of low interest rates not unlike those we've seen in recent years. It also succeeded when stock valuations were high (high valuations run before a market fall, eventually).[4] But we haven't yet been through a period like the recent one, with low interest rates and high market valuations running hand in hand. Many forecasters think that this combination foretells subnormal stock and bond returns over the next few years. For this reason, Wade Pfau, a professor of retirement income at the American College of Financial Services in King of Prussia, Pennsylvania, thinks it's more realistic to start your cash withdrawals at 3 percent if you intend to spend at a steady, inflation-adjusted rate. If, after several years have passed, the markets have performed better

---

4   A "valuation" purports to tell you whether a stock price is high or low, compared to some other measure of financial performance.

than the forecasters expected, you can raise your take. (Read Pfau's excellent analyses and advice at retirementresearcher .com.)

Should your withdrawal rate depend on the state of the stock market when you retire?

This approach requires some technical knowledge, as well as willingness to stay the course. Michael Kitces, of Pinnacle Advisory Group in Columbia, Maryland, bases his safe cash withdrawal rate on the P/E10. That's the ratio of current stock prices to the earnings of the 500 companies in Standard & Poor's stock index, adjusted for inflation and averaged over the past 10 years.

Fortunately, you don't have to figure this out yourself. You can find the P/E10 just by asking your search engine for the "Shiller PE Ratio."[5] It's also known as the Cyclically Adjusted Price Earnings Ratio, or CAPE. CAPE doesn't try to call market tops and bottoms so it's not a market-timing rule. Over- or undervaluation often persists for many years. If the ratio lies above 20,[6] the market is considered overvalued, implying lower, long-term returns ahead. In that case, your initial withdrawal rate shouldn't exceed the classic 4 or 4.5 percent, Kitces says. Between P/E10s of 12 and 20, where the market is "fairly valued," you might start withdrawals at 5 percent plus annual inflation increases. Below 12, the market is undervalued, suggesting higher returns ahead. With that prospect, your withdrawal rate could start at 5.5 percent.

---

5   This ratio was developed by Nobel Prize–winning economist Robert J. Shiller of Yale University.

6   As it does at this writing.

Following this system has, in the past, improved returns. But remember: The future is always, *always* unknowable.

Do these spending plans include the interest and dividends that your investments earn?

Yes, but don't treat them as extras. They have to be counted toward your 4 or 4.5 percent withdrawal. With mutual funds, you can take interest and dividends as quarterly payments. An easier way is to have them reinvested in your funds automatically and take your withdrawal all at once at the end of the year. Either approach works. What does not work is taking your 4 or 4.5 percent *plus* the dividends.

Is the "safe" 4 percent withdrawal rate too safe?

Probably yes. In 97 percent of the periods Bengen studied, retirees wound up—30 years later—with at least the same amount of money they had when they started and usually much more (sometimes three or six times more). If you follow that course, you'll favor your heirs over your personal standard of living. Why do that? Increase your spending. Live it up!

The problem, of course, is that you never know. That's why planners (and financial writers!) generally advise you to start with 4 or 4.5 percent, take your annual inflation raises, and see where you stand after five years or so. You can increase your draw if the markets have risen. If the markets fall at the time you retire, your modest spending rate should keep you safe until stock prices have recovered, at which point you might start taking more. Or start with 5.5 percent if the extra is discretionary money that you could temporarily do without. A common wish is to spend extra money on travel during your younger retirement years, while you're still physically able. That makes sense to me. Later in life, most retirees reduce spending anyway, so it's not such a chore to cut back.

What about taking 6 or 6.5 percent?

Normally, withdrawals this high could leave you broke after 15 years or so. But you can safely jack up your spending by adding a reverse mortgage (RM) in the form of a credit line (see page 323). The credit line supplements the income you're taking from your nest egg. If you're not interested in RMs, hold your initial withdrawals to 5.5 percent or less when you need your nest egg to last for 30 years or more. You can raise your withdrawals later, if the markets have been doing well.

What about planning for fewer than 30 years?

If you're older than 70 or in poor health, you might decide that your money will have to last for only 20 years. A withdrawal rate of 5 percent plus annual inflation adjustments should get you through. You could even start with 6 percent if you're able to reduce your spending in a bad market year. For a 15-year retirement, you might start with 6 percent (7 percent, if you're able to cut back).

Don't take this decision lightly. We're living to much older ages than any of us expected, even with chronic illnesses. If you're married, be sure to take your spouse's possible lifetime into consideration as well as your own. Guys sometimes run on their own clocks, forgetting that their wives, especially younger wives, will survive them by a decade or two.

Research suggests that if you establish a short payout period—say, 15 or 20 years—at a high annual withdrawal rate, you should reduce your stock allocation to perhaps 30 percent with the rest in short- or intermediate-term U.S. Treasury bonds. You need the extra protection in case the stock market takes a deep dive just when you're starting your

withdrawal plan. Treasuries usually go up in price when
stocks go down.

BUT, BUT, BUT REAL PEOPLE DON'T LIVE BY RULES

So true! It's unlikely that your own savings, investments, and spending needs fall into the simple patterns used to develop the safe withdrawal rules. Nevertheless, there are plenty of lessons to be learned
from the research.

**To use the classic withdrawal rules safely, you can't be aller-
gic to stocks.** If you keep all your money in certificates of deposit,
bonds, or bond mutual funds, and draw 4 percent (plus annual increases for inflation), your nest egg might last for just 18 years in
a low-interest-rate world. In an average-interest-rate scenario, your
money could last 25 years. But the odds increase that something
will go wrong, including unexpected expenses. You have no cushion
and no chance of drawing a higher income from your investments in
future years. If you feel comfortable only with a pure fixed-income
portfolio, you should drop your initial withdrawal rate to 2.5 percent, Pfau says. But remember: Over the next 30 years, the value of
America's corporations and their stock prices are going to grow—
providing investors with more financial flexibility in their later lives.

**You can't use any old stock or bond investment and expect the 4
or 4.5 percent withdrawal rules to work.** The research is very specifically based on the long-term price performance of large and small
U.S. stocks, a proxy for international stocks, and intermediate-term
U.S. Treasury bonds. Your own investments have to come very close
to matching those averages for your withdrawals to last for life.
There's only one way of ensuring this happy result: Put your money
into low-cost stock and bond index mutual funds (see pages 269 and

286). Index funds track the market, so your returns should generally match the returns that the research projects. By "low cost" I mean annual fees of 0.3 percent a year or less.

If you buy other types of investments, such as individual stocks, high-cost mutual funds, or high-yield bond funds, there's no guarantee that your long-term gains will equal those of the market every year. Perhaps you'll get lucky and do even better. In the real world, however, there's plenty of evidence that you will probably fall behind. If your investments don't at least match the market, withdrawal rates starting at 4 or 4.5 percent could deplete your money faster than you'd planned. The same is true if you pay high costs for money management.

Life runs more smoothly if you simplify. You probably approached retirement with a mixed bag of investments: a handful of individual stocks, a concentration of stock in the company you used to work for, assorted mutual funds, municipal bonds, high-yield bond funds, certificates of deposit, and who knows what. It's not at all clear that you're well diversified. Nor is it clear how to draw out your 4 or 4.5 percent. Which stock should you sell? Which mutual fund do you want to keep? What's the best way to rebalance?

Decisions come easier and you are more likely to succeed when you consolidate your investments into the smallest possible number of stock and bond mutual funds (see Chapter 9). This arrangement lets you take your annual cash withdrawals out of "stocks" or "bonds" generically without having to pick particular stocks or bonds to sell. Simplifying your investments also makes them easier to manage, especially for novice investors and even experienced investors in their older age.

Life also runs more smoothly if you maintain a two-year cash reserve. Cash reserves cover any gap between your retirement income, such as Social Security and a pension, and your daily bills. You need enough money to cover that gap for the next two years. If there's a storm in the stock market or bond market, you can skip your withdrawal that year and use your reserves to cover the grocery bills and other expenses. There's no need to return to your withdrawal plan until prices turn back up. This approach helps you avoid having to sell assets at a loss. For more on working with a cash reserve, see page 261.

You have to know what your savings and investments are currently worth in order to turn them into an orderly income for life. If you're simply tapping your nest egg for whatever amounts of money you need, you're flying blind. You don't know whether you're taking 2 percent or 8 percent so you can't make a solid estimate of how long your money might last. When planning your retirement budget, make a list of your total financial holdings, inside and outside any retirement accounts, and establish their current value. Revalue your nest egg annually to help you decide which funds to tap for your annual withdrawal.

You need the safest possible investments in the bond portion of your nest egg. When the stock market falls, you'll need to take annual withdrawals from bonds while you wait for stock prices to recover. That means holding the types of bonds that tend to rise in value or at least hold pretty steady when stocks decline.

Historically, the best choice has been intermediate-term Treasury bonds. You'll find them in government bond mutual funds with "durations" of about five or six years (see page 283). After a short hiccup, these funds performed wonderfully during the stock market dives of 2000–2003 and 2008–2009—going up in price when stocks collapsed. Short-term bond funds worked well, too. By contrast, risky, high-yield (junk) bond funds plunged right along with stocks. As a safety net, they failed.

None of the withdrawal-rate researchers tested high-quality,[7] tax-deferred municipal bonds to see if they could be substituted for intermediate-term governments. But they might work, for a portion of your money. If you'll be depending on munis for your annual withdrawal whenever stock prices fall, you should buy mutual funds, not individual bonds. Funds are your best guarantee of ready access to cash. (For more on bonds, see page 281.)

High-quality corporate bonds haven't been tested, either. They'd probably work better than junk bonds for reliable cash withdrawals but not as well as Treasuries. A mix of Treasuries with a small percentage of corporates in a general, high-quality bond mutual fund should meet the 4 percent test.

Rebalancing is important but not to the decimal point. To rebalance a portfolio means to bring it back to a predetermined asset allocation—say, 50 percent in stocks and 50 percent in bonds (see page 246). Some investors choose to rebalance to a lower stock allocation as they get older. That's comforting but not optimal—see page 250.

All the withdrawal-rate research assumes that you rebalance once a year. That's convenient for keeping track of your withdrawal plan but not critical. Your plan won't fail if, in a given year, you're off by 5 or 10 percentage points or so. There's a lot of give in the numbers because of the unpredictable way that markets behave. You could work your way back to an ideal balance over two or three years. Many 401(k) plans offer free automatic rebalancing if you sign up for it.

---

7   Both individual bonds and bond funds carry safety ratings. Those for investment-grade bonds and bond funds range from a high of AAA, Aaa, or A++ to a low of A, B++, or A1, depending on the designations used by the rater.

There are two reasons to rebalance:

1. Rebalancing makes it more likely that you'll be able to make your planned, annual withdrawals from savings over 20 or 30 years. Note that this strategy does *not* produce the highest long-term investment returns. That's because stock markets rise more often than they fall and rise by more than the previous decline. By selling when stocks go up and reinvesting the money in bonds, you are taking away from the very investments that will gain the most. If you don't rebalance, however, your portfolio will eventually contain more in stocks than you might be comfortable with. To keep up your withdrawals, you might have to sell them at a loss which, emotionally, is hard to do. Rebalancing saves you from yourself.

2. Rebalancing limits your investment risk. As an example, say that stocks rise to 60 percent of your portfolio and you don't rebalance. If the market suddenly falls, you'll take a larger percentage loss than if you'd rebalanced and were holding only 50 percent in stocks. When the market improves, of course, the 60 percent stock portfolio will recover faster and, long term, might produce better returns. But rebalancers generally don't care about that. Their interest lies in limiting loss so they can rely on their withdrawal plan each year.

Rebalancing of any sort matters the most during a plunge in prices for stocks. For example, say that stock prices are down, you've taken your withdrawal for the year, and the market continues to fall. The percentage you own in stocks is below your target amount. You're afraid that prices will fall even further. What to do?

The best answer is to hold your nose, shut your eyes, and rebalance. Sell more bond shares and use the money to buy stock funds at lower prices. When the stock market goes back up, you'll have more shares at work to capture the gains. Do the same thing if bond prices fall: Rebalance by selling stock-fund shares and reinvesting in bonds. Don't wait for the end of the year if prices have fallen fast.

But will you do it? Or will you find it too scary to buy stocks (or bonds) when they're down and you don't know where the bottom is? Small errors of rebalancing won't hurt your plan. But failing to take advantage of deep drops in price will make it harder for you to stretch your money over your life span. At the very least, don't sell in a panic. Hang on to the stocks and bonds you have and reconsider your withdrawal rate once the scare has passed. Then promise yourself to make rebalancing a habit. The more you do it, the easier it gets.

A new theory of rebalancing, arising from behavioral finance, doesn't require you to sell stocks when they rise in price. This idea comes from Meir Statman, professor of finance at Santa Clara University in California and author of *Finance for Normal People*. He calls it a "wants-based" approach. In the big picture, Statman says, investors want two things: to get rich (meaning having plenty of extra money available) and to avoid being poor (that is, failing to have a sufficient level of retirement income). In any investor, one desire will dominate the other but both exist in everyone at the same time.

Your personal asset allocation will focus on what you want most. For example, investors whose greater fear is becoming poor might decide to devote 60 percent of their portfolio to bonds and certificates of deposit with only 40 percent in stocks. They've done the math and know that the dollar value of their bond funds (taken at a modest, fixed withdrawal rate), plus their guaranteed retirement income, will cover their basic living expenses. If stock prices soar—say, rising to 50 percent of their portfolio—and bond prices remain roughly the same, they do not rebalance. The money held in bonds still takes care of their not-poor needs. By letting the stock portion rise, they're advancing their secondary goal, which is to get rich. If stock prices fall, Treasury bond funds will usually rise in price. Again, the wants-based rebalancer might do nothing, enjoying the added security that their bonds now provide while waiting for stock prices to come back.

If bond prices fall, of course, they would rebalance to bring their fund's dollar value back to the needed level—perhaps not at first, but if the damage to their bond-fund portfolio persisted. Using this approach, they focus on maintaining the safety portion of their money at whatever level they set and letting the risk portion fall where it may.

What about the get-rich investors? They might choose to hold 70 percent of their money in stocks. They've also done the math and know that their bond-fund withdrawals plus their other income will cover their basic expenses. If stocks go up, they're golden. If stocks go down, they're still okay because they can pay their bills with other money. By not rebalancing, they figure that, when the market turns up again, their higher stock allocation will pay off in the long run.

The downside is that both the get-rich and not-poor investor isn't taking the opportunity to buy stocks at lower prices. In this regard, the traditional way of rebalancing might be the smarter choice.

For tax management when you're rebalancing, see page 352.

How secure you feel about your withdrawal plan will depend on what happens to stocks in the first few years after you retire. That's the most critical period. If the stock market falls, your annual cash withdrawals will keep depleting your nest egg while you wait for the market to recover. You might even have the bad luck to suffer through two steep declines within just a few years (I'm thinking of 2000 and 2008). The 4 or 4.5 percent rule should still work but only if you have the fortitude not to sell. Investors who dumped stocks after the 2008 financial collapse and failed to buy back in 2009 when stocks started back up missed the huge price recovery that would have kept their retirement on track.

Conversely, you might enjoy a long, strong stock market rise during your early retirement years with only brief declines (an example would be 2009 to mid-2019). In this case, your nest egg should grow so fat that you won't have to worry if stocks weaken 15 or 20 years from now. It will be easy to stay the course. In fact, you'll have much more to spend.

Which type of market comes your way depends entirely on luck. You can weather either sequence of returns, financially, provided that you can endure emotionally. The withdrawal rules suit investors who buy, rebalance, and hold.

You won't have to worry about what happens to stocks right after you retire if you maintain a safety net. Your safety net is your two-year cash reserve plus a holding of short-term bond funds. With these in place, you won't have to withdraw any money from your stock funds until prices go back up. For more on this strategy, see page 249.

The withdrawal rules help you provide for a younger spouse. In almost all of the 4 and 4.5 percent withdrawal scenarios, the money lasts longer—sometimes much longer—than 30 years. You'll also be able to leave a legacy for your children or a charity if that's one of your goals.

When you have a much younger spouse, consider holding at least 50 percent in stocks and perhaps up to 60 percent. You'll need the money to last for your spouse's lifetime as well as your own. As long as you have a two-year cash reserve, you can skip withdrawals in years that stocks decline.

Always evaluate your stock, bond, and cash portfolio as a whole. You might rush to sell stocks if the market drops 30 percent. But if you have only half your money in stocks, and if the bond market rises (as Treasury funds usually do when stocks decline), your total portfolio might be down only 10 percent or so. That should be something you can live with. The reason you own both stocks and bonds is to keep the dollar value of your combined investments from dropping too far.

You could raise the amount you're taking out of your nest egg if your investments have done well for several years. Everyone makes midcourse corrections. You might reset your withdrawals at a moderately higher rate now that you have less time ahead, or take a lump sum for a special purpose.

Consider starting with a higher withdrawal rate if you unexpectedly lose your job at age 60 or so. A higher withdrawal could help you defer your Social Security benefits until you reach full retirement age. At that point, you'll get a larger check. Once Social Security starts, you could reduce your withdrawals from savings by the same dollar amount.

You might want to lower your take if you plan to reduce your stockholdings as you age. Bengen's original rule called for a 50/50 division between stocks and bonds, lasting through the entire 30-year period. But he found (no surprise) that a 50 percent allocation to stocks frightened many of his older clients. He began to advise that retirees start with 50 percent in stocks and reduce that amount by 1 percentage point a year. The less you hold in stocks, however, the less your opportunity for long-term growth and the harder it becomes to make your savings last for 30 years. If you follow this strategy, consider starting your withdrawals at 4 percent or less.

You can skip the annual withdrawal if you already have more than enough money in cash reserves to get through a couple of years. New retirees sometimes overestimate what they're likely to spend. Once you get settled, you might find that you don't need quite as much as you originally thought. Some of you will leave the extra money in your nest egg to grow. Others will start spending a little more, for fun (that would probably be me . . .).

You might not have to touch your nest egg during your early retirement years. Some retirees can live comfortably on Social Security, pension, and income from other sources, such as dividends, interest, rental real estate, or a part-time job. You tap your savings only for splurges, such as vacations, gifts, moving expenses, or unexpected health-care (often, dental) costs. When you finally get around to making withdrawals, you'll have a shorter remaining life span and, presumably, a larger nest egg. You could start spending at the rate of 5.5 or even 6 percent, plus inflation increases, and still feel pretty sure that your savings will last for life.

You might never need your nest egg, thanks to your moderate spending or other sources of income. In this case, you're managing the money entirely for your children. To build up their inheritance, you might put 90 percent in stocks. Money that you're required to take out of an IRA or other tax-deferred retirement accounts, after age 70½, can be reinvested for the kids in a taxable account.

You'll have to adjust your thinking when you reach 70½, if you have a tax-deferred retirement account. At that age, you have to start taking required minimum distributions (RMDs) every year. The distribution rate is designed to use up the money over your expected life span (in fact, it generally lasts longer due to long-term market gains). Your first RMD comes to about 3.7 percent of the assets in these accounts. You can take more, of course, but if you can manage on 3.7 percent, that's all to the good. The required percentage withdrawal rises a little every year. At 80, it's about 5.4 percent. You'll be taking more money, in dollar terms, if the stock market goes up, and perhaps less if the market goes down.

Whether this jibes with your 4 or 4.5 percent withdrawal plan, plus inflation adjustments, will depend on how much or how little your investments have grown over the years. If your RMD comes to more than your withdrawal plan calls for in the current year, and you don't need the money, reinvest it in a bank account or mutual fund. But if your nest egg is doing well, spend the money—maybe by taking your family on a trip. Or donate to charity. Savings are there to enjoy while you still have your health. For more on RMDs, see page 220.

Be sure to take income taxes into consideration when creating your retirement spending plan. You might feel rich because you have $1 million in your individual retirement account. But after state and federal taxes, a 4 percent withdrawal ($40,000) might be worth $24,000 or less. Match your standard of living to your annual income *after tax*.

YOUR ASSET-ALLOCATION DECISION IN A NUTSHELL

There's a tight link between a safe withdrawal rate and the amount of money you decide to allocate to stocks or bonds. I've mentioned it, here and there, as I reported on the new retirement-income research. Here, I've pulled it all together into a single section to help you make your own asset-allocation decision.

Your first consideration should be your cash reserve. How much money do you need to set aside to be sure that your bills are paid for the next two years? (Remember: This cash doesn't count when you're figuring your 4 percent withdrawal rate. A withdrawal rate applies only to your invested financial assets.)

Next, decide what percentage of your remaining money you want to keep in stock-owning mutual funds. A typical range would be somewhere between 40 and 65 percent, although that can be stretched to as low as 35 percent and as high as 70 or even 75 percent.

If you commit just 30 percent of your money (or less) to stocks, you might not be able to sustain an initial withdrawal rate of 4 percent (plus annual inflation adjustments) for 30 years. To be safe, the stock shy should start by taking out only 3 percent or even 2.5 percent of their assets in the first year they retire.

Holding more than 75 percent in stocks can be equally counterproductive. The higher your stock allocation, the larger your dollar loss when prices plunge. If you have to make a withdrawal from your stock funds that year, you'll lock in a loss that will be hard to make up. Those who want to be mostly in stocks should be able to live without touching that money during bear market cycles.[8]

Here's a surprise! For the purpose of creating a sustainable lifetime retirement income, there's not much difference between holding 40 percent in stocks or raising your stake to 70 percent. A 4 or 4.5 percent withdrawal rule works with both. To minimize the price swings in your portfolio, up and down, stay at the lower end of that range. If you can handle price swings and hope to leave a larger legacy for your kids or a younger spouse or a special charity, go toward the higher end. Always knowing, of course, that there are never any guarantees.

Once you've settled on a stock allocation, what's left of your investment fund goes into bonds. For flexibility, choose bond mutual funds. For income security, choose bond funds invested in intermediate-term Treasuries. Never mind the low interest rate. Treasuries tend to rise in price when stock prices fall. They give your portfolio a cushion so that, in bad times, you can sustain your regular 4 or 4.5 percent withdrawal rate.

Like all bond funds, intermediate-term Treasuries will fall in

---

8 In the taxonomy of the market, "bear markets" go down and "bull markets" go up. A bear market rally, when stocks start to rise but then fall again, is a "dead cat bounce."

market price when interest rates rise. To hedge against that risk, put part of your money into a high-quality short-term bond fund. It pays less interest but, when rates rise, it will lose very little in price. That makes it useful as a safety net. If you blow through your cash reserves and the general stock and bond markets are still in a slump, you can tap your short-term bond fund to help pay your bills. A two-year cash reserve plus two years' worth of expenses in short-term bonds keeps you safe for four years—usually, more than enough time for a bad market to pass. Financial planner Harold Evensky, cofounder of Evensky & Katz/Foldes Financial Wealth Management in Coral Gables, Florida, pushes his clients' short-term allocation up to enough to cover five years of expenses, including known future purchases such as a car or tuition aid for grandchildren. This approach emphasizes safety over long-term returns.

For specifics on the stock and bond mutual funds you might choose, see Chapter 9. From the point of view of your asset allocation, the fewer funds the better. That's because rebalancing doesn't apply only to the split between stocks and bonds. It also applies to the funds you choose for each class of investment. For example, say that you're holding four funds invested in stocks and want to keep 25 percent of your stock allocation in each. Whenever you rebalance, you'll have to realign those four funds among themselves to get back to your original stock allocation. Only then do you proceed to rebalance between stocks and bonds.

The more funds you own, and the more individual stocks you keep, the more math you have to summon when you rebalance and take your annual withdrawals. Personally, that's not my cup of tea. You can create a regular retirement income using the 4 or 4.5 percent rule with as few as two mutual funds—a U.S. Total Market Fund and a U.S Total Bond Fund. You have Bill Bengen's research to prove it.

THE RETIREE'S ULTIMATE ASSET-ALLOCATION GOAL: NEVER BOOK A LOSS!

This strategy comes straight from the desks of some very smart financial planners. It assumes that—in any year—your savings and investment fund contains some assets that rise in value or whose value doesn't change. Those are the ones you tap for your annual cash withdrawal. If the stock market falls, you won't have to raise money by selling securities at a loss.

As an example, say that year-end is approaching and you need to take your regular 4.5 percent withdrawal to pay next year's bills. Your retirement investments are divided into four parts: an indexed stock-owning mutual fund, an intermediate-term Treasury bond fund, a short-term bond fund, and a two-year cash reserve (the cash reserve is this strategy's secret sauce). Here's how your no-loss approach might work, depending on how the markets performed in the past 12 months:

- If stocks and bonds have both risen in price—your withdrawal comes out of the stock fund and the intermediate-term bond fund.
- If stocks are up but bonds are down—your withdrawal comes principally out of the stock fund, as well as any interest or dividends you've received in cash. If the gain isn't strong enough to cover your entire withdrawal, you can top it up with money from your short-term bond fund or your cash reserve.
- If bonds are up and stocks are down—your withdrawal comes from the intermediate-term bond fund.
- If both stocks and bonds are down or flat—your withdrawal comes out of the cash reserve. If the cash reserve is insufficient, you'd tap the short-term bond fund. That fund will

show a small loss but not enough to derail your plan. Fill up your cash reserve when the markets go up again.

By approaching your withdrawal choices this way, you have a good chance of preserving your capital. I'm not saying that a no-loss strategy works all the time. But if you follow it carefully, you have a high chance of success.

SHOULD YOUR ASSET ALLOCATION CHANGE AS THE YEARS GO BY?

There are three views on how you should handle the stock funds in your portfolio as you grow older: the traditional view and two better ones.

- **The traditional view calls for gradually reducing the percentage you hold in stocks.** Do it by taking money principally from your stock funds whenever you tap them for your annual withdrawal.

    The classic rule of thumb says that the percentage you hold in bonds should equal your age. For example, if you're 50, you'd hold 50 percent of your money in bonds with the rest in stocks. At 70, you'd hold 70 percent of your money in bonds. I think that advice is a little behind the times, given the increases in longevity. I prefer the rule of 110. It says that the percentage you hold in stocks should equal 110 minus your age. At 50, you'd be 60 percent in stocks with the rest in bonds. At 70, you'd be down to 40 percent in stocks.

    Gradually reducing your stock allocation feels pretty comfortable for people in midlife and later. It's also what most advisers recommend. Financially, however, it's generally not the best choice. You're slowing the rate at which your investment portfolio can grow. That adds to the chance that your money won't last for life or for the lifetime of a younger spouse. If you foresee this approach, you might start your withdrawals from savings at a rate lower than 4 percent.

- **A better decision would be to maintain the same asset allocation throughout retirement.** If you start with, say, 50 percent in stocks and 50 percent in bonds, you'd rebalance to those same percentages, after taking your withdrawal every year. You'll get higher returns and your money should last longer than if you gradually reduce the percentage of stocks you hold. If you adopt this steady-state strategy and are a little bit stock-phobic, you might decide to start with a more conservative allocation—say, 40 percent in stocks with the rest in bonds.

  Even if you're not stock-phobic, there's an argument for choosing a lower allocation for steady-state investing. The day you retire is also the day you face your maximum investment risk. At that point, you have the largest amount of money in your retirement accounts (because you haven't started withdrawals yet), and the longest number of days ahead. Holding less in stocks gives you more protection from bad markets at that critical time.

- **The newest idea (here's a curveball) calls for increasing your stock allocation after you retire.** This strategy is gaining adherents among sophisticated financial planners. It combines safety in your early retirement years with growth in your later years. Here's how you'd handle your assets:

  First, gradually reduce your stock allocation in the four or five years before you plan to retire. When retirement day comes, you should be perhaps 30 percent in stocks with the rest of the money in intermediate-term bond funds. That protects you from the risk of a stock market plunge in those first few critical years after your paycheck stops.

  Second, take your annual withdrawals mostly (or entirely)

from your bond-fund investments for the first few years. The percentage of your nest egg that you hold in bonds will shrink while the percentage in stocks will rise. Between your withdrawals and your rebalancing, you're aiming for your stock percentage to increase by, say, two percentage points a year.

Third, when stocks reach 50 percent of your portfolio, switch strategies. Rebalance regularly to hold your allocation at 50/50, stocks and bonds.

By taking this approach, you'll be using fixed-income investments to get you through the first part of your retirement while depending on long-term stock appreciation to fund the second part. If you're worried about rising interest rates, which would lower the market price of intermediate-term bond funds, Michael Kitces of Pinnacle suggests that you substitute Treasury bills or mutual funds invested in very short-term bonds.

It might go against the grain to hold a rising percentage of your savings in stocks as you grow older. We've been trained (me, too!) to think the reverse. But at age 60 or 65, we might have 30 years to live or even more. Stocks remain *the* investment for the long term.

REBALANCING AND TAXES

Your annual 4 or 4.5 percent withdrawal from savings will come from a mix of original capital, market gains, interest, dividends, distributions from mutual funds, and distributions from retirement accounts. How do you decide what to sell, and which taxes will you pay?

If you're making withdrawals from tax-deferred retirement accounts: The tax part is easy. All withdrawals are taxed as ordinary income. Rebalancing is easy, too, if you're invested entirely in mutual funds. You can shift money from one fund to another with no tax consequences. You can also use your withdrawals to bring your accounts into balance—for example, taking most of your distribution from stock funds if prices are up and stocks now represent a higher percentage of your assets than you want. If you're holding individual stocks and bonds, you will have to decide which stock or bond to sell and how much. Reduce the ones that appear to have the least promise (if you can tell!).

If you're required to make a minimum withdrawal, and it exceeds the amount you need to meet your spending plan, you might put the extra back into other investments. Or step up your spending if your investments have been doing well. Give yourself some treats.

If your annual spending amount comes from taxable savings (not invested in retirement plans): First, use the money that will be taxable this year—interest, dividends, mutual fund distributions, and realized capital gains. That might be enough to fulfill your withdrawal plan. If not, sell shares in stock or bond funds in ways that will roughly restore your stock/bond asset allocation. When you sell an investment, you're not taxed on the whole amount, only on the gain that your investment earned. You get a low rate on most dividends and long-term capital gains. If you're selling the shares at a profit, see if you can sell some losers, too. By offsetting your capital gains with losses, you avoid the tax. Don't rebalance by moving appreciated assets from one taxable account to another. That just adds to your tax. Instead, reestablish balance in the way that you take your money out. If you don't have enough in distributions and don't want to sell securities at a loss, come as close to balance as you can and try again the following year.

If you have investments in tax-deferred retirement accounts as well as in taxable accounts: Your overall asset allocation should include them both. To meet your spending plan, use the interest, dividends, and distributions from the taxable account. Anything more can come from your retirement plan or from selling shares in your taxable account, depending on your strategy.

HELP! I NEED HELP!!

Don't faint, I've already called 911. Emergency financial medics, schooled in asset allocation, rebalancing, withdrawal plans, taxes, and portfolio resuscitations, are speeding your way. Jump to page 295.

WHY I LIKE THE 4 PERCENT RULE AND ITS KISSIN' COUSINS

There's no such thing as an ironclad *safe* withdrawal strategy. *Safe* means "as far as we can tell." Markets and investor behavior are nothing less than changeable.

Still, the withdrawal percentages discussed here aren't casual rules of thumb. They're backed by research that can give you some comfort as you start to tap your capital to pay your bills. Your mix of investments probably won't exactly match the ones that proved the rules. But as long as you have a well-diversified portfolio, 4 percent or one of the other rules discussed in this chapter gives you a useful place to start.

WHAT ARE THE BEST INVESTMENTS FOR A RETIREMENT WITHDRAWAL PLAN?

Read on.

9

Investing for Income: Not What You Think

Nothing endangers your lifestyle more than to pile into "income investments."

I don't know about you, but I have a paycheck mentality. There's nothing I like better than a regular check deposited in my bank account. Or even an irregular check, as long as I'm sure that it will come.

In our 40s and early 50s, we live on our earnings and invest our savings primarily in stocks for long-term growth. Then one day we wake up, look in the mirror, and say, "Yikes." Retirement beckons, the paychecks will stop, and a switch flips in our heads. Suddenly, we decide that we need conservative investments that pay a regular income. Usually, that means bonds, dividend-paying stocks,[1] and—if

---

1   I've said this before and want to say it again: Whenever I say "stocks" I always mean stock-owning mutual funds, not individual stocks. For the reasons why, see page 279. "Bonds" means conservative intermediate- and short-term bond funds. "Mutual funds" includes exchange-traded funds (see page 275).

a salesperson gets his or her hands on us—investment annuities that pay lifetime benefits (ugh).

That belief stems from the ancient idea that we should spend only the interest and dividends from our savings. "Don't dip into principal" sounds like the polestar of retirement life. But unless your expenses are low enough, your savings high enough, and you have enough income from other sources (Social Security, pension, rent, royalties, a trust fund, yes, please, a trust fund), interest and dividends won't be enough—especially when rates are low. They not only produce insufficient income, they won't grow by enough in value, after inflation and taxes, to pay our bills over the next 30-plus years.

It's time for an attitude adjustment. You still need to be an income investor. But for success you have to think about income in a different way. Here's what the professionals say.

Sticking with traditional income investments makes your retirement nest egg riskier, not safer. Say, for example, that you focus on dividend-paying stocks. You'll hang on to "good" names too long (think General Electric or, worse, Pacific Gas and Electric). You'll be concentrated in a small number of industry sectors. (In 2007, the high payers were the financial stocks, and you know what happened to their dividends and market prices. Down, down, down.) You'll be ignoring the universe of growth stocks, smaller-company stocks, and international stocks, which leaves you even less diversified and probably earning lower returns. You'll also lose income in years that dividends go down.

When you think about it, taking a 3 percent dividend has roughly the same effect as selling 3 percent of the stock. Emotionally, it feels better to get the dividend (you didn't touch capital!). But the dollars are the same and you didn't have to limit yourself to a certain type of stock.

On the fixed-income side, you might lean toward high-yield (junk) bond mutual funds because they pay so much more interest than Treasuries do. But when stock prices drop, the share prices of those funds usually drop, too. They *add* risk to your portfolio, which isn't what bonds are supposed to do. Worse, the apparent high yields on funds invested in supposedly safe industries can be hugely misleading. As I write, I'm looking at a real estate investment trust that appears to be paying 9 percent. It's actually paying almost zero. Most of the current payout is simply a return of the investors' own capital. *Any* interest rate investment claiming to pay a fabulous annual dividend has a catch in it somewhere.

Traditional investments might get you through the first half of your retirement but probably not through the second half. When you're reasonably healthy or have a chronic condition that's under control, it's easy to reach your 85th birthday (an unimaginable age when you're 55 or 60). You have a good shot at 90 or older, especially if you're female. Intermediate-term bonds provide security during the first half of your retirement. At an initial 4 percent withdrawal rate,[2] plus annual inflation adjustments, they might last for 20 to 25 years, at 2 percent inflation. That could work, provided that you die within that time frame and stick to a strict lifetime schedule of withdrawing not a penny more per year. Your money would vanish faster if—as is likely—you have unexpected expenses or put part of these savings into short-term bonds and certificates of deposit. There's little or no potential for growth.

When you were younger, you chose stocks for money you didn't expect to touch for a decade or more. That guideline doesn't change when you reach 60 or 65. Rising stock prices in a growing global

---

2   For simplicity, I'll refer to a 4 percent withdrawal rule throughout this chapter. It assumes that you withdraw 4 percent of your assets in the first year you retire plus an inflation adjustment in each subsequent year. The discussion applies equally to higher or lower withdrawal rates, as outlined in Chapter 8.

economy are your best hope for funding the second half of your retirement starting 10 or 15 years from now, despite the occasional recession that comes along. Stocks *reduce* long-term portfolio risk.

"Income" is the money that flows into your checking account on a regular or irregular basis, regardless of source. It might be Social Security or a paycheck for part-time work. It might be interest and dividends. It might also be an annual withdrawal from an investment portfolio, as explained in Chapter 8. That portfolio will contain some stocks that don't pay dividends but do provide long-term capital growth. Growth in capital is a source of income, too.

Your regular withdrawals from your investment account amount to a "homemade paycheck." Conceptually, the money is drawn from the portfolio's interest and dividends plus capital gains, which means that it's also a homemade dividend payment. If that's not enough to fill out the 4 percent that you've budgeted for, your withdrawal will include some of your principal, too. Don't worry about nibbling at your principal. As long as you stick to a well-thought-out asset-allocation plan, future increases in the market will replace part or all of any principal you used. That's why the 4 percent rule works.

Hold your homemade paycheck steady at the withdrawal rate you planned. It's just like the paycheck you might have gotten at work—a fixed amount plus an annual inflation raise. You might be tempted to take extra money whenever the value of your investment portfolio goes up. The withdrawal-rate research, however, assumes that you'll reinvest those gains in order to cushion future losses. Wait to recalibrate when you're 5 or 10 years down the retirement road, with several years of market experience behind you. If you want extra money to spend in your early retirement while you're still young, consider the 5.5 percent withdrawal rule (see page 231) or the discretionary fund (see page 262).

There's an exception to this Steady Eddie rule. It comes into play at a time when the values of your stock and bond mutual funds have both declined in price. In that year, you'd skip the withdrawal and pay your bills from your cash reserve (an account that holds enough money to help cover your bills for the next two years). When the markets have at least partly recovered, start restoring your cash reserve by tapping your investments for more than your 4 percent scheduled amount. The extra money brings your cash reserve back up to the two-year level.

For long retirements, a portfolio of well-diversified, short- and long-term investments is both sensible and safe. That's because markets, properly used, have been more reliable than you might think.

Here's what we know:

- The major U.S. stock market falls and rises in cycles of varying length.[3] The time it takes for investors to recover their money—from the top of the market, to the bottom, and back up again—has averaged just 29 months, assuming that dividends were reinvested. The longest cycle lasted a little over five years (August 2000 to October 2006, after the tech-stock bust). The shortest one, starting in June 1998, took a mere five months.

  If you spent all the dividends instead of reinvesting them, the cycle averaged 39 months. In this case, the longest cycle lasted a little over eight years (December 1972 to July 1980 during the Great Stagflation). The shortest took five months, also starting in June 1998.

  The message is that average prices for the leading stock-market index have *always* recovered, and usually within

---

3   For the following data, thanks to Towneley Capital Management of Laguna Hills, California.

a reasonable period of time. The mutual funds that follow this index have always recovered, too. But individual stocks in the market do not necessarily recover. Sometimes they fly, but sometimes they underperform or even go to zero. That's why it's so risky to buy them. You can't predict, reliably, which the brilliant or pooper stocks are going to be.

- Bond markets rise and fall in cycles, too. They have gone through shorter-term cycles, like stocks, but very long-term cycles, too. For 40 years, up to 1981, bond prices zigzagged down. From 1981 to 2019, bond prices zigzagged up. In both periods, the 4 percent withdrawal rule worked. It's still working now.[4]

- No one knows when stocks or interest rates are going to rise or fall or by how much, no matter how professional or well informed your adviser sounds. The future is unknowable. Trying to follow "timing" advice is a loser's game.

- There is always turmoil and uncertainty somewhere in the country or the world. If you wait for "normalcy" to return before you invest, you will never invest.

- Your margin of safety, against investment risk, is a cash account that will help pay your bills for the next two years no matter what happens in the markets, plus short-term bonds as a safety net for the two years after that. You won't have to follow the news or daily stock prices to see if you're still okay.

- Your margin of safety against inflation risk and the risk of living a very long life is to hold a portion of your money in stocks. To help you allocate your money among cash reserves, current income, and capital growth, consider the system of investing known as "bucketing." It suits the way we think as well as the way we behave.

---

4 For guaranteed longevity insurance, you might hold an immediate or deferred annuity instead of bonds (see pages 152 and 153).

BUCKET INVESTING AND HOW IT WORKS

The concept of bucket investing works especially well for investors who manage their money themselves. It's a process that's easy to understand and carry out. You put your money into different buckets, with each one reserved for a specific purpose. There's one for cash, one for fixed income (bond funds and perhaps an immediate annuity), and one for growth (stock funds). The buckets can be separate accounts or you can keep a single account divided into mental buckets.

Every bucket strategy starts with one for cash. You hold enough cash to help cover your living expenses for the next two years. That doesn't mean all your expenses—only those that won't be paid from your other sources of income. For example, say that it's costing you $55,000 a year to live and, between you and your spouse, you're getting $30,000 in Social Security. There's a $25,000 gap. Your cash bucket has to cover that gap. A one-year bucket would hold $25,000. A two-year cash bucket would hold $50,000. You'd keep the money where you'd earn the most short-term interest—in a local bank or credit union savings account, a high-yielding online bank, a money market mutual fund, or a very short-term (one- or two-year) bond mutual fund. Think of it as a permanent reserve. You might tap it from time to time, but you will always fill this bucket up again, using proceeds from your growth investments. Ignore the low returns. This is purely safety money.

If you work with a professional money manager, you will probably follow a two-bucket strategy. One bucket holds your two-year cash reserve. The second one holds all your financial investments, both stocks and bonds. You and the manager will agree on a stock/bond allocation, which will appear on your quarterly statement. The account is rebalanced regularly. Once a year, the manager takes money out of your investment account, following the 4 percent rule, and deposits it into your cash reserve. You draw on that money every month to help pay your bills. Some managers will send you monthly checks if that's what you prefer.

When you're managing your own money, you'll probably use a three-bucket strategy. The first bucket is your cash account. The second bucket holds short- and intermediate-term bond mutual funds—effectively, your "income portfolio." The third bucket holds stock funds. Each fund should be reported separately on the statement you get from your mutual fund company. To rebalance your investments, you move shares from one account to another (in a tax-deferred retirement account) or you take interest and dividends as well as selling some stocks or bonds (in a taxable account). You can accomplish that directly if you manage the money through an online account. Or ask the firm's telephone rep to make the changes for you. For simplicity, your money should be consolidated at a single financial institution. If you're holding your retirement investments in a 401(k), ask if the company plan will rebalance it for you, automatically.

Consider the value of a fourth bucket for a separate discretionary fund. That good advice comes from Jonathan Guyton of Cornerstone Wealth Advisors. Almost inevitably, you're going to "want" or "need" money for things your homemade paycheck doesn't cover. "People will rationalize extra withdrawals every which way till Sunday," he says, "and they put a chink in your armor." His solution: Put only 90 percent of your investments into the stock and bond buckets that support your inflation-adjusted withdrawal plan. The other 10 percent goes into a discretionary fund, invested conservatively in bank CDs and short-term bond funds. If you want or need more than your regular withdrawal allows, take it from this fund. When it's gone, it's gone. You might reconstitute it after 10 years or so if your long-term investments have done well.

This bucket might include any lump-sum expenses that you know will come up soon. For example, you might be planning to replace your car two years from now or put a down payment on a vacation condo. You'll need a specific amount of cash on hand. That's a job for a bank certificate of deposit.

Some planners advocate a super-conservative two-bucket strategy known as "safety first." You hold the usual two-year cash bucket in a checking account or money market mutual fund. For your second bucket, you buy Treasury Inflation-Protected Securities (TIPS) in tax-deferred retirement accounts (see page 287), bank or credit union certificates of deposit, and a short-term bond fund. Maybe an intermediate-term bond fund, too. You expect (hope!) that the earnings from your second bucket, plus Social Security and any other guaranteed income, will cover a bare-bones budget for the rest of your life. At this writing, the safety-first portfolio would pay only about 1.5 percent a year, so your budget would have to be bare indeed. Your main risk is inflation. Fixed-income portfolios are more likely than other portfolios to force cuts in spending when inflation turns up.

To raise your safe income, you might add an immediate-payout annuity (see page 152). I'd also suggest a *multiyear guaranteed annuity* or MYGA, bought from an insurance company. These are simple savings products that pay a bit more than insured certificates of deposit. The minimum investment ranges from $5,000 to $100,000. You're paid a fixed rate of interest for the number of years you choose— usually three years and up. Insurers charge penalties for quitting the annuity early although you can usually withdraw a certain amount every year, penalty free. (Note that there's a 10 percent tax penalty on earnings withdrawn before age 59½.) Income taxes on your earnings are deferred until you take the money out. For a list of multiyear annuities, go to ImmediateAnnuities.com and put "MYGA" into the Search box. At this writing, three-year investments range from 2.5

percent to 3 percent and five-year investments, from 3 percent to 4 percent. These are not lifetime pension annuities, although you can turn them into a lifetime income if you want.

If it takes all your savings to fund the second bucket, so be it, the safety-firsters say. Your lifestyle will be modest but reasonably secure. You'd add stock funds only if you have money to spare, earmarking any gains for luxuries—travel, gifts, and entertainment that you presumably could do without.

If you've been a black belt saver all your life, a safety-first strategy might produce enough income to cover luxuries, too. In general, however, this approach works only for people who are willing to cut their spending significantly—and why would you do that if you don't have to? Better to include the bucket that owns stocks.

HOW MUCH RISK CAN YOU AFFORD?

Whether you're buying investments directly from a mutual fund company or dealing with a financial adviser, you'll probably fill in a risk-tolerance questionnaire. It's supposed to help guide your decision about how much money to keep in stocks and how aggressive or conservative your investments ought to be.

Sorry—risk-tolerance questionnaires are generally bunk. You'll lean toward more risk if stocks are going up, you've had a good day at the office, and your shoes don't pinch. If you've had a bad day because stocks went down and your unemployed child is moving in, you'll suddenly feel more conservative. In either case, the risk questionnaire will probably steer you toward "income and growth," which covers just about any mix of investments on the planet.

When choosing investments, don't start with your imagined tolerance for risk. Instead, consider your *capacity* for risk. Capacity measures whether you can afford the risks you take. A retiree with a pension, Social Security, a paid-up house, low expenses, and a multi-million-dollar IRA has a high capacity for risk. It won't cripple your lifestyle if you're suddenly hit with a large, unexpected expense or a temporary stock market loss. Conversely, if you're living on Social Security plus a small amount of savings, your capacity for risk is zero no matter how willing you are to gamble. You might suddenly need some cash for home repairs or health-care expenses. You aren't in a position to risk a market loss.

If you have the capacity for risk, you can expand into stocks. If not, stay with safe investments and cut your spending to fit.

I don't mean to dismiss risk tolerance entirely. You might have the capacity to keep 90 percent of your money in stocks but wouldn't dream of doing so because your tolerance for risk is poor. These retirees choose very low stock allocations because they can't stand the stress of watching the market rise and fall.

You don't need a questionnaire to tell you this. By the time you approach retirement you'll have been through several stock market cycles and should have a general idea of where your pain point lies.

Creep up on risk slowly, however, if you've never managed important money before. Maybe you just received an inheritance or took a large lump sum from a 401(k). Invest just a modest amount at first, keeping the rest of the money safe. You need to discover how well you hold up in sunshine and in rain.

Consider your personal circumstances when picking a stock allocation. Anything from 40 percent to 65 percent is typical, with the rest in bonds.[5] But you might keep 90 percent in stocks if you won't need the money (because you're rich or your expenses are low) and you're managing it for the next generation. You might put zero in stocks if you're in poor health, your savings are modest, and you'll need cash to pay for care over the next 10 years. Even if you're healthy and comfortable with risk, you might stay with 35 or 40

---

5   This excludes your two-year cash reserve.

percent in stocks if your future depends largely on a closely held business you intend to sell in the next couple of years. Wait until the sale goes through and you've cashed the check before stepping into the market any further.

Choose a bond allocation that minimizes risk. You do this by dividing your money between high-quality short-term and intermediate-term bond mutual funds.

Short-term funds pay less interest but are pretty stable in price. That makes them useful as a safety net. Say, for example, that you're keeping two years' worth of your cash needs in the bank or a money market fund. Say, further, that market conditions are poor, you skip your annual 4 percent withdrawal for two years, and use your cash reserve to pay your bills. If conditions remain poor, you can start taking withdrawals from your short-term bond fund with little risk of a serious loss. Some planners advise that, between your cash reserve and your short-term bond fund, you hold enough money to protect yourself for four straight years, no matter what happens in the economy.

The remainder of your fixed-income money goes into high-quality intermediate-term bond funds. Intermediates pay higher rates of interest than short-term funds, which increases your income. They also rise and fall more in price when interest rates change. For more on bonds, see page 281.

When you're holding a cash reserve, your investment portfolio is more conservative than you think. Your reserve should be counted as part of your fixed-income allocation. So should your discretionary fund (the "fourth bucket"), if you have one. What looks like 50/50 in your investment account (50 percent stocks, 50 percent bonds) might actually be more like 40/60 or even 30/70, including the reserves. When you hold that much cash as a safety net, you should be putting more of your investment portfolio into stocks.

Repeat after me: After bear markets, the broad stock market has always recovered. Always. Individual stocks might not, which is why it's so risky to be a stock picker. But the price of a broad-based mutual fund will go back up. Selling the stock market when it falls is like feeding your money to the squirrels. It's gone for good. If you simply do nothing, and wait, the money will eventually return.

On this point, you had an object lesson in 2007 when the financial system almost collapsed. The average S&P stock lost 50 percent of its value over 24 months. Investors fled and some of you didn't return. Had you been in the market at its bottom in 2009, however, you'd have earned back all of your losses by 2013, then gained another 88 percent by mid-2019. Unfortunately, no one rings a bell when prices are starting up. You just gotta be there.

Sometimes markets zigzag for years without a net price advance. An example would be 1966 to 1982. During such periods you can still earn an average annual 5 percent or so by reinvesting dividends and rebalancing. You earn little or nothing, after inflation, by retreating and putting your money into a bank.

RISK AND THE OLDER INVESTOR

When you're pushing 80 or 85, should you still be in stocks? The answer depends on your temperament, financial resources, and when you're likely to need the money.

If you're sure that you have enough income and savings to cover your expenses for life (for healthy people that could be 95 to 100 or more), nothing requires you to take any risk at all. You've won the game. You can drop out of stocks, switch to short-term bond funds and certificates of deposit, and draw down your nest egg year by year. Taking some risk—with, say, 20 or 30 percent in stocks—becomes a matter of choice. It can also serve as a reasonable hedge against future inflation.

If you have more than enough to cover your lifetime needs and want to leave money for your kids, maintain a higher stock allocation—perhaps 40 to 80 percent. Growth becomes important when you're managing money for the next generation. You might also have to grow your assets to help support a longer-lived spouse.

If you aren't sure that you have enough money to cover your bills for life, consider switching part of the savings that you're holding in bond funds into an immediate-pay annuity. The annuity will provide a much higher income than your bonds yield now, and it's guaranteed for life. With that guarantee, you might feel better about keeping at least 40 percent of your money in stocks for growth.

If every stock market decline sends a shock to your heart, stick with short-term bonds, CDs, and multiyear guaranteed annuities (see page 263). You're giving up the potential for growth but that's better than losing serious savings if you're likely to panic and sell when the next bear market strikes. If your super-safe savings aren't large enough to cover your expenses for life, you'll have to downsize in some way.

If you do commit to stocks, keep enough money in cash and short-term bond funds to ensure that you can pay your bills for at least the next four years. That protects your standard of living while you wait for a bad stock market to turn around.

CHOOSING THE RIGHT STOCK AND BOND INVESTMENTS FOR YOUR HOMEMADE PAYCHECK

Deciding how much to allocate to stocks and how much to bonds is just the start of your retirement investment decision. The next question is which of the thousands of stock funds and bond funds to choose. You need diversification within your buckets. The fewer and more streamlined your choices, the simpler and surer investment management will be.

What's in Your Stock Bucket?

You hold stocks for growth. Not growth next year (that's always a gamble), but growth over 10 or 15 years. You're betting that the U.S. and world economies will have expanded substantially by that time, with corporate profits and stock prices up. It's a good bet, even if a steep recession intervenes.

With dividends reinvested, Standard & Poor's 500 stock average has never lost money over 15-year periods and rarely over 10-year periods. Over the 15 years ending in March 2009, which covered the market collapses of 2000, 2008, and 2009, buy-and-hold investors still reaped 6.5 percent. And that's before the 2009–2019 stock market recovery.

If you own a stock index mutual fund that follows the market as a whole, the only way you can lose money—as a long-term investor—is to bail out when stock prices drop. If you buy and hold, history says that your investment will succeed. If you buy and rebalance from time to time, your returns could be even better.

The case for buying stock-owning mutual funds. A mutual fund is a big pool of money contributed by thousands of people just like you and me. That money is invested in the stocks of many different companies. Your share in the fund gives you a tiny ownership interest in every one of them. You're spreading your money around, which is the right thing to do.

Fund shares can be purchased, cashed in, and switched around whenever you want. That makes it easy to construct an asset allocation, rebalance your investments, and take regular withdrawals. It's much harder to make a rebalancing and withdrawal plan work when you own a portfolio of individual stocks.

The case for buying index funds that track the performance of the stock market as a whole. The financial researchers who

developed the 4 and 4.5 percent withdrawal rules based their findings on how the total market performed. They used specific, well-
known indexes of stock and bond prices. You can't buy an index
itself, but you can buy a low-cost mutual fund that mimics the index.
That's the only way of feeling reasonably sure that the withdrawal
rules will work. Besides, index funds have a terrific track record for
investment success.

   What's an index? It's a way of measuring changes in price. For
stocks, the media follow the Dow Jones Industrial Average, which
tracks the price performance of 30 large American companies. When
a talking head tells you that prices are up or down for the day, it's
always the Dow. For investors, however, the most important index is
Standard & Poor's 500, a composite of 500 leading American companies (S&P 500 for short). It's the measure tracked by professionals
when they evaluate how well or poorly the general market performs.
Hundreds of other indexes cover narrower parts of the market, such
as small companies, real estate, commodities, and international
stocks. There are bond indexes, too.

   An index mutual fund is designed to track the price performance
of a particular index. For example, an S&P 500 fund effectively owns
all 500 of the index's stocks and in the same percentage amounts. If
the index rises by 5 points, so does the mutual fund (plus dividends
and minus fees). Another term for indexing is "passive investing."

   There are index funds for every market you can think of. An international fund might follow the MSCI EAFE Index (that's Morgan
Stanley Capital International, tracking the developed countries of
Europe, Australasia, and the Far East) or one of the FTSE indexes
(originally, the Financial Times Stock Exchange, now run by the London Stock Exchange). Funds invested in small U.S. companies might
follow the Russell, MSCI, or CRSP indexes (CRSP is maintained by
the Center for Research in Security Prices).

   All the funds following the same index—say, the S&P 500—are
essentially investing exactly the same way. The principal difference

among them is cost. The lowest-cost fund will provide the best return—and, yes, it's that simple. As long as you buy low-fee funds and rebalance your investments, your annual withdrawals should last as long as the research says they will.

Vanguard, the granddaddy of the index fund business (Vanguard .com), offers the longest list of low-cost funds, covering various market sectors (at this writing, its S&P fund costs 0.04 percent a year with a $3,000 minimum investment). Charles Schwab (Schwab. com) charges 0.02 percent, with no minimum investment. Last year, Fidelity Investments (Fidelity.com) swept the field by offering four well-diversified U.S. and international stock funds at zero—yes, *zero*—cost, also with no minimum. (Fidelity expects to make money through these funds by selling you additional investment products that do carry fees.) These are all no-load funds, meaning that they charge no commissions if purchased from the firm directly. Funds that follow major market indexes are also highly tax efficient. They don't trade their investment holdings as often as do funds that follow narrower indexes or funds run by active managers. So you don't wind up with a lot of taxable distributions at the end of the year. To the extent they own exchange-traded funds (see page 275), you shouldn't get taxable distributions at all.

Financial advisers who earn commissions sneer at index funds and have a patented method for talking you out of them. "Why would you want *average* returns?" they ask with a superior smirk. "Average is for the ordinary schlub. You can do better than that!"

Before you nod and say, "Yes, please, please take my money and make me rich," think what a "market average" means. It has nothing to do with "the middle." It's more like par in golf. Only the best golfers can beat par and even then only occasionally. The average golfer never does. In the stock market, the index is "par." The miracle of index funds is that they let all investors, regardless of skill, score par all the time. Meanwhile, those brokers and advisers who pick stocks are almost certainly falling behind.

By the way, there's not a material difference in cost between Schwab's and Vanguard's index funds and the Fidelity Zeros. If you invested $10,000 at 8 percent for 20 years, a 0.02 annual fee costs a total of $173. If you invested the same amount of money in the average equity mutual fund, you'd pay 1.1 percent, for a total of $8,480. That comes right off the top of your fund's performance.

Which of the many index funds should you choose? Index funds come in many, many varieties. The most useful today are known as total market funds because they invest in smaller companies as well as large ones. For sophisticated investors, they've mostly replaced the original S&P 500 funds, which owned only the 500 companies (mostly big ones) in the S&P index.

You can also find indexes for growth funds, containing stocks whose earnings are expected to grow faster than average; value funds, whose stocks are out of favor and down in price; small-stock funds, including small-stock value funds, a group with a good long-term performance record; international funds that cover the developed world; emerging-market funds for the developing countries; total international funds, for large and small companies in every foreign market; funds that specialize in various industries such as energy, health care, precious metals, real estate, and commodities; and socially responsible funds for investors seeking companies that treat workers well, improve the environment, diversify their workforce, and avoid dangerous products such as tobacco and guns.[6] A common piece of advice is to buy a total market fund, then add a couple of other funds that you hope will beat the market. As an example, take energy stocks. Energy companies are included in a total market fund, along with companies from every other sector of the economy.

---

6   Vanguard's FTSE Social Index Fund has held its own against the S&P 500 for the past 10 years. For information on social investing, see SocialFunds.com.

If you add an energy fund, you have placed an extra bet on that part of the market. That's called "tilting" your portfolio. Some investors tilt to tech stocks or health-care stocks.

I don't tilt, myself. I'm not smart enough to know which industry will do the best. But if you like to gamble, tilting might make index investing a bit more fun.

It's less fun, however, when you start making regular withdrawals. Every year, you will have to decide how much of each specialized fund to sell and whether you ought to rebalance. If you own five stock funds, that's five rebalancing decisions before you even start thinking about your bonds. The diversification might or might not improve your performance. It will definitely test your skills in math.

Personally, my inclination is always to make things easier. I'd vote for holding one or two broadly diversified stock funds rather than a large collection. That's because your risks and returns are governed mainly by the total percentage you hold in stocks as compared with bonds. Beyond that, your allocation among different types of stocks—large, small, value, growth, foreign, domestic, and so forth—doesn't matter very much, says William J. Bernstein, author of *The Four Pillars of Investing: Lessons for Building a Winning Portfolio* (EfficientFrontier.com). Over time, the various percentages chosen all come out about the same.

Remember that it takes just *one* low-cost total market U.S. stock fund (for large and small stocks) and *one* total market U.S. bond fund to make Bill Bengen's 4 or 4.5 percent withdrawal rules work.

You might add an international stock fund. Vanguard's Total International Stock Index Fund includes both large and small stocks; Fidelity's focuses on large stocks.

That's three funds. Just three. Everything else is decoration.

What about all those stock funds run by brilliant/famous/rich professional managers who pick individual stocks? Supposedly, they can beat the market thanks to their technology and expertise.

But study after study, year after year, shows that they don't beat the broad market index over time. I'll give you just one example, from Rick Ferri, founder of the investment management firm Portfolio Solutions, and Alex Benke, vice president of advice and investing for Betterment.com, the online investment advisory firm. In "White Paper: A Case for Index Fund Portfolios,"[7] they tested a three-index-fund portfolio against 5,000 simulations of similar and randomly chosen managed portfolios. They covered periods between 1997 and 2012. As benchmarks, they used three Vanguard funds: the Total Stock Market Index Fund for 40 percent of the money, the Total International Stock Index Fund for 20 percent, and the Total Bond Market Index Fund for the remaining 40 percent. The index fund portfolio outperformed the stock pickers' portfolios more than 80 percent of the time.

In truth, there might be a manager who beats the market over the length of time you'll be invested. My advice is to find out right away who that person is going to be. Famous stock picker Bill Miller, formerly head of the Legg Mason Capital Management Value Trust, beat the S&P 500 for 15 years straight—the longest streak for publicly traded funds that I'm aware of. Then his returns fell off the cliff. The only Value Trust investors who beat the market invested early, around 1982, before they had any idea of the returns they were going to get, and stayed with it. Those who came late, after Miller became a star, would have been better off in the S&P.

At this writing, only one-quarter to one-third of managed stock funds have beaten the indexes over one-, three-, five-, and ten-year periods, according to the financial research firm Morningstar, *and they're almost never the same funds.* The three-year winners are not also the five-year winners. They rotate as their luck changes. This

---

7   Available from RickFerri.com.

year's top funds will drop back to the middle of the pack or worse.[8] Over periods of 20 years or so, the average managed fund has underperformed a comparable stock market index by about two percentage points a year.

One of the reasons for the lag is that managed funds carry higher expenses. To outperform, they not only have to beat the market, they have to do it by more than enough to cover their costs. The few managed funds with persistent good records have low costs, including some that Vanguard runs. Morningstar's research identifies cost as the only—repeat, *only*—dependable predictor of a mutual fund's future performance.

Another reason managed funds underperform is the complete unpredictability of stock prices. The market is far too surprising for any one manager to guess which combinations of stocks, out of the billions possible, will actually outshine.

Why do managed funds keep attracting buyers? Because they usually have one lucky market-beating period to brag about, which makes us imagine that they'll always be on top. Or because they're sold by brand-name firms that dazzle us with their famous-ness. And, finally, because we the suckers hate to give up the dream that someone, somewhere, possesses secret stock market knowledge that will make us rich.

The only "secret" is index funds. You are paying your fancy fund manager to lose.

What about using exchange-traded funds instead of traditional mutual funds? Exchange-traded funds, or ETFs, are mutual funds in a different form. They almost always follow an index—a traditional

---

8   Perhaps because, instead of following a broad index, they bought hotter stocks or riskier bonds, to attract money by looking better than their peers . . . and then the inevitable happened.

one, such as the S&P 500, or a niche index, for special goals. Their main difference lies in the way they're bought and sold.

Traditional index funds are purchased from the mutual fund company. They're priced at the end of each day. You pay the average net asset value[9] of all the securities in the fund. There are no sales charges if you buy directly from a no-load fund company, by phone or online. There *will* be a sales charge if you buy from a commissioned broker or financial adviser—probably a charge that lasts for many years. A registered investment adviser might charge a flat 0.5 percent.

ETFs, by contrast, are bought and sold on the stock exchange and are priced like stocks. You need a brokerage account and will pay commissions on trades unless you use the commission-free ETF services of firms such as Charles Schwab, Fidelity, TD Ameritrade, and Vanguard. You can trade whenever the exchange is open. There's a "spread" between a share's buying price and selling price—perhaps a small one, but it's still a cost. Spreads will be tiny on ETFs tracking broad indexes such as the S&P but wider on more specialized ETFs that trade less. Depending on the market, you might pay a little more than the ETF's underlying net asset value, or you might pay less.

Management fees for both traditional mutual funds and ETFs are plunging toward zero, as the industry competes for the most cost-conscious investors. Two small ETF sponsors have already issued zeros. At the larger firms, annual ETF fees run about the same—in the 0.02 to 0.04 percent range—if you stick to the broadest-based indexes such as the S&P, says Dave Nadig, managing director of ETF.com, the go-to site for information on ETFs. For more specialized index investing, ETFs charge a bit less than traditional funds, although brokerage and trading fees might offset those savings. The big difference lies in when your gains are taxed. Both ETFs and traditional funds distribute, to your account, your annual share of taxable

---

9 The fund's price per share. It's calculated by dividing the value of all the stocks in the portfolio into the number of shares outstanding.

interest, dividends, and capital gains. With traditional funds, you pay the tax even if you sell no shares. With ETFs, you'll usually pay the tax only if you sell shares personally. That makes ETFs attractive for taxable accounts. The difference is immaterial, however, if you're investing with a tax-deferred retirement account. Even taxable accounts might not receive taxable capital gains from well-diversified traditional funds that are managed for tax efficiency.

The leading ETFs follow the same broad indexes that many traditional index funds do. Under the iShares label, for example, you might choose iShares Total U.S. Stock Market or iShares Core MSCI EAFE (for the whole list, see iShares.com). The SPDRs label (us .spdrs.com) includes SPDR S&P 500 and SPDR Gold Shares. Charles Schwab offers Schwab U.S. Broad Market and Schwab International Equity. A popular ETF for smaller-company shares is iShares Russell 2000. At Vanguard, you can buy ETFs based on exactly the same portfolios offered by its traditional index mutual funds, such as Vanguard Total Stock Market and Vanguard Total International Stock.

ETFs come in hundreds of other flavors—value, growth, commodities, real estate, energy, health care, small company stocks, stocks in a single country or region, stocks in specific foreign industries, bear market stocks, and on and on. Most of them follow standard indexes. Specialty ETFs follow indexes created by their sponsors. In effect, those sponsors are stock pickers, trying to replicate certain aspects of market behavior. Some ETFs are run by active managers who don't follow an index. As with their traditional mutual fund counterparts, they all complicate your retirement life. For easy rebalancing and withdrawal purposes, two or three broad-based ETFs are plenty—Total Market U.S., Total Market International, Total Bond U.S. You'd buy them in place of their traditional index fund counterparts.

So, which should you use—ETFs or traditional index funds? You might as well choose what's most convenient. Traditional fund investors will stick with their fund companies. People who invest primarily through discount brokerage accounts or have taxable accounts will probably use ETFs. Just be sure that you aren't paying sales commissions when you rebalance your ETFs or take your annual withdrawal. The more you buy and sell through a commissioned broker, the more expensive ETFs become.

There's more than one type of index tracked by mutual funds. Traditional funds and ETFs, like the ones above, use indexes that are *capitalization weighted*. The more a stock is worth in the market, the greater its weight in the index. When you buy a cap-weighted fund, a larger portion of your money goes into its priciest or largest stocks and a smaller portion into smaller or undervalued stocks. The S&P 500 is a cap-weighted index, as are most of the other indexes followed by the leading funds.

Critics call that wrong-way investing—buying high instead of buying low. In a new approach, some exchange-traded funds track indexes that give more weight to smaller or less popular stocks. *Fundamental index funds* follow stocks that meet specific tests of operating value, such as cash flow, dividends, sales, and book value. They tilt toward value stocks. *Equal-weight indexes* spread your money evenly over all the covered stocks, giving you a smaller-stock tilt. *Dividend index funds* collect stocks with a history of raising dividends; they appeal to income seekers but leave you unexposed to growth funds, small-company funds, and tech stocks. Dozens of other differently weighted indexes currently vie for investor attention, all of them claiming they'll beat the traditional S&P 500 because they're constructed in a smarter way. And they might, if you hold them for very long periods of time. Hard to know.

In the meantime, they'll outperform the cap-weighted market in some years and underperform them in others. When they outperform, they do so by taking more risk, not because of the magic of their special form of indexing. They're generally less diversified than the broad market, rebalance more often (which raises costs), and rely on a stock picker's idea of what the best performing companies are likely to be. If you want to tilt your total market index fund toward smaller or value stocks, you can do it just as well by adding a small-stock or value mutual fund or ETF to a traditional fund.

What about diversifying with individual stocks? To be truly diversified, you have to own stock in at least 50 companies of different sizes and in different industries. That's not how individuals invest. What's more, if you owned all those stocks, how would you decide which ones to sell when taking your annual withdrawal, and once you sold them, how would you stay diversified? You'd almost certainly miss some of the meteor stocks that produce a decent chunk of an index fund's return. You'd also miss stocks you never heard of that outperform the more famous names.

You've probably owned some of these meteor stocks in your time. But you've bought a lot of losers, too, or sold good stocks too soon. If you averaged your winners with your losers and the stock holdings you'd call blah, you'd find—and I say this with confidence—that your personal performance has lagged the S&P 500. You've left a lot of money on the table over your investing life.

When you look in the mirror, you'll probably have to concede—unless you're a deeply experienced investment analyst—that you know very little about any of the individual stocks you own. Can you say how good the company's business is right now? What are the trends in profit margins, sales rates, and inventories? What earnings growth do you project and how much are you paying for it? What are the company's problems and how are they being handled? For each of its lines of business, is the market share rising or falling? What's the competition up to, at home and abroad? You probably can't answer these questions, so you have no idea whether holding the stock makes sense. Keeping it just for dividends isn't good enough. When the company faces headwinds, the dividends might be cut.

If you're investing with a taxable account, you might want to keep a stock that has risen substantially in value. If you sell, you'll owe a capital gains tax on the profits. If you don't sell, the tax vanishes when the stock passes to your heirs. But a lot can happen to a company over 20 years. If you're looking at a long life span, it generally makes more financial sense to sell, pay the tax, and diversify into mutual funds.

Stocks are amusing if that's what you'd like to play with during your retirement. You might put 5 percent of your investment portfolio into your entertainment budget. But do it as a single lump sum. If you lose it, don't throw good money after bad. Maintain a careful index fund allocation for the money you'll rely on for the rest of your life.

Some almost-great advice from Warren Buffett. Buffett, chair of Berkshire Hathaway, is best known for saying that you should buy good stocks and hold them forever. But in real life, he doubts very much that you and I know what a "good stock" is. He judges a company by whether he can estimate an earnings range for the next five years or more and whether those earnings can be bought today at a reasonable price. In his 2013 letter to shareholders, he wrote that people like you and me can't possibly do that. But he goes on to say that, luckily, we don't have to:

> The goal of the non-professional should not be to pick winners—neither he nor his "helpers" can do that—but should rather be to own a cross-section of businesses that in aggregate are bound to do well. A low-cost S&P 500 index fund will achieve this goal. . . .
>
> What I advise here is essentially identical to certain instructions I've laid out in my will. One bequest provides that cash will be delivered to a trustee for my wife's benefit. . . . My advice to the trustee could not be more simple: Put 10%

of the cash in short-term government bonds and 90% in a very low-cost **S&P** 500 index fund. (I suggest Vanguard's.) I believe the trust's long-term results from this policy will be superior to those attained by most investors—whether pension funds, institutions, or individuals—who employ high-fee managers.

P.S. from me:

Dear Mrs. Buffett,

Your smart husband got it almost right. His advice about indexing is right on. I'm guessing the trust is being managed for your children or grandchildren so 90 percent in stocks is fine. But, hey, why would you want all the money only in the S&P 500? How about all the rest of American stocks and then the world? You can be smarter than Warren. Tell the trustee that you want to own U.S. and international total market funds instead!

Sincerely yours,
Jane

What's in Your Bond Bucket?

Everything in a retirement portfolio has a specific job to do. For stocks, it's growth. For bonds, it's ballast. All the safe withdrawal plans assume that you own high-quality bonds that hold reasonably steady or rise in price when the stock market falls. Bonds also contribute to your retirement income, but their safety is more important than their interest rate. Even when quality bond markets fall, they never lose anywhere close to as much as you can lose in stocks.

Finally, you need bonds for liquidity in case stock prices decline for a couple of years and you have to come up with money for your annual 4 percent withdrawal. For this reason, you'd hold a generous helping of short-term bond funds along with intermediate-term funds.

Here's a very quick bond market primer:

- A bond is a loan. The issuer pays interest, usually quarterly, and promises to return your money after a certain number of years have passed. The safest bonds, in terms of default risk, are those issued by the U.S. Treasury. High-rated AAA or AA bonds issued by corporations and municipalities have a history of safety, too. If you're investing through a tax-deferred retirement account, you'd choose Treasuries or bond mutual funds that include both Treasuries and high-quality corporates. If your account is taxable and your income is high, you'd favor top-rated tax-exempt municipal bonds or funds. High-income investors might buy Treasuries, too. You owe federal income taxes on the interest that Treasuries pay but no state and local income tax.

- Bonds are issued in various maturities, from one year to 30 years. "Short-term" generally means one to three years; "intermediate-term," four to 10 years; "long term," over 10 years. Their fixed interest rate is called a *coupon rate*. The *yield to maturity* tells you your annual percentage gain if you hold for the bond's full term and reinvest each interest payment at the same coupon rate that you're earning from the bond. If you spend the interest payments, your yield won't be as high.

- The main thing that you need to know about bond prices is that they move in the opposite direction from interest rates. When interest rates fall, bond prices rise. When interest rates rise, bond prices fall. You see this relationship clearly when you own bond mutual funds because their posted prices change every day. The prices of any individual bonds you own are changing, too, but you don't notice it—that is, unless you want to sell a bond before maturity. At that point, you'd get whatever price the market set.

- How much a bond's price rises or falls as interest rates change depends on the bond's *duration*. Duration is a calculation that includes such things as the bond's coupon rate, current yield, and final maturity.

  Bonds with longer durations rise and fall more sharply in price than bonds of shorter durations. For example, assume that interest rates change by 1 percentage point. Bonds with 15-year durations will rise or fall by about 15 percent. Those with six-year durations will rise or fall by about 6 percent. Those with two-year durations rise or fall by about 2 percent. It's important to understand duration because it helps you choose a bond mutual fund. Of two funds with the same average maturity (say, two intermediate-term funds), the one with the longer duration will rise and fall more in price when interest rates change. A shorter duration fund gives you a slightly smoother ride. No-load mutual funds show their durations on their websites. You can find this information for all bond funds, free, at Morningstar.com.

- Interest rates, hence bond prices, are also influenced by inflation expectations. Starting in 1980, inflation generally cycled down, lowering rates and lifting bond prices up. Holders of bonds and bond mutual funds received excellent returns. At this writing, the big institutions that drive the market foresee only moderate inflation over the next decade—the kind of cycle that bond investors have been through before and lived. For the effect of rising interest rates on bond mutual funds, see page 285.

- Yes, but . . . Government spending! National debt! Hyperinflation! Treacherous Federal Reserve! Destruction of our way of life! Not impossible, I suppose. But don't let the rowdy, freaked-out forecasting crowd mess with your mind. The link between federal debt levels and long-term interest rates is, on average, exactly zero, a Vanguard study says. There's only a weak link between price inflation and budget deficits. During some quarters in 2015, average consumer prices declined in real-dollar terms. Wage inflation is nowhere in sight.

- You have two defenses in case the future brings us an inflation surprise. Own short-term bond funds, whose prices normally fall only a small amount when interest rates go up. (You should own them anyway, as a backup to your cash reserve.) And invest in some Treasury inflation-protected securities. TIPS are merely inflation hedges, not all-out investment bets because, well, you never know. Rant about debt and hyperinflation all you like but invest agnostically.

The Case for Buying Bond Mutual Funds

With a mutual fund, you're buying into a pool of bonds. The share value of your fund will rise or fall every day as interest rates change. If you sell your shares when rates are up, you might get less than you originally paid. You'll get more than you paid if rates are down. There's no guarantee.

But successful retirement withdrawal portfolios don't run on guarantees. They need *liquidity*, which means access to cash at any time without having to take a steep discount from the current market price. That's what you get from mutual funds. Funds also make it easy to rebalance your investments, especially if you're holding them in a tax-deferred retirement account. You simply move money from bond funds to stock funds and vice versa. Life isn't anywhere close to this easy if you hold individual bonds.

Investors worry about the share value of their bond funds at times when interest rates are going up. But during those periods, they do better than you think. The managers will invest the fund's continuing cash flow in bonds that pay the higher rate. As a result, the income you receive from the fund goes up. If you're spending the interest, you'll have a little more in your pocket. If you're reinvesting it, you'll be purchasing shares in your fund at a lower price. When interest rates go down again and bond prices rise, those additional shares will provide you with an extra gain. You don't get these market advantages if you own individual bonds.

Funds have another edge over individual bonds in a period of rising rates. If you buy, say, a $10,000 individual bond paying 3.5 percent, you'll earn $350 this year. That's not enough to reinvest in a new bond. You'd probably spend the money or put it in a bank at almost zero percent. If you own a bond mutual fund, by contrast, that $350 can be reinvested in the fund at the same 3.5 percent (or whatever new rate the fund currently pays).

Bond funds are also diversified. That's not important if you're buying Treasuries. But for general bond funds that include corporates or tax deferred municipals, safety lies in spreading your risk. You do have to pay the fund's management fees. That cost is at least partly offset by the fact that the managers can buy bonds at low institutional markups. If you buy individual bonds, you have to pay retail.

Treasury funds serve you better than funds primarily invested in investment-grade corporates when you're making regular withdrawals from your investment account. That's because Treasuries usually rise in price when the rest of the market is drowning in fear. The price of any corporate bonds you own usually goes down.[10]

Speaking of fear, don't panic and switch your money into a bank when interest rates rise and the value of your bond fund falls. If you

---

10 Fee-only financial planner Jon Luskin of Define Financial in San Diego, California, compared returns of two 50/50 stock/bond portfolios over multiple periods. Stocks paired with long-term government bonds did better than those paired with high-quality corporates, adjusted for risk.

do, three bad things will happen. You'll lose current income because banks usually pay less than you earn from bonds. The capital loss that you took on the sale is permanent. And you'll lose the future capital gains that the funds will rack up when the cycle turns and interest rates decline again.

The Case for Buying Bond Index Mutual Funds

In general, all the funds that contain bonds of the same duration and type will perform about the same. The principal difference will be fees. Need I say that low-cost bond index funds almost always beat the pack? To do better than the index, a managed bond fund has to take higher risks, and why would you want that? This is the portion of your retirement portfolio that's supposed to be relatively safe.

In a tax-deferred account you could own a single fund— Vanguard's Total Bond Market Index Fund (costing 0.05 percent a year) or Fidelity's U.S. Bond Index Fund (0.25 percent, both about two-thirds invested in government-backed securities). They're intermediate-term funds.

For price stability, you'd also want to own a short-term fund. All bonds fall in value when interest rates rise, but a high-quality short-term fund falls by only a small amount. You could use it for your annual withdrawal if stock and bond prices are down and you don't have enough money in your cash reserve. Short-term funds also recover quickly, as the bonds mature and are replaced with new ones paying higher rates. That makes them a good inflation hedge.

Don't bother buying long-term bond funds in addition to intermediates. Over time, they do modestly better than intermediate-term funds but are much more vulnerable to loss when interest rates rise. They also complicate rebalancing. The total bond index funds, mentioned above, put about 15 percent of their money into long-term bonds, which is enough.

International bond funds provide you with currency diversification against the dollar. But they cost more to own and, again, complicate your investment plan. The simpler your bond bucket, the easier it is to rebalance.

What about funds that own Treasury Inflation-Protected Securities (TIPS)? TIPS pay a fixed rate of interest plus an increase in principal value that matches the rise in the consumer price index. You buy them to hedge against unexpectedly high inflation. The "expected" inflation rate is already built into the price.[11] TIPS mutual funds distribute the interest and inflation adjustment monthly, which you can reinvest in additional shares.

TIPS funds don't protect you from normal market risks. Like other bond funds, they rise in price when interest rates fall and fall in price when interest rates rise—and by greater percentages than comparable Treasury funds do. They perform especially badly when rates rise and inflation goes nowhere.

The TIPS market can be unstable, subject to sudden price hits whenever big institutional investors or hedge funds get alarmed. During the 2008 financial collapse, for example, intermediate-term TIPS funds shocked investors by dropping 12 percent in a month. (If you were a faithful rebalancer and bought TIPS during the panic, you were up 15 percent over the following year. But how many people actually did that?)

TIPS have just one purpose: to deliver inflation-adjusted income, which is what you'd want if inflation escapes to unexpectedly higher

---

11 To calculate the current expected inflation rate, compare the TIPS yield with the yield on a comparable Treasury bond that is not adjusted for inflation. For example, if a 10-year TIPS yields 1 percent and a 10-year Treasury yields 3 percent, the expected annual rate of inflation is 2 percent a year over the next 10 years. If inflation exceeds 2 percent under this scenario, TIPS will do better. If it's less than 2 percent, regular Treasuries will do better.

levels. As usual, the time to buy is when expected inflation lies low. Short-term TIPS funds carry less risk than intermediate-term funds, but they also provide inflation protection for a shorter period of time. At this writing, Vanguard's short-term TIPS fund has an average duration of just 2.6 years.

Adding TIPS to your investment portfolio would give you a three-fund fixed-income bucket—a short-term fund for stability, an intermediate-term fund for more income, and a TIPS fund for inflation protection. That's three funds for bonds plus, perhaps, two funds for stocks—still not too hard to rebalance, but if you're a simplifier, you're pushing the envelope.

Sometimes TIPS sell at negative yields. That means they'll pay you less than the expected inflation rate. This reversal occurs during periods of low interest rates and high demand for an inflation hedge. At such times, short-term Treasuries that are not inflation adjusted would generally sell at a negative real yield, too.

What about high-yield bond funds otherwise known as "junk"? Junk bonds are issued by low-quality companies and municipal entities. They're beloved by investors because they pay high interest rates. Unfortunately, their default risk rises when the economy turns down. They often fall in price right along with stocks, so they can't provide you with safe withdrawals in bad times. What's more, there's good research showing that their higher rates of interest are offset by defaults and other losses, so they don't actually do any better than quality bonds. Don't punch holes in your bond bucket. Stick with high quality.

What about tax-free municipal bond funds? If you're in the 24 percent federal tax bracket or higher and are investing with a taxable account, use part of your money for funds that own tax-exempt municipal bonds. They're issued by government entities for public purposes. As long as you buy a top-quality fund (not a high-yield "junk muni" fund) you should be okay. These are all managed funds, not index funds.

National muni funds own the bonds of many states. You pay no federal income tax on the interest income you receive. States tax only the portion of the income earned from out-of-state bonds. You can skip state income taxes entirely by buying a fund invested only in your state's bonds but single-state funds charge higher fees. They're also not diversified. An apparently top-quality state could lose value in the next recession.

By the way, muni funds are only *income* tax free. You can be taxed on any realized capital gains.

What about owning no intermediate-term bonds at all? During periods of low interest rates, some advisers suggest holding 60 percent in stock funds and balancing that higher risk by putting the other 40 percent into Treasury bills and short-term bond funds. High-quality, investment-grade short-term funds don't pay very much, but they're solid protection against rising interest rates and inflation, if that's your worry. (Quality is critical. Some broker-sold short-term bond funds, peddled for their higher yields, have lost 10 to 15 percent during bond market meltdowns.)

Alternatively, you might also look into bank and credit union certificates of deposit for the safety portion of your portfolio. A five-year CD might yield more than a bond fund with a five-year duration. For high-yield CDs, insured by the Federal Deposit Insurance Corporation, check Bankrate.com.

Ginnie Mae funds invest in mortgages insured by the federal government. You earn higher returns than you would from other funds whose investments are government insured. Dividend income rises when mortgage interest rates go up and falls when rates go down. There's a complication. With each check, you receive part of your principal back as well as an interest payment. If you spend it all, you're spending principal, which should count toward your annual 4 percent withdrawal.

Bond "alternatives" are not bonds. When interest rates hang low, income investors reach for higher yields. These include real estate investment trusts (REITs), which invest in real estate companies and distribute rental income to shareholders; master limited partnerships (MLPs), which buy natural resource companies such as gas pipelines; preferred stocks that pay high dividends but carry more market risk; and mutual funds invested in floating-rate bank loans that rise and fall with interest rates and the economy. Alternative investments provide diversification for investors willing to increase their risk and complicate their rebalancing strategies. But the extra income they provide in good times could be overrun by their loss of market value during bad times. They don't perform the proper function of bonds in a retirement portfolio—namely, as a source of cash in bad markets without having to sell stocks at a loss.

The case against buying individual bonds. At first blush, buying individual bonds sounds like a no-brainer. You know exactly what you're getting in advance. There's a fixed rate of interest. If you hold the bonds to maturity, you'll get all your money back. If you buy Treasuries, there's no default risk (and a vanishingly small default risk for top-quality five- to ten-year corporates and tax-exempt municipals). You don't have to worry about the bond market's ups and downs.

But you do have to worry if there's a risk that you might suddenly need extra cash.

Individual corporates and tax-exempts aren't liquid when owned in amounts of less than $100,000 or so. You can sell them but will take a haircut on the price. If you buy such bonds, you have to be very sure that you can afford to lock up that money until they mature.

Individual Treasuries can be bought, with no commission, from

TreasuryDirect.gov. To sell before maturity, however, you'd have to transfer them to a brokerage firm.

Individual TIPS have a special disadvantage compared with TIPS mutual funds. The inflation adjustment[12] is taxable every year but not paid until the TIPS mature. You can defer the tax by keeping TIPS in your retirement fund but there they don't produce current income. By contrast, TIPS mutual funds distribute the interest and inflation adjustment every month.

Newly issued individual municipal bonds can be bought from a broker with no commission. But brokers prefer to sell you older munis that already trade in the market. They mark up the price of those older bonds by 2 or 3 percentage points, which is close to what you'd earn in interest the first year. Some brokers hit you for even more. You're unlikely to know the size of the markup because the muni market is so opaque. Investment expert William Bernstein calls older munis a vehicle for transferring wealth from investors to brokers.

If individual bonds have a place at all, they're for wealthy people with large amounts of money to invest, not portfolios of small or medium size.

What about building ladders with individual bonds? A bond ladder is a series of bonds arranged so that one of them matures each year. A five-year ladder would start with bonds coming due in one, two, three, four, and five years. In theory, this answers the liquidity problem. On every due date, you'd have cash if you needed it for your annual withdrawal.

If you don't need the cash when the one-year bond comes due, you'd invest the money in a new five-year bond. If you always reinvest

---

12 In a deflation, your principal would be adjusted downward and interest paid on the reduced amount. At maturity, however, you'd get the bond's full face value back.

the principal, you'll soon own five five-year bonds with one coming due each year. Most bond ladders use Treasuries. You can do something similar with certificates of deposit. You need at least $100,000 (some say $500,000) for a well-diversified ladder of municipals.

But how does a ladder really help? If, in one of those years, you find that you need the cash for your annual withdrawal, you'll leave a hole in your ladder that you'll have to fill in some future year. Each time your broker sells you another muni, you pay another big markup in price. If interest rates rise, the payments from your ladder will lose value. And because of the inflexible maturities, it becomes difficult to rebalance your portfolio every year.

Wealth managers create million-dollar ladders for clients with a super-high net worth at a minimal markup. For the rest of us, ladders waste our time and interfere with sensible withdrawal plans. Use mutual funds instead. When you think about it, ladders could be called bond mutual funds in disguise, except with less diversification.

What about exchange-traded funds that own bonds? Bond ETFs work like stock ETFs. You need a brokerage account and might have to pay commissions when you rebalance or make withdrawals unless you choose a firm that provides free trades. Bond markets aren't as liquid as stock markets, which hurts the ETF price if a selling panic hits. If you use ETFs, stick entirely with funds that buy Treasuries or track the total U.S. investment-grade bond market. Low-cost possibilities include Vanguard ETF or iShares Core U.S. Aggregate Bond.

USING TARGET-DATE MUTUAL FUNDS

Target-date mutual funds are a terrific invention for people building wealth. All you have to do is pick a fund designed for the approximate date that you plan to retire (2025, 2030, 2035, 2040, and so on). After that, the fund solves the asset-allocation problem for you.

If your target retirement date is far away, your fund will be invested primarily in U.S. and international stock funds with a small amount in bonds. As retirement draws closer, the managers will gradually reduce the stock allocation and raise the amount in bonds. Accounts are rebalanced automatically. If you're in a 401(k) plan, you can roll your target-date fund, intact, into the fund company's individual retirement account when you leave your job.

Target-date funds work well for people who agree with their manager's investment philosophy. They usually hold roughly 50 to 55 percent of their assets in stocks on the day you retire with the rest in short- and intermediate-term bonds. As the years go by, the stock allocation will generally continue to decline. By the time you reach 70 or 80, the stocks in your fund will level out at roughly 20 to 30 percent with the rest in bonds. That's a pretty traditional progression (called a "glide path") for a retirement portfolio intended to last for 30 years or more. Vanguard's Target Retirement Funds, Fidelity's Freedom Funds, Charles Schwab's Target Funds, and T. Rowe Price's Retirement Funds all follow this general pattern. Declining stock allocations support an initial 3.5 percent withdrawal rate, plus annual inflation adjustments, but perhaps not 4 percent if the markets turn down when you first retire.

Target-date investing is poorly understood, even among savers who chose these plans for their 401(k)s. They thought "target date 2020" meant "safe in 2020 and every previous year, besides," and were shocked when the stock portion of their fund lost half its value during the 2008–2009 financial collapse. Savers who stayed in their funds recovered wonderfully. Their accounts were rebalanced, adding more stock at lower prices. At this writing, stock prices are up more 335 percent from the 2009 low. But some people couldn't stand the stress. They sold their target-date funds and switched into fixed-income funds—a choice that permanently reduced the amount of monthly retirement income that their savings will support.

If it feels too risky to accept 50 percent in stocks in the year you'll retire, but you like the automatic rebalancing that target funds provide, you could choose a fund with an earlier target date than the year you'll actually retire. For example, say that you're 55 in 2020 and will retire at 65 in 2030. Ten years from now, the 2030 fund—apparently your predestined choice—might plan to be 50 percent in stocks. If that's too much, you could choose the 2025 fund, which, 10 years from now, might be only 40 percent in stocks. It's not that you're planning to retire in 2025, you're simply choosing a fund meant for people older than you are and, hence, is invested more conservatively.

Conversely, you might think that 50 percent in stocks is too little. In that case, you'd choose a fund with a later target date, say, 2035, which might be 60 percent in stocks 10 years from now. (Note that the date is just a title. These funds continue to be managed for many years past their target date.)

You might not want to keep your target-date fund after you retire. You're stuck with the stock/bond allocation that the fund decrees. If you're making withdrawals, the money will come proportionately from the fund's stocks and bonds, regardless of how well or poorly each performed. There's a better choice: Roll the money into a low-cost stock index fund and a low-cost bond index fund. That way, you can decide for yourself how much money to allocate to each. You can also choose whether to take your regular withdrawals from stocks or from bonds, depending on how well each investment has done. As a bonus, the index funds might cost a bit less than the target-date fund.

A few target-date funds take your stock allocation down to around 10 percent at retirement, on the assumption that you will drop the fund and choose something else.

WHERE CAN I GET HELP?

You can manage a retirement account yourself if you keep it really simple—say, just two or three low-cost index funds. You rebalance when necessary and take your annual withdrawal from the appropriate accounts (see page 249). If you don't want to do the rebalancing yourself, you have a few options:

- Hold all your savings in a target-date fund. The manager does the rebalancing for you. At year's end, you simply take the total withdrawal (according to the 4 percent rule) in a single amount. Useful, if you agree with the stock/bond allocations that the fund makes or if you want to keep things simple.

- Some 401(k) plans offer personal services that advise new retirees on how much money to withdraw each year, taking into consideration their Social Security benefits and other investments.

- Use Quicken Financial Planner online. It has a rebalancing program that tells you how to move your money around each year (assuming you're investing with a tax-deferred account, so there are no tax consequences to the adjustments). Once you've rebalanced, it's up to you to take the proper percentage from each fund.

- Move your money to an online investment service such as Betterment.com. It will create an asset allocation for you, manage the money, rebalance, and advise you on a sustainable lifetime withdrawal plan. Cost: 0.25 percent a year plus the price of the underlying ETF investments. Many larger brokerage firms now offer robo-advisers, too, but mainly for money management, not for advice.

- Use one of the following two online services for a holistic approach to your lifetime income planning. You enter your financial information into a sophisticated software program that shows you how to maximize your income from the assets you have. You can enter different spending and savings scenarios, to see their likely effect on your future. If you're still working, you'll get advice on how much to save in order to reach the retirement standard of living you'd like. The planning projections take taxes, Social Security, and Medicare into account and suggest the most efficient way of drawing from savings of all types—traditional and Roth IRAs as well as taxable accounts.

IncomeStrategy.com offers three levels of service. For $20 a month, you get a proposed lifetime income plan, which you can adjust as you please. A "get cash" button tells you which investments to liquidate to receive the retirement income you want. For $50 a month, you get access to model investment portfolios, investment recommendations, and a rebalancing tool. At either level of service, you can talk to a planning expert for $125 an hour. Finally, you can let IncomeStrategy manage your money and send you checks. Cost: 0.3 to 0.8 percent annually, depending on the size of your account.

MaxiFiPlanner.com offers two levels of service. Standard, at $99 a year, provides access to its comprehensive planning software, including strategies for spending, saving, investing, insurance, and maintaining your lifestyle in retirement. You can click a button to see the potential results of various Social Security and retirement withdrawal strategies. Premium service, at $139, adds access to preset investment portfolios and risk analysis, so that you can test how changes in your investment plan add or subtract from your future income security. Personal advice is available for $250 a session.

- A fee-only financial planner will give you asset-allocation advice in addition to providing other personal financial services. Some will manage your money and send you monthly checks. A wealth manager should be a registered investment adviser (RIA). Choose one who sells no financial products, agrees in writing to act as a fiduciary at all times, and charges under 1 percent (including the cost of your investments).

- The big no-load mutual fund companies offer low-cost planning services to customers. Vanguard Personal Advisor Services provides money management, portfolio rebalancing, retirement-withdrawal plans, and ongoing personal finance advice to its customers for just 0.3 percent a year and an automatic robo adviser for 0.15 percent. Schwab Intelligent Advisory, which also offers personal planning, charges 0.28 percent a year. Fidelity Investments, T. Rowe Price, and others offer advice as well. Check their websites. Also check the underlying cost of the investments these advisers use. They should all be low-cost mutual funds or ETFs.

FEES MATTER!

However you decide to invest, fees matter! The more you pay—for money management or for investments you choose yourself—the less cash you'll have in your pocket to spend. Traditional, broad-based index funds and exchange-traded funds cost the least and allow the 4 or 4.5 percent rule to work as planned. As cost benchmarks, use Vanguard's index funds, at 0.04 to 0.14 percent a year or Fidelity's, at zero. Add 0.25 to 0.5 percentage points if you work with an online adviser or one of the advisory services offered by the big mutual fund groups. Add 0.5 to 1 percentage point if you choose to work with a fee-only financial planner or wealth manager. Note that, while fees for mutual funds and ETFs are dropping like stones, fees for personal investment advisers are *not* going down.

You will not earn the net income you expect if you pay high sales commissions to a financial adviser, including the commissions hidden in high-cost fixed-index and variable annuities. The more famous the firm and the fancier the offices, the more they will extract from you in fees. They have no conscience. Trust me on this. A variable annuity with a guaranteed lifetime withdrawal benefit might cost 3.5 percent or more. A "wrap account" or "fee-based" account, where the broker or financial advisory firm oversees your money, might cost 2 to 3 percent. For each percentage point you pay in fees, the amount you can safely withdraw from your nest egg drops by about 0.4 percent. Even with an efficient investment strategy, costing under 1 percent, you have to be cautious when starting with anything over a 4 percent withdrawal.

So quit talking yourself into thinking that a high-cost adviser is doing you some sort of favor. Do the math. The lower your fees, the more money you will earn and the higher the income you can take from your retirement investments.

EARNING RETIREMENT INCOME FROM RENTAL REAL ESTATE

Real estate is a different world. If you buy rental properties, intending to add to your retirement income, you are starting a small business. You can't check your statement once a year and then go back to your favorite retirement pursuits. Running your rental real estate *is* your pursuit.

It's harder than you think to draw real personal income out of your property month after month. Your rents have to cover your costs with a decent amount left over. That's a reasonable expectation if you're renting an apartment carved out of your personal residence and the tenant pays on time. It's certain if you buy a rental property with cash so you have no mortgage payments. If you take a mortgage, however, your rental income will probably fall short. You might wind up dipping into savings to support the property every month. That's not what you had in mind. Your risk rises exponentially if your income drops after you retire and you're having to dig even deeper into savings to support your properties.

Rental real estate investors get into trouble because they overestimate their likely net income from the property, underestimate their expenses, or both. Among your expenses are mortgage payments, taxes, insurance, fix-up costs before the house can be rented, any utilities the renter doesn't cover, trash hauling, unexpected repairs, advertising for tenants, reserves for repainting and replacements, fix-up costs when you're in between tenants, legal advice when preparing a lease, and a dozen other things. You need reliable service people on call if you can't make emergency repairs yourself. On the income side, you have to account for the weeks or months you're between tenants if the market is poor or you have to take the house off the market for repairs. If the heat goes out and you're slow with repairs, the tenant might not feel required to pay the rent that month.

Bad tenants can be your largest cost of all. They pay late, quit paying, resist eviction, and might trash your property on the way out. They'll probably have an illegal cat that pees on the carpet. It's all the more painful if those tenants are in an apartment over your garage.

Before renting to anyone, do a credit check and call his or her previous employers and landlords. Get cash or money orders for the first month's rent and the security deposit (that gets rid of people whose checks bounce after they move in). Jack Reed (johntreed .com), author of *How to Manage Residential Property for Maximum Cash Flow and Resale Value,* advises that you also spend an evening watching the movie *Pacific Heights,* a dark and cautionary tale about landlording gone wrong.

Not everyone has the temperament to be a landlord. You have to be cheerful about taking calls at any time of day or night, keep your temper with rude tenants, and handle problems right away. Know your local eviction laws and move to evict the first time the rent comes late. A good tenant will apologize and never miss the date again. A bad tenant will find excuses, not just once but again and again.

Ask yourself, honestly, do you have the guts to demand the rent on time? To demand rent at all if someone gives you a sob story? Can you throw out a single parent who has lost his or her job? Even if the child is small? And sick? And has a puppy? If you can't answer all those questions with a hard-boiled yes, don't even try to be a landlord. In this game, nice guys get their clocks cleaned. You might set out to be the best landlord in history and discover, too late, that you were just incompetent. Buying any sad story, from any tenant, could cost you not only your income and profit but your principal and—if you have a mortgage—your credit rating, too. Grrrr.

Nouveau landlords commonly overinvest in the rental houses they buy. They choose homes they might want to live in themselves and bring them up to their own high standards. It could be a long time before you recover those costs. The condition of rental properties needs to be adequate for the market and nothing more. The same is true for small apartment houses. Here, you might run into unexpected costs, such as heating or plumbing problems that your real-estate inspector didn't catch before you bought.

Cash flow is the name of the game. Selling the house at a profit, if that happens, won't cover your grocery bills today. You might be able to raise the rent as inflation rises, but taxes and other costs will go up, too. Furthermore, real estate isn't liquid. Even highly desirable properties might not sell and close in less than six months. You'll need cash on the side, in the bank or in short-term bond funds, in case a tenant flees and you need ready money to pay your bills.

Rental income is taxable. But you can deduct expenses, including depreciation, which will offset part of the gain and possibly all of it. If your expenses exceed your rental income, the loss is deductible on your current tax return, up to certain limits, once the property has been sold. Assuming that you manage the rental house yourself and your modified adjusted gross income doesn't exceed $100,000, you can write off up to $25,000 in losses, which tax-shelters some of your regular income, too. At higher incomes, the allowable deduction gradually phases out, terminating at $150,000. For more detailed information from the IRS, enter "Tips on Rental Real Estate Income, Deductions and Recordkeeping" into your search engine. Also, ask your accountant if you qualify for the 20 percent deduction on qualified business income, included in the tax law that took effect in 2018.

A vacation home that you treat as a rental property is considered a personal residence if you use it more than 14 days a year or more than 10 percent of the time it is rented, whichever is less. It's also considered personal use if you rent to a relative or friend at less than the going rate. You'll have to prorate the expenses between days of business use (deductible) and personal use (not deductible).

Before getting into rental real estate investment, study up. It's not like buying index funds. Read books on real estate finance, learn about property values in various neighborhoods, analyze your local economy (have people been moving in or moving out?), and set rules for yourself, such as the amount you're willing to spend on fix-up expenses. Successful real estate investors have to get their fingernails dirty. If your game plan relies mainly on prices going up, rather than on generating positive cash flow, buy a real estate mutual fund instead.

If you already own rental real estate, consider developing a plan for getting out. Landlording becomes more difficult as you age. The cash tied up in your properties might generate more income in a different type of investment.

YES, THEY'RE OUT TO GET YOU!

Willie Sutton robbed banks because that's where the money was. For the same reason, greedy financial salespeople go after the retirement accounts of people in midlife and later. They're selling products that carry high commissions and conceal your annual costs and risks. You're on their list if you're rolling over a 401(k) into new investments, choosing a lump-sum pension payout instead of a monthly lifetime income, or looking for higher returns on your savings than you're getting from banks and bonds.

These modern-day Willies are especially eager to meet you if you haven't had much investment experience outside the protected world of 401(k)s and are looking for someone to help you make your money grow. Also, if you're older, single, and lacking someone to protect you, you'll find the Willies soooo smart, sympathetic, and nice. They'll help you right out of the savings you worked so hard for. When you complain that you didn't understand what you were getting into, they'll say they disclosed the risks (which they probably did, in the contract's fine print). Their firm will back them. Selling high-cost products is what their employers expect them to do.

Take special care when your adviser buys you mutual funds. For broker-sold funds, there is not just one price. There are various "share classes" in the fund, which carry different fees and different commissions to advisers. It's all too common for advisers to saddle you with the class that costs the most—sometimes through up-front fees, sometimes through annual maintenance fees, sometimes through fees called 12b-1s that pay the broker a "trailing commission" of up to 1 percent every year. You could have bought exactly the same fund for less. Hiding the overcharge is not just bad form, it's illegal. In 2017, the Securities and Exchange Commission waived penalties for firms that admitted their wrongdoing. At this writing, 79 firms have come forward, agreeing to refund $125 million to clients. Several big-name firms have been fined individually. No one is safe! If you're holding mutual funds in a brokerage or advisory account, find out if you're paying 12b-1 fees and whether cheaper versions are available. If so, demand a refund. Your "adviser" has effectively been clipping your investment returns.

Unfortunately, many of you deliberately fall in with the Willies' plans. You beg them for "safe, high-yielding" investments so that you won't have to touch your capital to live. With happy smiles, they serve you an expensive, complex "conservative" portfolio that appears to yield more than average market rates. Please. *Nothing* that pays substantially more than market rates is safe; it's only constructed to look that way. In order to avoid touching capital, you're setting yourself up to lose capital. The menu of sweet-sounding perilous products is long. Here are a few of the ones you might run into:

- **Nontraded real estate investment trusts.** REITs invest in commercial properties such as shopping centers, apartments, and hotels. Most of them trade on a stock exchange so you know what their real market value is. The red-alert word here is "nontraded." Unlike similarly invested REITs, you have no idea what the actual market value might be. The sponsoring companies can name their price. Nontraded REITs appear to pay high dividends, but part of that "dividend" might come from the capital you invested (in other words, you're just getting your own money back). Often, the managers borrow money to pay the dividend, which increases your costs and risks. Sometimes, they skip the dividend, and there's nothing you can do about it. You're usually told that you'll have to wait seven years (or more) to get your full investment out. At that point, the REIT is supposed to sell the properties and distribute the proceeds or else go public so you can sell your shares on the open market. They might not be able to do either one, however, if market conditions are poor. Instead, they'll have to liquidate. If they do go public, the shares might trade for much less than you paid. You might be allowed to sell your shares back to the company before the seven years are up, if you have a financial emergency. In that case, you'll take a steep discount from what you thought was the market price. Even if your REIT distributes its properties successfully at the end of the term, you'll probably never be able to find out what it actually returned on your investment. In some cases, the answer has been zero.

Front-end fees and sales commissions on nontraded REITs run as high as 15 percent, which explains why they're so popular among brokers and financial advisers. You're also paying high annual management fees to the sponsor of the REIT. Three years ago, the Securities and Exchange Commission started to require that nontraded REITs do a better job of disclosing costs. They're also supposed to provide you with periodic estimates of what your shares are worth. That estimate, however, will be far above the price you'll actually get if you want to sell early. One good sign: When brokers started disclosing costs, sales fell.

In real life, nontraded REITs cannot do better than publicly traded REITs. In fact, they are almost bound to do worse because they charge so much more in commissions and fees. If you want a REIT, buy one that's publicly traded and sold by a no-load mutual fund.

- **Private placements and nontraded business development companies.** You're buying into some sort of business—energy, cell phones, restaurant chains—which is supposed to pay high, periodic distributions with handsome profits at the end. The regulators pretty much ignore these placements because they're supposedly sold only to "sophisticated investors." The managers don't even have to provide you with financial statements, which makes them a hotbed for fraud. All too often, they come to naught. You'll discover that it's hard to bring suit because, in the offering document you signed, you agreed you were sophisticated and understood the risks. You might even find that the document prevents you from suing or requires you to pay the adviser's legal costs. As for those exciting venture capital funds invested in startups—a

2018 analysis found that the average fund underperformed Standard & Poor's 500 stock average.

- **Collateralized loan obligations (CLOs).** They're very similar to the collateralized mortgage obligations (CMOs) that set off the financial collapse of 2007–2008—except that, instead of investing in high-risk mortgages loans, you're investing in a package of loans from various high-risk companies. You'll also find them peddled as "leveraged loans." CLOs are lightly regulated. In 2018, they were exempted from some of the investor-protection covenants passed after the collapse. They offer high (and floating) interest rates which, in a strong economy, can be paid. In a deep recession, who knows?

- **Leveraged exchange-traded funds.** You're gambling. If all goes well, you can make two or three times the return of a particular index. Or you can lose twice as much, and more. For your right to gamble, you pay a high fee. Last year, Vanguard barred leveraged ETFs from its trading platform because investors didn't understand the risks.

- **Any high-rate investment "crowdfunded" to innocents on the Internet.**

- **Cryptocurrencies of any sort.** That includes crowdfunded Initial Loan Procurements. What? You don't know what they are? Believe me, ignorance is bliss.

- **Funds of hedge funds.** What are called hedge funds don't really hedge against anything. They're pools of sophisticated money that invest in different, complicated ways. They take annual fees plus 20 percent of the profits in a year that the value of the fund goes up. If it goes down, all the losses are yours. Hedge funds have an undeserved reputation for making their investors rich. Some of them do, but those funds don't sell to the hoi polloi. Before you take the plunge, you might want to know that the average hedge fund underperformed the S&P 500 over the past 10 years. CalPERS of California, the country's largest public pension fund, has ditched its hedge funds and put two-thirds of its stock allocation into low-cost index funds. With experience, even big institutions get smart.

- **Inappropriate IRA investments.** Shares in nontraded REITS, private placements, and similar investments can't readily be sold. If you invest most of your IRA money there— as the greediest salespeople propose—you might be in trouble when you reach 70½. At that age you're required to start withdrawing a certain percentage of your IRA's value every year. To raise the money, you might have to sell these illiquid investments at steep discounts. If you can't sell them at all, the IRS will fine you 50 percent of the money you failed to withdraw on time.

- **Inappropriate rollovers from 401(k) plans.** When you retire, you might have the option of leaving your money in the company's 401(k). Costs might be low and you'll have enough mutual fund choices to create a well-diversified portfolio. Alternatively, you might switch to an IRA in a no-load mutual fund. Financial salespeople, however, want you to switch your money into an IRA with their firm. "Take control of your financial destiny," they'll croon. "Our IRAs give you more investment choice." Well, yes . . . you could choose the kinds of bad investments not allowed in company 401(k)s, including high-cost mutual funds.

There's No Clear Way of Knowing Whom to Trust

Savers and investors have been duped by advisers recommended by close friends, members of their social group, advisers who come into corporations to give talks to preretirees, accountants who handle their taxes, and close relatives. Even experienced investors can be talked into terrible investments by persuasive salespeople.

You can check on an individual broker's or commissioned adviser's conduct at the website of the Financial Industry Regulatory Authority (FINRA.org, click on "Broker Check"). You might find past settlements and complaints. Most complaints against brokers don't make it into the record, however, so you can't be sure. While you're there, check on the firm itself. Under "Firm," scroll wa-a-ay down, to "Disclosure Event Details," to find the sorts of complaints brought against its brokers. A lot of similar complaints suggest that the firm likes the money that the bad apples bring in. For the types of investments that the regulators worry about, go to FINRA's Investor Alerts. Similar services are provided by the federal Securities and Exchange Commission. At SEC.gov, scroll down to "Protect Your Money! Check Your Investment Professional," for broker checks, and "Investor Alerts & Bulletins".

I don't mean to scare you unduly. Many commissioned advisers work well with their clients. But they also have to earn a living and keep their jobs, so they're always in conflict. I'd suggest an adviser whose firm does not accept sales commissions—a fee-only planner or the advisory services listed on pages 295 and 296.

If you keep your investments simple and use low-cost index mutual funds, you will only have to trust yourself.

10

Home Sweet Income-Producing Home

Your house is a piggy bank. This might be the moment to break it open.

There's money in your house. Those friendly walls are packed with legal tender just waiting to be released. You can take the cash now or take it at some point in the future. The decision hinges on how you'll want to live in early or later retirement, and whether you'll need more income to maintain the style of life you want.

If you don't need more income, you can leave your home equity locked up for your heirs, in your current home or in an equal or fancier home that you buy somewhere else.

On the other hand, if your budget already looks tight, the equity in your home might fill the gaps perfectly. You can tap it while staying in place by getting a reverse mortgage, or release it by moving somewhere else.

If you move, you don't have to choose a new home for life. The right place for people in their mid-50s to mid-70s might be the wrong place when you reach 80. There could be two moves in your future, not just one.

Young retirees who move generally want to live among active, like-minded people. That might be a home in an adult community, with scheduled activities and near golf and tennis (check some of them out at 55places.com). Or a university town, where you can audit courses and attend football games. Or a city with plenty of theater, concerts, and access to jobs if you want part-time work. Or a place near your grandchildren (provided that you're not expecting your son or daughter to keep you entertained). Or it could be a smaller house or apartment in the town where you live now, so that you can keep up with old friends.

Older retirees seek a friendly social atmosphere, too, but their priorities lean toward health care, good public transportation, proximity to adult children who can provide help if needed, and easy-care apartments where someone else mows the lawn. A rising trend among boomers is the two-step retirement—first, downsizing to a smaller place, then, later, moving to a full-service retirement community. Even those who hope to age in place should be open to assisted living, financed, in part, by the equity in their homes.

WHATEVER YOU DO, TAKE THE LONG VIEW

Right now, my health is good. I hope yours is, too. But I wonder where I'll live when (and if) I start to need help with the daily business of living. I don't want to wait for my children to open "the conversation" in carefully casual tones of voice. ("Ahem, Mom, we were wondering . . .") I want to open that conversation myself. Their input will influence what I think, but I want the decision to be mine.

Most of us want to "age in place"—whichever place we choose—with occasional side trips to other nice places. That works fine as long as we can take care of ourselves. If we slip, however, we'll have to depend on someone else. Who will be there to help and what can we do in advance to ease the transition? I don't want to be stubborn about aging in place if it's going to create caregiving problems for my children (not to mention medical risks for me).

Doing nothing is itself a decision. You're relying on someone else to step up and make the changes you failed to make yourself.

If you don't have children (or children you can depend on), the question becomes even more important. Kindly neighbors running errands isn't a permanent solution.

People hoping to stay in their homes should look at the floor plan as if they were already on a walker. You might have to add a bedroom downstairs with a bathroom whose door can accommodate a wheelchair. Your pretty front porch will become a trap if there's nowhere to build a ramp to the sidewalk. Plan on renovating while you're still healthy, before an emergency crops up.

Besides renovation, consider your community access. What happens if it's no longer safe for you to drive? In car-centered suburbs, you'd have to depend on others to do your shopping or take you to doctor's appointments. Maybe it's impractical to age in place.

Eventually, you might need caregiving services if a spouse or child isn't constantly available. You'll also need someone you trust to supervise home care aides to be sure they're always doing right by you. Who is that likely to be? Do you want to lay that responsibility on your kids, and if so, how will they handle it? This shouldn't be a snap decision made under duress. The whole family should plan.

My own parents set an example for me. In their late 70s and in reasonably good health, they decided to sell their house and move to a lovely apartment in a continuing care retirement community (CCRC—see page 315). In a CCRC, you live independently among a group of like-minded people. If you start to fail physically, you can move to an assisted living or skilled care unit. These communities not only lift burdens from you, they relieve your adult children of the minutiae of parent care. The children will be especially grateful if they live far away and can't stop by to check on your needs every day or two.

For people who stay in their homes until they are frail, the best option—when you finally move—might be a residence for assisted living (see page 318). There you live as independently as possible but can get help with basic physical needs such as dressing and bathing. Like CCRCs, they provide activities and a social life. There might be a nursing home wing attached.

The key is to plan ahead. What can you afford—today and in the future? What's a reasonable way to live? Do you expect your children to help (and do they know that)? Should you stay where you are or move?

THE GOVERNMENT PRACTICALLY PAYS YOU TO MOVE

A house is not only a piggy bank, it's a tax shelter, too. If you're married and sell it, you can take up to $500,000 in profits tax free. This tax break applies only to your principal residence, not a second home. By "profits," I mean any money you make on the house after subtracting the price you originally paid, the cost of all home improvements over the years, and fix-up costs and real estate commissions when you sell. If you're single, the first $250,000 in profits comes tax free.

If you expect to sell, do it sooner rather than later. The older you get the harder it becomes, emotionally, to make a move, and the more you'll have spent on upkeep—furnace, roof, paint, repairs, and lawn work, along with real estate taxes and insurance. That money could have gone straight into a savings account instead. Why be house poor in retirement? Shake loose some of that cash.

You have several choices when you want to move and take equity out of your house.

1. **Buy a less expensive house or condo.** Add the money left over from the move to your savings and investments. That beefs up

the current and future income you can afford to withdraw from your savings every year.

But take care: If you buy another house, it will come with the same kinds of upkeep costs that your old one did. If you renovate and redecorate, the move might not save you any money at all. A modern, easy-to-care-for, one- or two-bedroom condominium or town house might be a better choice. If your children come to visit from far away, you can put them up in a motel for much less than the annual cost of maintaining a large home. (When I sold my four-bedroom house and moved to a co-op apartment, I solved short visits from family by buying pull-out sofas and topping them with feather beds.)

Big question: Should you pay cash for the new place? I'd say yes, *if* you'll have enough money left over to provide yourself with a comfortable income for life. Owning a paid-up home confers great peace of mind. But if paying cash would squeeze your budget, put 20 percent down and take a 30-year mortgage to cover the rest.[1] Long-term mortgages make sense, even at older ages, because they hold down the size of your monthly payment.

For an estimate of the dollars that downsizing can add to your income, use the calculator "Figure Out How Moving Changes Your Finances" under the headings "Tools," then "Housing," at SquaredAway.bc.edu. It's one of a series of calculators backed by the Financial Security Project at Boston College.

Warning about applying for mortgages today, especially if you're no longer working: You can't just waltz into a bank and waltz out with a loan, as you might have done 20 years ago. There's stepped-up paperwork. Lenders are demanding proof

---

1   Interest on loans up to $750,000, used to buy, build, or improve a home, is tax-deductible. But odds are, you won't use this deduction. The standard deduction will probably be more advantageous.

of every penny of income as well as its sustainability. Pensions, Social Security, interest, and dividends are acceptable as income. So is a portion of your retirement assets, such as an individual retirement account or 401(k), provided that you can put 30 to 40 percent down. You also need a good, current credit rating, so don't give up your credit cards and pay everything with cash. Keep at least one card, use it regularly, and pay on time.

What if you want to move but don't have much home equity? You may be stuck—for a while, at least. You can keep making mortgage payments and hope your home's market value goes up. The monthly cost might be less than you'd pay in rent somewhere else. Worst case: You owe more than your home is worth. If staying in the house becomes untenable, let it go to foreclosure and move on.

2. **Rent instead of buying something else.** The cash you'll get from selling your home might appreciate faster in a diversified investment account than it will in another house. You'll have more money to spend every month, counting a percentage of your enhanced savings, and the landlord will handle the property chores. Rent will go up, but if you buy another place, so will your property taxes, homeowner's insurance premiums, and upkeep costs. The mortgage interest and property tax deductions aren't worth much anymore, thanks to the caps imposed in 2018. You might resist renting because it's "money down a rat hole." But not if it frees up cash to keep you living well. Why own a house and build equity for your heirs if housing expenses crimp your income and limit what you can do during your freedom years? Renting is liberating. You can shut the door and leave. That's especially important if you moved to be closer to one of your adult children. What if the child gets a new job and moves away? You'll want to be free to move as well.

3. **Hit the road.** For younger retirees, these can be years of experimentation. You might buy an RV and tour the country, live on

a boat, or find a warm nest in Costa Rica or Panama. Your new setup should cost only a small portion of the proceeds of your home sale, leaving you with extra income to live on. (But don't spend it all. Most likely, you'll come home again.)

4. **Move in with a willing adult child.** Use the proceeds from the sale of your house to put an addition on the child's house. Or renovate his or her existing house to create a separate bed/sitting room with bath, TV, microwave, and refrigerator. Or build your own cottage on the property, if the zoning allows.

Co-living takes a lot of careful planning. Will you be expected to cook or take care of the grandchildren? Will your adult child be on tap to take you shopping or to the doctor if you can't drive? Will you go on family vacations? Which household expenses will you cover? What's an acceptable mix of privacy and family time? If you need daily assistance, who will help and who will pay? Do you need a home health aide? Can you have a separate social life—say, visits from friends? If you're single, what about sex (yes, grandparents do it!)? Will your children freak if you stay out overnight?

Check on medical coverage before moving to a new area. If you bought an individual policy through a broker or on one of the health-care exchanges, it won't cover you in a different city or state at in-network prices. It might not cover you at all except for emergency care. So shop for health insurance at the same time as you're shopping for a new home. Apply for the new plan in the month you move. Your current insurance company will tell you how to make the transition without opening a gap in coverage.

There are no gaps in coverage when you're on Original Medicare. That plan follows you wherever you go in the United States. By contrast, the Medicare Advantage plans generally limit you to local network doctors. If you expect to move, you might switch to Original Medicare plus a Part D drug plan during the open enrollment period in the year before you move. Add a Medicare Supplement plan, if you can pass the health test. Alternatively, find out if there's a good Advantage plan in your new town. If so, apply for it the month you move so you can go directly from your old Advantage plan to the new one. These plans include Medicare Supplement coverage, so you won't have to risk going without.

Consider a continuing care retirement community, if you can afford it. You'll live in your own town house or apartment and can take your main meals in a community dining room. There's usually a fitness center, along with movies and other social activities. As long as you're well (and you have to be in good health to move in), you carry on with your independent life. If your physical abilities start to fail, you'll move to a part of the campus that offers assisted living, such as help with bathing and dressing. Those who become seriously ill switch to the CCRC's nursing home or Alzheimer's ("memory care") unit. The community should be Medicare certified in case you need skilled nursing care.

Married couples often move to a CCRC to ensure that the survivor is in a safe place when one of them dies. The attraction for singles, besides the social life, is knowing that you've arranged for any long-term care that you might need. I count it a further plus that you've made your own decision rather than dragging your heels until your kids or other relatives have to choose for you.

Typically, you'd use the proceeds of the sale of your house to buy into a CCRC. There's an entrance fee (the median was $335,000 in 2019, meaning that half cost more and half cost less). You'll also pay a monthly maintenance fee (median: $3,500) that will rise a little every year. The contracts vary a lot but fall into three main types:

> *Type A*— the most expensive choice. You buy lifetime hous-
> ing, meals, amenities, and long-term care in a single
> package. Your fees won't rise if you transfer from

independent to assisted living. You can generally remain at the CCRC even if you run out of money.

Type B— a moderate fee up front with the possibility of higher costs later. You buy housing, meals, amenities, and a limited number of days in the assisted living or nursing home wing. If you need more care, your monthly fee will rise. If it turns out that you can't pay, you will have to move.

Type C— a pay-as-you-go arrangement. You get the same housing-and-meals arrangement as the other contracts offer, but if you need comprehensive health care, you pay for it at the market rate.

If you already have long-term care insurance, discuss your options with both the CCRC and your insurer. How does the CCRC bill for its assisted-living and memory-care wings? What portion will your insurer pay? You might consider a B or C contract if your policy will cover most of the CCRC's long-term care charges. Even if you go for a Type A contract, you might want to keep the insurance if it covers private home care in your unit or in the CCRC's health center if you're bedridden.

Visit more than one CCRC to get a sense of the spirit of each place. See the various types of living quarters, have some meals, talk to the residents, check the activities list, and visit the wings that provide assisted living or custodial care. What medical services are available to help residents on-site—perhaps weekly visits by an internist, podiatrist, hearing-aid specialist, or other health professionals? Is there room service for meals if you're down with a cold? If the CCRC doesn't have an Alzheimer's unit, will you be given priority to enter another home for care? Consult with family members as you go along.

There have been a handful of bankruptcies among CCRCs, but in almost all cases the facility was reorganized without affecting the residents' investment. To feel sure that you're buying into a financially strong community, have the contract evaluated by an accountant or real estate lawyer. One source: the National Academy of Elder Law Attorneys (naela.org). Among the things you need to check:

- The full list of services covered by the entry fee plus a list of the fees for extras.
- A five-year history of the community's monthly fees. Moderate annual increases are good. You want the CCRC to keep up with inflation. If it doesn't, large increases might have to be imposed in the future.
- The audited financial statement. Is the line labeled "fund balance" or "net assets" in the black?
- Cash on hand. The CCRC needs at least 150 days of cash on hand. The community probably carries bond financing, which might require much more. Is the facility meeting all its bond covenants? Are the community's bonds rated "investment grade" (AAA to BBB)?
- Operating costs. They should be covered entirely by the monthly fees that the existing residents pay. You don't want a community deeply dependent on new sales, which might not be forthcoming, or having to chew into its cash reserves.
- Actuarial soundness. A CCRC that mainly sells Type A plans needs enough younger, healthier residents to ensure that the costs of the sicker residents can be covered. The facility should provide you with a letter from an actuary saying that, demographically, the community is on a sound financial footing.
- Any lawsuits against the CCRC.
- Accreditation. As a quality measure, the facility should be accredited by CARF International (formerly the Commission on Accreditation of Rehabilitation Facilities).
- Any plans for improvements that might require a financial assessment on the residents.

- Your financial protection if the community that you're buying into hasn't been completed yet. You'll want to be able to get your deposit back if construction is held up too long. To check the financial soundness of new CCRCs, ask for the track record and financials of the developer. Avoid a developer that has never built a CCRC before.
- Your financial options if you decide to leave. With some types of contracts, you simply move out. For those willing to pay higher monthly fees, the CCRC will give you part or all of your entry fee back. You might have to wait for your refund until your unit is resold.
- The quality rating of the CCRC's nursing home section. Go to Medicare.gov, type "nursing homes" into the Search box, and look for "Nursing Home Compare."

You will have to disclose some information, too. The CCRC will ask for your financials to be sure that you can afford the place, and you'll have to pass a health exam. You won't be accepted if you need assisted living right away or don't appear to have enough income to pay the fees for life.

For checklists on how to evaluate CCRCs, visit CARF.org. Type "Financial Performance" into the Search box and scroll down to the free booklet called "Consumer Guide to Understanding Financial Performance & Reporting in Continuing Care Retirement Communities." CARF.org and LeadingAge.org can help you find CCRCs in or near specific towns or cities.

Consider a home for assisted living. These facilities enter the picture if you've stayed in your home until you can't manage anymore, even with home health care. I beg you to be realistic about your capabilities. If you wait until you fall, you might be delivered to a nursing home with a broken hip rather than walking into an assisted-living place where you can still live a mostly independent life. In general, you have to pay for assisted living out of pocket—a good use for home equity. Some states provide limited Medicaid assistance for people with low incomes and few assets. Go to the website of the National Association of Area Agencies on Aging (n4a .org) to find your state's agency. It will tell you what sort of help is available, if any. You might consider checking out the local possibilities in advance, perhaps with the help of a child or friend. If assisted living becomes inevitable, you'll know what the facilities offer and which ones you prefer.

SQUEEZING YOUR HOME FOR INCOME IF YOU DON'T MOVE

You might refinance your current mortgage. At this writing you can get a low fixed rate for 30 years. The payments due might be smaller than those on the loan you have now. You also might take in a boarder or roommate or add a rental apartment over the garage. This works best when the layout provides some privacy for you both. If you're splitting expenses with a roommate, the two of you should prepare a written signed and dated agreement—who pays for what, how are chores divided, and what are the rules on splitting up your partnership?

Before becoming a landlord, check your legal position. Does your zoning law allow boarders? Are you subject to rent control or eviction laws that might make it hard to move a bad boarder out? Is the boarder covered by your liability insurance? What are the tax implications of using part of your house as a rental property? Have you prepared a sound written lease? Do you have the temperament to deal with renters in your home and the spine to turn them out if they misbehave (even if they are, or were, friends)? If you live in a popular tourist spot, you might operate like a motel, if local law allows. Airbnb.com will send you renters who need only a room and bath and will stay a night or three at a time.

Another option is selling your house to one or more of your children and leasing it back from them. This strategy is more talked about than consummated, but here's a quick peek at how it works: The children give you a down payment, which adds to your cash. You give them a mortgage for the rest of the money they owe. They send you a mortgage payment every month. You pay them rent and cover the utilities, which, together, should come to less than the amount of the mortgage payment you receive. So, your spendable income goes up. The children pay the insurance and taxes and see to the maintenance and repairs. For them, it's a rental property so they get deductions for their business expenses.

A sale/leaseback should be worked out with a lawyer. The house price, interest rate, and rent all have to be set at fair market value. Before getting into anything like this, however, consider the risks. What if one of your children loses his or her job and can't make mortgage payments or repairs? What if the children disagree? What if there's a divorce? What if you and your children have a fight? Remember *King Lear.* . . .

Another choice might be a reverse mortgage with regular payments that raise your retirement standard of living. These loans don't get good press, but you should take another look.

NEW WAYS OF THINKING ABOUT REVERSE MORTGAGES

I've changed my mind about reverse mortgages. I used to see more risk than reward for most borrowers. But the risk has diminished. New federal regulations make reverse mortgages safer for people in their late 70s and 80s who need extra money to help them stay in their homes. New cash-flow strategies also make them interesting for people in their early 60s and 70s who want to improve their monthly retirement income.

I'll have more to say about these strategies a little further on. First, here's a general explanation of reverse mortgages and how they work.

Reverse Mortgages Defined

A *reverse mortgage* is a loan against the equity you hold in your home. You don't have to repay it as long as you're living in the house. Instead the lender makes payments to you, entirely tax free. Your only obligation is to cover the cost of homeowner's insurance, property taxes, and general upkeep.

Eventually, the house will be sold—because you move, enter a nursing home permanently, or die. The proceeds of the sale will be used to repay the loan plus all the accumulated interest and fees. If the house sells for more than what's owed, the remaining money goes to you or your heirs. If it sells for less, you or your heirs walk away—you get nothing, but you're also not responsible for any additional money owed.

You can get a reverse mortgage, individually, as early as age 62. If you borrow jointly with a spouse or domestic partner, only one of you has to be 62. The younger your partner, however, the less money you will get. Almost all reverse mortgages come in the form of a Home Equity Conversion Mortgage (HECM). It's issued by private lenders and insured by the Federal Housing Administration (FHA). A handful of financial firms provide their own reverse mortgages, often at a lower cost. You can borrow against a single-family house, a two- to four-unit home provided that you live in one of the units, an FHA-approved condominium, and most manufactured homes that sit on property you own. Mobile homes are out. So are vacation homes. Reverse mortgages can be used only for your principal residence. These loans work best when your home is completely (or substantially) mortgage free. But you can use them to help pay off an existing mortgage, too.

Reverse mortgages are *expensive* compared with traditional loans. Not only do you pay more in up-front and annual FHA fees but the total amount you owe goes up every month because the cost of the interest and fees compounds within the loan. Paying these fees makes sense only if the loan is part of a carefully thought-out plan.

How Reverse Mortgages Work, Step by Step

1. A lender agrees to make the loan. How much you can borrow depends on the appraised value of your home, current interest rates, the age of the youngest borrower, and how much (if anything) you still owe on the home. These loans work best for people who own their homes free and clear or who have only small mortgages. If you have little or no equity, you won't qualify. The older you are and the less you still owe, the more money you can get. Appraised values are capped at $726,526, which limits the amount of money you can borrow on more expensive homes. For a quick estimate of the potential size of your loan, use the reverse mortgage calculator at mtgprofessor.com.

2. As part of the deal, you have to pay off any remaining mortgages on the house, including home equity loans. If you don't have the cash, you can use the proceeds of the reverse mortgage to help make the payoff. Any liens or court judgments secured by the house have to be repaid as well. The loan is off the table, however, if you're delinquent on any federal debt, including student loans that you might have cosigned.

3. Before you can close the loan, you have to reveal the size of your income and savings. The lender must be satisfied that you can pay the ongoing costs of homeownership (insurance, property taxes, condominium fees, upkeep) and still have enough left to live on.

4. You're required to go through reverse mortgage counseling, by phone or face-to-face. The lender will give you some names. You can also search for counselors online or call the counseling line of the U.S. Department of Housing and Urban Development at 800-569-4287. Be warned that the counselors won't help

you choose the best option for your circumstances. Their job is merely to ensure that you understand the terms of the loan and what it means, to you and your heirs, when you spend home equity. They're also required to tell you about alternatives to the reverse mortgage, such as local programs that help low-income homeowners. A HECM counselor's advice is free or of modest cost.

5. You pay little or no cash up front. All closing and FHA insurance costs can be included in the loan.

6. You can receive the money from your reverse mortgage in one of several ways:

  • **A credit line that you can borrow against at any time.** This is normally the best choice because it's not an ordinary credit line. The amount you can borrow rises every year at the same rate as the interest rate you're paying on the loan. If you use very little of the money during the first few years, you'll be able to access much more cash when you are older. That makes your HECM credit line an excellent hedge against future inflation or increased medical costs. If you borrow too much too fast, however, you might be entitled only to smaller amounts in your later years. For more on this magical credit line, see page 329.

  • **A check a month, for a fixed amount, paid as long as you're in the house.** The lender will calculate the size of the check based on the total sum you're allowed to borrow. The checks will keep coming even if they exceed your original borrowing limit.

  • **A fixed number of checks, up to your borrowing limit.** Once you've received them all, the game ends. No more money will be paid. These checks can be for larger amounts than the check-a-month deal because the lender knows—in advance—when its obligation will end.

- **A lump sum.** This is the most tempting choice because it's nice to have so much cash in hand. But it also makes it more likely that you'll run through the money and still won't be able to keep your house. Lump-sum borrowers have to settle for smaller loan amounts than other borrowers get. They also pay higher fees.
- **A combination of the above.** For example, you might take $25,000 up front, $800 a month for as long as you live in the house, and a $60,000 credit line.

7. Each reverse mortgage check looks and feels like income. But it isn't income, it's a loan. You owe no taxes on the money. Also, you don't have to count it when figuring whether your Social Security is taxable or whether you owe a higher Medicare premium. It might affect your eligibility for Medicaid, however (Medicaid pays for nursing home care if you run out of money).

8. You don't have to repay a penny as long as you stay in the house. The loan normally comes due only if you sell the house and move somewhere else, enter a nursing home for a long stay (usually 12 months or more), or die. If you own the house with a spouse or partner, and you're both on the HECM, these terms apply to you both. If one of you enters a nursing home, the other one can stay in the house and keep using the HECM credit line or receiving scheduled monthly payments.

9. You can be forced out of the house if you fail to pay real estate taxes or homeowners' insurance, or if you let the house run down. People run this risk when their income is too low to cover their projected living expenses. They take a HECM in a lump sum, spend all the money, then go broke. They default on their insurance and taxes and lose the home.

     A new regulation, first effective in 2015, is greatly reducing this default risk. If your income is marginal, the lender is no longer allowed to give you the whole loan amount. Part of it will be set aside in a special fund that's expected to cover your housing expenses (insurance, taxes, upkeep) over your lifetime. Sometimes these set-asides leave you with hardly any additional spendable income. In that case, skip the HECM. The lender is effectively telling you that you can't afford your home. Best to sell right away and downsize.

10. When the house is sold, the HECM is repaid out of the proceeds. If there's money left over, it goes to you or your heirs. If the proceeds of the sale aren't large enough to cover the loan, you or your heirs owe nothing but also get nothing. You'll have spent the entire value of your home. Anyone who strongly wants to leave a debt-free home to children is not a candidate for a Home Equity Conversion Mortgage.

Tell Your Heirs about the Loan!

Please, please involve your adult children in this decision if they're your heirs. In spending your home equity, you're using what could have been their inheritance. You're absolutely entitled to do so. You worked for that house, and responsible children should agree that maintaining your standard of living comes first. But they shouldn't be taken by surprise after you die, learning suddenly that this piece of their expected inheritance is gone. What's more, your children can make a good sounding board while you consider your choices. One of them might have financial expertise.

If you borrow in the form of a lump sum, the odds are high that there will be no equity left when you die. When the loan is front-loaded, the costs build up fast. There's a better chance of getting some value out of the house if you borrow in the form of monthly payments or a credit line that you tap at a slow pace.

At your death, your legal heirs have an opportunity to buy the house themselves or sell it to a third party. The price to heirs is either the amount due on the loan or 95 percent of the appraised market value, whichever is less. For example, take a house worth $100,000, where the loan against it has grown to $150,000. An heir could buy it for $95,000. There's no equity left, after fees, but he or she could live there without having to repay the remaining loan. If the same house is worth $200,000, the heirs might want to put it up for sale. If they find a buyer, they could repay the $150,000 owed to the bank and pocket the rest. They generally have six months to sell. If they can't, the lender will foreclose or take a deed in lieu of foreclosure.

Some heirs have complained about the way that various lenders handle HECMs that come due. They might seize the house too quickly, or lose documents sent by heirs who are trying to buy the property, or give them the runaround when they're trying to find out the status of the loan. The more your heirs know about the loan in advance and during its term, the better prepared they will be to handle the sale or foreclosure process in the end.

What Does a Home Equity Conversion Mortgage Cost?

HECMs come with fixed interest rates or variable rates. You don't pay the interest monthly, as you do with regular mortgages. Instead, it's added to the amount of your loan, where it compounds. Both principal and interest fall due when the house is finally sold.

From a current income point of view, it makes no difference how much interest accumulates. You always get the amount of borrowing power that you signed up for—the lump sum, the monthly checks, or the credit line. The cost shows up in the amount of money you (or your heirs) realize from the proceeds of the sale. The more interest you owe and the less your house appreciated in value, the less money will be left over for the family. Here's how the two versions of the HECM work.

- *A fixed-rate HECM* is of interest only to people for whom the fixed rate matters more than the cost or the amount of money they receive. You're normally given no more than 60 percent[2] of the total allowable amount in the first year. That's all. You can't come back for the remaining 40 percent in the second year. You have to take the money in a lump sum; you can't get monthly payments or a credit line. The interest rate might be nearly double that of a new variable-rate HECM. At this writing, many lenders aren't even writing fixed-rate HECMs.

- *A variable-rate HECM* also sets a normal borrowing limit of 60 percent of the allowable loan amount in the first year. But thanks to the lower interest rate, that might add up to more dollars than you'd get from a fixed-rate loan. Twelve months later, you can come back for the remaining 40 percent.

That is, assuming that you want to take as much cash as possible up front. You can also take the loan in the form of monthly payments or a credit line. The interest rate is usually linked to LIBOR (the London Interbank Offered Rate) plus an additional amount (the "margin") set by the lender. For example, if LIBOR is 2.4 percent and the margin is 2.5 percent, your opening rate would be 4.9 percent. The rate changes every week and can't increase by more than 10 percentage points above the starting rate. Some loans have lower caps. Remember that rising rates do not affect the income you receive from your loan. Instead, they reduce the amount of equity left in the house when it's finally sold.

You can pay the fees on HECMs out of pocket but usually they're added to the cost of the loan and accumulate over time. Here's a list of your costs:

---

2 You can borrow more if needed to cover mandatory payments related to the home, such as the current mortgage, tax liens, and the up-front HECM fees. In this case, you could also get up to 10 percent of the available proceeds in cash.

- An up-front loan insurance fee, charged by the Federal Housing Administration (FHA). You pay 2 percent of the appraised value of your house. For example, on a $300,000 house you'd pay $6,000. Appraised values are capped at $726,525, so the most you'd pay is $14,530. Yes, it's a lot.
- The annual FHA mortgage insurance premium. You pay 0.5 percent a year on the outstanding balance of the loan.
- The loan origination fee. Some lenders charge this up front; others charge zero up front but raise your interest rate a little bit. Fees are capped at 2 percent of the first $200,000 of your home's appraised value and 1 percent of the remaining amount, up to a maximum fee of $6,000. On a $300,000 home, that's $5,000 up front.
- Repair costs. Before you can borrow, an appraiser has to certify that the house is sound. If the cost of repairs will amount to no more than 15 percent of the value of the house, you can take the reverse mortgage and use some of the proceeds to make the necessary fixes. If the cost will be higher, you have to make the repairs yourself before closing the loan.
- Closing costs. You pay many of the normal closing costs that you would for any other mortgage, such as document fees, courier fees, title insurance, recording fees, credit report fees, fees for sending your lender on a world cruise (well, maybe not that last one, but close).
- Annual service fees. These are usually included in the interest rate, but some lenders charge them separately.
- Compounding costs. You pay interest on all the fees added to the loan. These costs build up fast, making it less and less likely that you'll have any equity left when the house is sold.
- TALC calculation. Reverse mortgage lenders are required to calculate a total annual loan cost, or TALC, based on all projected costs over specified holding periods. You can use TALC to compare two loans. But I wouldn't call it an effective form

of disclosure. More customized cost estimates can be had from a reverse mortgage counselor (see page 322) working with specialized software. To make the best use of the software, you should talk with the counselor face-to-face, not just over the phone.

The HECM's Magical Credit Line

When you take a HECM in the form of a credit line, the only money you borrow—at first—is the amount of the settlement costs. That might run $12,000 to $15,000 or more. Beyond that, the lender has simply granted you a pot of money to use whenever you want. You will owe interest only on the amount that you actually borrow. For example, say that you take a $150,000 credit line and spend $12,000 of it every year. You pay interest only on the $12,000 annual increments. The annual 0.5 percent FHA fee is also assessed only on the borrowed amount.

Here's the magical part. The amount of credit available grows every year by the rate of interest you pay plus the FHA insurance fee. For example, say that in the first year your loan costs a total of 4.25 percent. Interest rates rise in the second year, bringing your borrowing cost to 4.5 percent. The amount of your credit line will also grow by 4.5 percent. By taking the credit line at age 62 *and not using it much*, it will grow and grow. You'll have much more borrowing and spending power by the time you're 70 or 75. That gives you a good inflation hedge.

The credit line grows even if you borrow against it heavily in the early years. But in that case, interest costs will be accumulating. If you're not careful, the credit line might run out.

Using a Home Equity Conversion Mortgage Strategically

A reverse mortgage puts extra money in your pocket right away. But always consider the endgame before signing up. What if you're unable to stay in your home for life? When you sell, you might net little or nothing after repaying the loan. That would be harmful if you needed cash to buy an apartment or enter an assisted living home. Ideally, you should manage the loan so that you'll always have home equity left or, alternatively, always have a pot of savings on the side.

Here's how to think about the most common reasons for taking a HECM:

Borrowing as part of a 20- or 30-year spending plan. This savvy use of a HECM is catching on with financial planners. It's what changed my mind about the potential value of HECMs for people in their early 60s and 70s.

Say that you're planning for a 30-year retirement. In Chapter 8, you saw that you should generally spend no more than 4 or 5 percent of your savings in the first year you retire, plus annual inflation adjustments, if you need the money to last for at least 30 years. For a 20-year retirement, you might take 5 or 6 percent. But what if that rate of withdrawal doesn't deliver the standard of living you want? A HECM can help you increase your annual income by combining your savings and home equity into a single spending pot.

To do that, take a reverse mortgage as early as age 62. Set it up as a standby line of credit and—at first—don't borrow against it. Instead, pay your bills by drawing, say, 6 percent out of your savings in the first year (for a 30-year retirement) and raising that amount by the inflation rate in each following year. When your savings run low, switch to taking the money you need from your reverse mortgage credit line. By now, the credit line will be much larger than it was when you started.

There are other ways of setting up your HECM-linked spending plan. You might pay bills from your savings in a year that your investments rise in value and pay them from the HECM credit line in a year the market falls. That saves you from having to sell stocks at a lower price. Or you might pay your bills entirely from the credit line for several years, leaving your investments alone to grow.

A well-planned rate of withdrawal from both pots of money raises your current income and can lengthen the number of years your money will last. The combo might even raise the amount of money you leave to heirs, if that's a concern.

The longer you wait to take the reverse mortgage, the less efficient it will be. You need 15 to 20 years to spread out the effects of the high up-front cost. Adopt this strategy only if you've determined that you're going to stay in your home and will need a higher income to keep you there.

Borrowing to pay the bulk of your living expenses. This is the classic—and riskiest—use of a reverse mortgage. You live on your savings for as long as you can. As a last resort, you take a reverse mortgage so that you can pay the bills and stay in your house. If you borrow in the form of a lump sum and run through the money, you're stuck. You might not be able to afford the taxes and insurance anymore. At that point, the HECM lender can call in the loan and force you to sell your house. The sale price might not be high enough to cover the loan repayment. You'd be on the street without enough cash to buy something else.

People with modest incomes do have some protection against eviction, thanks to a new regulation that took effect in 2015. The lender will now set aside part of the loan proceeds to help pay your future housing expenses if there's a risk that you might not be able to afford them.

If you find yourself facing set-asides, however, perhaps you shouldn't borrow at all. Consider selling the house and using the proceeds to settle in another, lower-cost form of housing—a condominium, a rental apartment, or an apartment attached to an adult child's home. If a reverse mortgage still appeals to you, choose monthly payments or the credit line to stretch out the loan for as many years as possible.

Borrowing to eliminate your traditional mortgage. Depending on how large your mortgage is, you might be able to use the proceeds of a reverse mortgage to wipe out everything you still owe. That ends the monthly payment and raises your spendable income. This use of a HECM, however, can also be risky business. Presumably, you're taking the loan because you're having trouble meeting the mortgage payments and other bills. The new loan will help you stay in your home only if you have enough cash flow to pay your expenses from now until the horizon, inflation included. If this is another form of last-resort borrowing, you should think about selling right away and finding less costly housing somewhere else. Always consider the future. What will you have left if you have to sell the house and enter a nursing home in your older age?

Borrowing to buy a new house. You can buy a new house or condo with the proceeds of a reverse mortgage plus some money of your own. Like the strategy above, this eliminates monthly mortgage payments. One potential problem is that you generally have to borrow in a lump sum. That increases your interest costs, which reduces your chance of maintaining any future equity in your home.

Borrowing for major home improvements. These loans will be worthwhile if you remain in the home for 15 or 20 years. But think about the cost and effort of maintaining your house as you age. Five or 10 years from now, you might decide that your future lies in an easy-care condominium. Over short terms, the reverse mortgage isn't worth its cost.

Borrowing to get rid of large amounts of credit card debt. You'll wipe out burdensome monthly payments but that won't help much if you run up consumer debt all over again. It's better to work with a credit counselor to cut your expenses than to spend your precious home equity on the cost of clothes, furniture, and meals that you bought in the distant past. If you take the HECM and sell the house in just a few years, the reverse mortgage will have cost you more than the credit cards did.

Borrowing for fun and grandchildren. I've seen celebrity TV ads aimed at the early-60s crowd, urging you to borrow a lump sum against your home and spend it while you're still young. Take a cruise! Buy an RV! Send your grandchildren to college! All worthy goals, but will you be blowing your home equity too fast? Can you pay your bills for the rest of your life when that form of savings is gone? Taking a reverse mortgage is an expensive way of paying for a vacation. Instead of the lump sum, consider taking a credit line and using modest amounts each year to give yourself a more comfortable life. (Note that lenders love you to take lump sums because they collect high interest on all the money from the first day. That's why they pay all those aging celebrities to shill.)

Borrowing to buy a variable or fixed annuity. It's illegal for a financial adviser to pitch you directly on buying annuities with the proceeds of a reverse mortgage. But nothing stops you from taking the loan and then buying an annuity or other investment at a later date. To do so, you'd probably take your loan in the form of a lump sum. That's the most expensive way to borrow and leaves you with no flexibility. Proposals like these come very close to being scams (the "adviser" makes out like a bandit thanks to the high sales commission on the annuity). Anyway, why bother? The reverse mortgage itself can provide you with a monthly income and at a lower cost than the mortgage-plus-annuity deal.

When You Sell the House, What Then?

Don't leave yourself stranded with no cash on hand. If you decide to leave your house (or have to leave for reasons of health), you'll want enough savings or home equity to set up new digs. If you'll need nursing home care, you'll find better choices when you can pay the bill yourself for at least the first few months before going on Medicaid (see page 129).

So, don't borrow every possible dime against your home. Take the reverse mortgage in the form of a credit line and monitor how much savings and equity you have on hand each year. Maybe your house will rise in value, adding a bit to your equity, but don't rely on that—especially after paying the reverse mortgage fees. If your total pot of savings looks threatened, downsize while you still can extract some cash from the sale.

Spouse Alert! What Are Your Rights If Your Partner Dies?

When couples decide on a HECM, each partner's financial security will depend on who owns the house.

If both your names are on the deed you'll both sign the loan agreement. Its terms apply to you equally. If one of you dies or enters a nursing home, the other spouse (or co-owner) can continue to draw payments from the HECM, as before.

If only one of you is on the deed, however, things change. Only the homeowner will be granted the HECM. The other partner will be listed as a "nonborrowing spouse."

As a nonborrower, you run a risk if the borrowing spouse dies or enters a nursing home. You can stay in the home, provided that you keep up with the taxes, insurance, any condominium fees, and repairs. But payouts from the HECM stop. A nonborrower cannot receive monthly checks or tap the credit line. You will have to pay all the household bills from whatever other money you have. If that's not possible, the loan will fall due. If you can't repay, the lender will foreclose and you'll have to move out. Eviction is almost certain if you took the loan because you couldn't pay your bill and the income you got from the HECM stops.

The right to continued occupancy belongs only to spouses (or official domestic partners) who were in place when the HECM was made. A spouse who entered the picture later will have to buy the house, pay off the loan, or move out if the borrower dies or leaves.

Please note! Nonborrowing spouses have the right to stay in the home only if the HECM was made on August 4, 2014, or later. If the loan was earlier, a nonborrowing spouse can usually stay in the home. But he or she has no occupancy "right." It's up to the lender to decide. If you want to stay, always ask. For good strategic advice, go to mtgprofessor.com, click on "Reverse Mortgages," then "Read Articles on Reverse Mortgages," then scroll down to "Managing a HECM Reverse Mortgage When One Spouse Is Significantly Older Than the Other."

Alert to parents who have an adult child at home, perhaps a child who's impaired: The child can't be made part of the reverse mortgage contract. If you die or move to a nursing home permanently, the child will have to buy the house or move out. If the child inherits the house, there might be no home equity left to assist with his or her support. For you, a HECM might be a mistake.

Where to Find Tons of Information and Advice on Reverse Mortgages

- Go to the website mtgprofessor.com. Jack Guttentag, real estate expert and professor of finance emeritus at the Wharton School of the University of Pennsylvania, has put together the best package of information and guidance I have found anywhere. You get a sophisticated calculator showing what you can borrow at different ages and with different options. You'll also find offers from loan advisers who agree to follow best practices when arranging a reverse mortgage. They'll suggest a package of up-front cash, fixed payments, and a credit line intended to meet your needs and hold down your costs over the period you'll keep the loan. The advisers might not serve all states.

- Go to nrmlaonline.org, the website of the National Reverse Mortgage Lenders Association. You'll find more info on reverse mortgages and a glossary of terms. NRMLA also posts estimates of current reverse mortgage prices. But they're consistently higher—sometimes much higher—than the prices offered by lenders on mtgprofessor.com.

CONTEMPLATING THE PAID-UP HOUSE

If you have enough cash to pay off the mortgage, should you or shouldn't you? This is one of those questions that can only be answered, "It depends."

If you have spare cash, put it first toward paying off any high-rate consumer debts. If you're still working and have wiped out your credit card debt, use the money to raise your contributions to your tax-favored retirement account such as a 401(k), IRA, or Roth IRA. If you've maxed on these contributions, go ahead, and reduce your mortgage by making extra monthly payments. It's bliss to own a paid-up house by the time you retire. If you still hold a mortgage at retirement, the calculation changes. Should you take a lump sum from your savings to pay off the remaining mortgage debt? The answer is no, if you'd have to take the money out of an IRA or 401(k). That would cost you a ton in taxes and deprive you of using those savings gradually and strategically. Also no, if repayment would seriously deplete your cash reserves. You need to maintain enough savings so that, at modest withdrawal rates (Chapter 8), you'll have enough money to pay your daily bills, including mortgage bills, for life.

If you have enough savings to live on comfortably, however, and have savings outside a retirement account, consider using them to eliminate the loan. A paid-up house reduces your living costs, saves you interest payments, and makes you feel secure. What's more, due to the tax law of 2018, you might not even be using the mortgage interest deduction anymore.

Some financial advisers think that, instead of paying off the mortgage, you should invest that extra money in the hope of earning a higher return. That won't work if you primarily hold bonds or bank certificates of deposit. At this writing, repaying the mortgage yields more than you'd get from high-quality bonds or CDs. You might do better, however, by using the money to buy stock-owning mutual funds and holding them for 10 years or more. With that as an option, the prepayment question becomes a matter of temperament. Are you happier trying to make some extra money in the market? Or happier getting rid of those monthly mortgage bills?

How to Prepay

If you have a fixed-rate mortgage, it's easy. Just add money to your monthly payment. That automatically shortens the term of the loan.

If you have a variable-rate mortgage, it's more complicated. Prepayments don't automatically shorten the term of the loan. They generally reduce the size of your monthly payments, but the number of years you have to pay remains the same.

As an example of how this works, say that you have a 30-year loan and the lender resets your variable interest rate once a year. You decide to prepay and start adding an extra $500 to your monthly payment. It's duly applied to reducing your principal. Next year, your schedule of payments will be based on that reduced principal, stretched over the loan's remaining term. The monthly amount that you have to pay will probably go down. But you'll still be in debt for 30 years.

You *can* reduce the term of a variable-rate loan but it takes some calculating. First step is to decide how soon you want to pay it off—say, in 12 years. Using an online mortgage calculator, find out how much that will cost per month and start paying it. Next year, when your interest rate changes, fire up the calculator again. Enter the new interest rate and the amount of principal owed, and say that you want to repay over 11 years. The calculator will give you a new monthly payment, perhaps higher than the last. Do the same in each subsequent year. Result: Your mortgage will end in the year you wanted to be clear.

DOWNSIZED LIVING, RETIREMENT STYLE

Maintaining a home will probably be your largest retirement expense. The better you are at holding down these costs, the more money you'll have to spend to keep yourself happy and entertained. It's surprising how pleasant a stripped-down life can be. No boxes in the attic. Fewer rooms to clean. And passports at the ready, to see the world.

11

Living on Your Life Insurance

There's money in a life insurance policy and you don't have to die to get it.

What should you do about your life insurance policy when you retire? Keep it or use the money for something else?

When you were younger, you bought insurance to protect your family. It would have replaced your paycheck if you died.

Motives change, however, when you retire. You don't have a paycheck anymore (or only a small part-time paycheck), and your children are grown and gone (with luck). There might be no point to owning life insurance. That's especially true for singles, including widows and widowers. Often it makes more sense to stop paying premiums so you can increase your spendable income. If your policy has cash value, maybe you should take that money out.

On the other hand, maybe you do need insurance for the rest of your life to meet your family obligations. In that case, you should find out immediately if your policy is secure. Some term insurance might not be renewable without a medical exam if you wait too long to act. Policies that include a savings element, known as "cash value," might lapse unless they're restructured in some way. Most owners of cash-value insurance have no idea that their policies might not last for life. You simply assume that your family is safe, then wake up one day to discover that your "safe" policy is about to blow up.

This chapter shows you how to extract more value—in cash or in coverage—from any life insurance you own. Just hop to the section that covers your type of policy. If you're not sure which type you have (which is pretty common in the confusing cash-value insurance world), your policy's cover sheet or annual report will usually tell you. It will be one of the following:

- *Term insurance:* pure insurance with no cash value. It's designed to protect your family during the years you're working and end when you retire. (See page 344.)
- *Guaranteed universal life*: designed for older people who want to buy coverage for life at the lowest cost. There's little or no cash in the policy. It's also called no-lapse universal life (see page 346).
- *Whole-life insurance*: designed for people who decide, at an earlier age, that they will want coverage for life. The policy builds up cash value and is generally guaranteed, provided that you pay the premiums on time (see page 352).
- *Universal policies with cash values:* these policies are not usually guaranteed and might not last for life. Whether they do or not depends on the amount of premium you pay and the investment return you receive on the savings element. If your cash value runs out, your policy will lapse (see page 355). The universal group includes *universal life insurance*, whose cash values earn varying rates of interest; *variable universal life insurance*, whose cash values are invested in

a variety of mutual funds; and *indexed universal life insurance,* whose cash values are loosely (very loosely) linked to stock market performance and generally yield bond-like returns.

WHO STILL NEEDS LIFE INSURANCE?

You don't need coverage anymore if you have no financial dependents or if your dependents are well provided for. You'd generally be better off using the premium money to add to your income, savings, and investments.

There are several circumstances, however, when you do need (or might want) insurance for life. Consider keeping or restructuring your policy if:

- You're married, but the family assets aren't large enough to support your dependent spouse if you die first. Work out how much money each spouse is likely to have if left alone and compare it with his or her probable expenses (see Chapter 2). If the survivor's likely retirement budget looks tight, hang on to the insurance for now. You can reassess at a later date.
- You married or remarried late in life and still have young children to support.
- You're responsible for a child with special needs. The insurance should be payable into a special-needs trust that supplements the support the child will get from government programs. An organization that specializes in your child's type of disability can refer you to a lawyer who understands this important branch of trust law.
- You want to leave a special legacy to a nonprofit organization.
- You own a valuable business or some illiquid real estate and

will owe an estate tax. You want your heirs to be able to pay the tax without selling out.[1]

- Your health is so poor that your life span probably will be short. The insurance payoff will be well worth the remaining premiums paid.

- Your policy is an attractive tax-deferred investment (see page 369), paying enough to compete with bonds. When you die, that investment goes to your heirs income tax free.

- You have plenty of money to live on, can easily afford the policy's premiums, and want to leave even more money to your heirs (the lucky sperm club).

If you plan to continue holding life insurance, take steps to ensure that the policy stays in force! There are three main reasons why it could lapse: (1) It's term insurance. You'll need to take timely steps to renew or replace it. (2) It's universal insurance and your investments haven't done well enough to maintain the cash value. You'll have to put more money into the policy or else restructure it. (3) You grow forgetful and stop paying premiums. Consider having notifications sent to one of your beneficiaries or your financial adviser or trustee if you have one, if you forget to pay. He or she should also be asked to check every annual policy statement you get (see page 365), to be sure all is well. The last thing you want is to lose a policy that you thought you were leaving to your heirs.

---

1 Not much of a concern anymore on the federal level. In 2019, singles could leave their heirs $11.4 million tax free and couples, $22.8 million. Those numbers are indexed to inflation. Some states, however, levy meaningful estate taxes on smaller estates.

THE MISSING INGREDIENT IN MOST OF THE INSURANCE MARKET: GOOD ADVICE

Whether to keep a policy, ditch it, or restructure it is a huge decision, potentially worth tens of thousands of dollars to you today or your heirs tomorrow. Your choice will depend on your family and financial situation, your health, how the policy works, how much cash value you have, and whether you think life insurance is a good investment. It will also depend on the soundness of the advice you get.

There's the rub. You can handle the questions related to term insurance pretty easily (see page 344). But cash-value policies have multiple moving parts that can be impenetrable to laypeople. If you ask an insurance agent for advice, he or she will almost certainly try to earn a commission by selling you something new. The same will be true of commissioned financial planners. They don't earn any money by advising you not to make a change or by helping you restructure your current coverage. At their urging, you might abandon a policy that it pays to keep and buy an expensive one that's not worth its price.

The following pages give you a feel for what you might do with an existing cash-value policy. But I strongly—*strongly!*—recommend that you get specific advice from a fee-only insurance adviser. These advisers don't sell policies or take commissions, so they have no conflicts of interest. You pay them to evaluate your current coverage and help you decide how to manage any changes you want. If it pays to get a different policy, they'll work with an agent to design one that will meet your needs at the lowest possible cost.

For the names of fee-only advisers, start with the website of adviser Glenn Daily in New York City. Daily believes so strongly in spreading the word that he generously publicizes his fee-only competitors (go to GlennDaily.com and click on "Links"). A run through their websites will tell you the type of service that each of them offers. Fee-only advisers usually charge by the hour (in the $350 range), with the maximum number of hours agreed to in advance. Exception: James Hunt (EvaluateLifeInsurance.org) of the Consumer Federation of America charges a low fixed fee for calculating your cash-value policy's current rate of return on investment and suggesting whether to keep it or switch. All these advisers work by phone and email, hold "face-to-face" meetings online, and have clients all over the country.

Another source of advice is a fee-only financial planner. His or her office might include a life insurance specialist or might work with one of the fee-only advisers.

It helps if your adviser also consults on annuities. One option for a cash-value policy that you don't need anymore is to convert it to a low-cost annuity, which earns you a tax advantage (see page 371).

To make decisions yourself, get what's called an "in-force policy illustration" from your insurance company. It shows you whether or not your policy is currently financially sound. For information on how to use this illustration, see page 366.

MANAGING TERM INSURANCE

Odds are, you're holding at least one large term insurance policy that you bought for family protection at a younger age. Term is pure insurance with no cash values. You're paying only to keep your spouse and kids financially safe. Most policies are sold with fixed premiums and for fixed terms, such as 5, 10, 15, 20, or 30 years. When the term is up, some policies lapse. Others continue, with premiums rising sharply each year. Whenever your need for insurance ends, you just stop paying premiums.

So, what if you're reaching the end of the term and find that you still need coverage? You have four options. Hint: The fourth is the worst.

1. If you're in good health and need coverage for just a few more years, you can shop the term insurance market for a new 5-, 10-,

15-, or even 20-year policy. Prices are still reasonable in your 50s and early 60s, especially if you don't smoke. You might not need as much coverage as you had before. For a look at prices, go to the website Term4Sale.com. Check that the policy is convertible into permanent insurance if you should ever need it.

2. If you're in good health and will need at least some coverage for the rest of your life, switch to permanent insurance—either cash-value or no-lapse (see next page). A fee-only life insurance adviser or fee-only financial planner who works with an adviser will help you get good value for your money.

3. If you aren't in good health and can't buy coverage on the open market at a reasonable price, you can generally convert your existing term policy into permanent insurance. There's no medical exam. You'll be offered whatever types of conversion policies your insurer decides to provide—not necessarily good ones (ask about no-lapse if you're sure you want coverage that lasts for life). The premiums will be much higher than they were for term but you probably won't need as large a policy. On flexible policies, you might be able to reduce the premiums in the early years. Timing is important! You must convert within the time period that the policy requires, usually in the weeks just before it expires but sometimes earlier. If you miss that window, you've lost your chance.

4. If you're in poor health, can't pass a health exam, and miss your chance to convert your term policy to permanent insurance, you'll be really, really sorry. You can renew your expiring term insurance regardless of health but only at an incredibly high premium. Worse, the premium will jump every year by large amounts until you can't afford it anymore. You'd keep such a policy only if you're likely to die soon. Very soon.

Be open with your insurance adviser about your state of health if you want to convert to permanent insurance. He or she should be able to tell you whether you're insurable on the open market and at what rate. If your only choice will be to convert your current term policy before it expires, you'll want to get it done.

GREAT NEWS!

If term policies are all you've ever had or will ever need, stop reading here. You're done! Skip to Chapter 12 for tips on getting started with your lifetime income plan.

Read on, however, if you own cash-value policies or need permanent insurance guaranteed for life. Your existing policies might or might not be working out. You need to know their status and what, if anything, to do about them.

GUARANTEED NO-LAPSE UNIVERSAL LIFE: PERMANENT INSURANCE AT THE LOWEST COST

If you want to convert your term insurance to permanent lifetime coverage, see if your insurance company offers a type of policy called *guaranteed universal life* or *no-lapse universal life*.[2] To distinguish this form of coverage from other types of universal policies, I'll always refer to it as "no-lapse." It's designed to last for life and its death benefit is guaranteed. The policy's selling point is its low premium cost compared with the other forms of permanent insurance available. As an example, take a man, 55, in excellent but not perfect health, needing $500,000 worth of coverage. His guaranteed premium for traditional whole-life coverage might run $16,000 a year. A blended policy combining whole life with term might cost $8,000 (blended policies are generally custom designs created by fee-only insurance advisers). Guaranteed no-lapse might be had for only $6,100 a year.

---

2   These policies might also be called *universal life with secondary guarantees* or something else that the insurance company made up.

No-lapse coverage is cheaper than whole life because it offers fewer benefits. In most cases, you get almost nothing in the way of cash values. You can't borrow against the policy or make cash withdrawals. If you cancel, you'll probably get no money back. On the other hand, it's a low-cost way of buying lifetime insurance at an older age. Effectively, you're buying late-age term insurance with a lifetime guarantee.

No-lapse can also be helpful to people who hold universal policies that are underfunded and in danger of collapse (see page 349). You could switch their remaining cash values into a no-lapse policy using a tax-free exchange (known as a 1035 exchange). You might also switch if you want to reduce your premiums while maintaining the same amount of coverage.

The insurance agent or adviser will propose a premium structure for your no-lapse policy, depending on whether you want to roll over money from another policy, pay regular premiums, or mix the two.

Salespeople sometimes misuse no-lapse policies. They sell them as replacements for sound cash-value policies that are providing decent investment returns or could be restructured as "paid up" with no more premiums due. In most of these cases, you're probably better off with your existing coverage. Consider no-lapse as an emergency buy—for essential lifetime coverage when your term policy ends, or you have universal policies that are likely to fail.

There's not much to say about managing no-lapse insurance. Buy it only if you intend to keep it for life. You lose most or all of the money you invested if you eventually drop it. The policy should be structured for lifetime coverage, beyond age 100 (current practice is for the coverage to last to age 121!). Pay the premiums on time, so as not to risk losing your guarantee. For certainty, set up automated payments from your bank account.

THE VARIETIES OF CASH-VALUE INSURANCE: WHOLE-LIFE, UNIVERSAL LIFE, AND "CONFUSION LIFE"

I'm really sorry to have to put you through the following pages. Trying to make a good decision about existing—and *complicated*—cash-value policies can drive you nuts.[3] What's more, there aren't many people around who will give you objective advice. For this chapter, I've asked some fee-only advisers what they might suggest for people in various personal and financial situations. Look for the heading that describes the type of insurance you have (it will say on your policy's cover sheet if you aren't sure). Then jump to the sections that describe how to use the money stored in the policy to achieve your particular goal.

> *But first, here's what you have to know about all cash-value policies regardless of type:*

Cash-value policies can cover you for life, no matter how long you live. They're sold as insurance combined with an investment. The "investment" develops because of the way the policy works. Essentially, you overpay for your coverage during the policy's early years. Your overpayment goes into the policy's cash reserve. The insurance company will draw from that cash reserve in your later years when your premiums alone aren't high enough to cover the rising cost of keeping your policy in force.

Your cash reserve or "cash value" earns an annual investment return, income tax deferred. You can withdraw some of that money or borrow against it, depending on the type of coverage you have. When you die, your heirs will collect the death benefit income tax free. If you cancel the policy and pocket the cash value, you'll usually pay income taxes on any amount that exceeds the premiums you paid.

---

3   Reporting, writing, and checking this chapter drove me nuts, too.

There's a difference between the policy's death benefit and its face amount. The "face" is the amount of insurance that you contracted to buy—say, $500,000. The death benefit is the amount the policy actually pays. It could be higher than the face amount if you used the policy's earnings or dividends to buy more insurance. It could be lower if you've borrowed against the policy or made cash withdrawals.

Cash-value policies come in two general types: *whole-life insurance*, which carries guarantees (see page 352), and a family of policies called *universal life insurance*[4] (see page 355), which depend for success on the size of the premiums you pay and the policy's investment returns.

You have to keep your policy's cash values up. Otherwise, your coverage might lapse. For many policyholders, this comes as a nasty surprise. You assume all is well as long as you pay the premiums on time. But the level of cash in your policy is critical, too. The insurance company taps that cash, year by year, to cover the policy's internal costs. If the cash value shrinks to a low enough level, the costs will be higher than the cash available. At that point, your policy will collapse.

The premiums for cash-value policies are generally set at a high enough level to pay for the coverage as long as you live. But sometimes, things happen that undermine that grand design. Here are the three most common:

1. *You take a loan against the policy.* Often, insurance agents sell this as one of life insurance's virtues. Policy loans are supposedly cheap. On the surface, they might appear to cost just 1 or 2 percent. But insurers can raise the loan's internal cost in ways

---

4   Excluding guaranteed universal (or no-lapse) life, which generally has no cash value.

that you won't notice because you're not paying them out of pocket. That loan is probably costing you 4 to 6 percent, compounded every year. The cost comes out of your cash value. After many years, the size of the loan (including interest) could endanger your coverage, as well as leaving you with a nasty tax bill if the policy lapses. You can reduce this risk by paying the loan interest out of pocket, but few people do. Loans also reduce the policy's death benefit.

2. *You make cash withdrawals.* With universal life policies, you can take money directly out of the cash value without paying interest. If you take too much, however, your cash value might eventually drain away. Withdrawals also reduce the death benefit the policy will pay.

3. *The investment gains on your cash value are insufficient.* Universal life policies depend on specific investment gains to maintain a high enough cash value to keep the coverage in force. If your investments do poorly, you'll have to add cash to the policy yourself, either in a lump sum or by raising the amount you're paying in premiums.

If your cash value runs down, for whatever reason, you'll face an unpleasant choice. Either bulk up the cash in your policy again—by repaying the loan or replacing some of the withdrawals you took—restructure it, or else let the policy lapse. If it lapses and you can't afford to repay the loan (the amounts might be large), you'll get even more bad news. If the size of your loan or withdrawals exceeds the amount you paid in premiums, you'll be taxed on the difference at ordinary income rates. If your policy is worth less than you paid, you won't have a tax bill but will wind up with no insurance, no death benefit, and a big nondeductible investment loss.

Insurance policies don't get into trouble right away. It might be 15 or 20 years before you reach the danger point. But by then, you might be 80 or 85 and counting on the coverage to support a dependent spouse. So, keep track of your cash values (see page 367). There are creative ways of addressing the problem if you start early enough.

Don't buy a cash-value policy as a primary source of future tax-free retirement income. These policies should be purchased *solely* to provide yourself with insurance for life. Often, however, they're sold as a tax-avoidance scheme. On paper, it works in three steps: (1) Buy a large policy and let the cash build up tax deferred. (2) When you retire, start taking loans or direct withdrawals against its cash value. That "income" will also be tax deferred. (3) When you die, the remaining proceeds of the policy (minus your withdrawals) will pass to your family income tax free. The agent will give you a beautiful illustration showing how everything works. It looks like a perfect way to beat the IRS.

But is it? There are two risks to this retirement-income strategy, and they're big ones. First, you might live longer than you'd planned and second, your policy's gains might turn out to be lower than you'd hoped. You start out happy—taking regular loans or withdrawals and using the money to pay your retirement bills. A few years later, however, you might discover that the policy's cash isn't going to last. Unless you start repaying the loans or replacing the cash, you and your heirs could lose the life insurance that you carried all these years. You'll be pretty peeved at your insurance agent for not being clear about this possibility. But you're stuck, with no good way out and perhaps a large income-tax bill. (You can rescue the policy by dying, but that's not recommended.) Personally, I think that selling insurance as a "free" way of getting retirement income is a disgrace.

Don't underestimate your longevity! For healthy people, taking policies that end at age 90 or 95 isn't safe anymore. If you live to that age, the insurer might pay you the face amount of the policy in cash, net of any loans or withdrawals. If that happens, the proceeds become taxable to the extent that they exceed the premiums you paid.[5]

MAKING DECISIONS ABOUT YOUR CASH-VALUE INSURANCE POLICY

What should you do with your cash-value policy after you retire? Drop it and reinvest the money somewhere else? Keep it? Restructure it? Switch to a different type of policy? Your decision will depend entirely on your personal financial needs. Look for the type of cash-value policy you own in the following pages, then read what you can do with it. If your agent pooh-poohs these choices and tries to sell you a new (and costly) policy, please, get another agent (or preferably, a fee-only insurance adviser).

Whole-Life Insurance: How It Works

A *whole-life insurance policy*—the most conservative kind—guarantees you coverage for life provided that you pay the premiums on time and don't take unsustainable loans against the cash value. You pay a fixed premium every year. Alternatively, you can choose to pay higher premiums up front so the policy will be paid in full by a certain age, such as 65. The company usually pays bond-like interest on your cash values but only if you hold the insurance long enough. The interest rate isn't always specifically disclosed.

The best whole-life policies, called "participating policies," pay dividends and are mostly sold by mutual life insurance companies.

---

5   Policies sold since about 2004 last to age 121. If yours stops at 100 and you're close to that age, ask your insurance agent for options. Some companies extend the maturity date or keep the policy in force while stopping the premiums when the cash value equals the death benefit.

You can use those dividends to buy additional paid-up insurance, which raises the death benefit that your survivors will receive. Alternatively, dividends can be paid to you in cash or used to reduce your premiums.

Nonparticipating policies, sold by companies without "mutual" in their names, pay no dividends. Policyholders simply pay their premiums, earn interest on their cash values, and at death provide heirs with the fixed payout that was contracted for. These are generally the types of policies sold by mail or on TV. Most agents stick with participating policies.

You *must* pay whole-life premiums regularly, with no interruption and on time. If you miss a month or more, the insurance company will usually collect the premiums through automatic loans against your cash values. The loan interest will compound. If that goes on long enough, the cash value will run out and the policy will lapse—even though you thought it was guaranteed. "We see this often," says Michael Kitces, of the Pinnacle Advisory Group. "It's one of the ugliest insurance scenarios and the hardest to fix."

Whole-life policies are less flexible than universal life policies, but that's an advantage. There are fewer ways of getting your policy into trouble. "Judging by the policies that we fee-only advisers see," says adviser Glenn Daily, "whole life has performed better over time than universal life."

What You Can Do with Existing Whole-Life Policies

If you decide that you don't need life insurance anymore: You can stop paying premiums on your whole-life policy, cancel it, and pocket the cash value. Ask the company whether any income taxes might be due. If the policy is worth less than the premiums you paid, you might convert the cash value, income tax free, into an annuity (see page 371).

If you don't need life insurance, but your policy is paying an attractive rate of interest: A few whole-life mutual insurance companies are paying a tax-deferred 3.5 to 4.5 percent on your cash values after all expenses. That's an attractive addition to a fixed-income portfolio. You might keep the policy for a few more years with plans to harvest the gains at some point in the future. For a quick way of calculating the current gain, see page 369.

If you need some insurance coverage but don't want to pay premiums anymore: You can use your cash value to fund a smaller, paid-up policy from the same insurance company. Or see what you can do with dividends. If you've been using dividends to buy paid-up additions to the policy's face amount, start applying them toward lowering your premium costs instead. Some companies offer a partial surrender—reducing the face amount, premium, and cash value proportionately. If you're insurable, shop around. You could use the cash value in your whole-life policy to buy a lower-cost, paid-up no-lapse policy guaranteed for life (see page 346).

Large whole-life policies often are blends of whole-life, term-insurance, and paid-up additions bought with your annual dividend (often, holders don't realize that they own a blend). With blends, you can lower the premiums and death benefit by reducing or dropping the term portion. Be sure to keep track of your cash values in a blended policy. If the dividends aren't sufficient, your cash value could run down (but it can't be exhausted; at some point, the insurer will ask you to pay a higher premium or reduce the term amount).

If you want to keep the coverage but need more income: You can collect the dividends in cash. Or cash out the value of the extra, paid-up insurance that you bought with previous dividends.

If you have policy loans: The interest is accruing inside the policy. If the loans are large or go on too long, your net cash value could be reduced to zero. In that case, you'll lose your guarantee. Your whole-life policy will lapse. Anyone with a loan should immediately get an in-force policy illustration to see if you're headed for trouble (see page 366). It's often cost-effective to pay off the loan rather than let the policy lapse, especially if lapsing will create income tax problems. To reduce the lapse risk, use your dividends to pay the loan interest or pay the interest out of pocket.

If you're in poor health: It pays to find a way to keep the full policy in force. If you live just a few more years, the return on your investment will be high—not for you but for your heirs, who will remember you fondly. If it's impossible to keep the full policy or even a reduced policy in force, consider putting it up for sale (see page 372).

UNIVERSAL LIFE INSURANCE WITH CASH VALUES: HOW THESE POLICIES WORK

Universal life policies are flexible—perhaps too flexible. There is usually no guarantee that your coverage will last for life—a point that the agent might have forgotten to mention. There's no fixed premium. You decide how much you want to pay, subject to certain minimums and maximums. Your cash values will earn varying rates of return depending on changes in the stock or bond markets. When setting your premium, you have to make an assumption about what those future returns are likely to be. Together—the premiums and the investment returns—have to add enough to the policy's cash value, year by year, to cover the rising cost[6] of keeping you insured. If that doesn't happen, the coverage will eventually lapse.

Clearly, universal policies have to be monitored regularly to keep

---

6   Class-action lawsuits have been filed against some insurers alleged to have raised their policies' internal costs beyond the limits the contract allowed.

them on track, and most of them aren't. Your original agent is probably out of the monitoring business. Many such policies are failing even as we speak. One of them might be yours.

The good news is that you can keep your policy healthy or manage it back to health once you know what to look for.

Universal life policies usually start on a firm financial footing. Your agent or adviser will suggest a premium that, hypothetically, could keep the policy in force until you reach some advanced age— say, at least 110. That premium level assumes that your cash values will earn a certain investment return (for example, 5 percent a year) and that there will be no unexpected rise in the policy's future costs.

You can choose to do one of two things with your policy's earnings. *Option 1:* Hold the death-benefit level and use the earnings to create a larger cash value—good for your personal future. It's the choice that advisers generally recommend. *Option 2:* Use the policy's earnings to raise the death benefit over the years—good for your heirs. This choice will cost more as you grow older. At some point you'll probably want to switch to the level benefit, Option 1.

You don't have to accept the agent's suggested premium for either option. You might decide to pay more to protect your policy in the event of higher costs and poorer investment returns than your agent predicts. Or you might pay a lower premium because, at the moment, your budget is tight. Your insurance agent might even have advised you to choose lower premiums, based on a rosy assumption about how much your cash value is going to earn, such as 8 percent or 10 percent (good luck with that, after paying costs!). You might stop paying premiums for a while and then start again. If you stop, however, you will probably have to pay higher premiums later, to catch up.

You're allowed to make cash withdrawals against universal life policies. No interest is charged (there might be a $25 fee). Withdrawals are income tax free up to the amount of premium that you've paid into the policy. After that they're taxed as ordinary income in the current year (you'll get a 1099-R). Once you've reached the tax-free limit you could start taking loans. Both withdrawals and loans reduce your policy's death benefit and cash value.

However you decide to pay the premiums or make withdrawals, one thing remains true: Your cash values need to keep going up. If they start declining, your policy could eventually lapse. To be sure that it lasts for your lifetime, you might have to restructure it or put more money in.

There are two ways to check on the status of your policy's cash value. (1) Every year, the insurance company sends you an annual statement (see page 365). Some statements tell you precisely how much longer your policy will last if everything continues as is. If you're healthy and the statement shows that the policy will fail before you reach at least 100, you should act right away. The sooner you focus on the problem the easier and less expensive the rescue will be. (2) If your statement doesn't give you this information, and you see your cash values going down, don't try to puzzle out an answer. Call the insurance company and ask for an in-force policy illustration that will show how sound your policy is.

You should pay particular attention if you bought your universal life policy 10 or 20 years ago. Back then, insurance salespeople were illustrating higher rates of interest than have actually occurred and higher long-term returns on stocks. They also might have projected lower expenses than your insurance company is actually charging. If you have raised the amount you're paying in premiums, your policy is probably still doing fine. If not, your coverage could be at risk.

There are three types of universal life policies. They all follow the general rules explained on page 355, but offer different ways of investing your cash values. Here are your choices:

1. **Fixed universal life insurance.** Its yield depends on the interest rate, after expenses, that the insurance company pays each year. When you first bought the policy, the interest rate might have been projected at 6 or 7 percent. Now it's probably around its

guaranteed minimum of 3 or 4 percent. Please note: The stated interest rate, including the guaranteed minimum, is not necessarily what your cash values actually earn. It's merely the credited rate *before expenses are taken out*. You're earning less than you think—perhaps not even enough to keep the policy alive.

2. **Variable universal life insurance.** This policy ties your cash value, and sometimes your death benefit, to the investment performance of stock and bond mutual funds. You decide how to invest the cash by picking from a menu of funds (called "subaccounts") that the insurance company provides. If the markets do well, after policy expenses, your cash value rises. Your cash value falls if your investments underperform.

There's a hidden catch to the returns you might be expecting on variable universal life. The salesperson will show you what the policy pays if it earns an average of, say, 8 percent over 30 years. But no stock market rises at a steady pace. How well your investment does in actual dollars depends not on averages but on how much the market rises or falls each day. Every time the market drops, your cash value goes down and—without your knowing it—the policy's internal cost of keeping you covered might go up. That extra cost leaves you with less cash in the policy when the market turns around, making it harder to get your cash value back on track.

That said, buyers of variable universal life should move most or all of their money into its stock-owning index fund options (if offered) or two or three stock funds that are similarly broadly based. Forget the bond funds. Their returns probably won't cover their share of the policy's costs. Going big on stocks is the most likely way of making variable universal insurance work. If you'd rather not hold stocks, you shouldn't be in this kind of policy at all. (Note: You might want to switch into the fixed-interest account, despite its low return, if you're in late retirement. You'd want to avoid a large market loss that might require you, suddenly, to put up more money to keep the policy alive.)

3. **Indexed universal life.** Here your cash values are linked, indirectly, to the performance of a stock market index, not counting dividends. You're credited with a gain when stock prices go up over a certain period of time. When stock prices go down, you don't take a loss; instead, your cash values are credited with zero for that period. That's the sales pitch: all gain, no loss.[7]

You don't get the whole gain. There's an annual cap on how much you can earn, which the insurance company can lower whenever it wants (subject to a minimum). Dividends are not included, which historically have accounted for about 2 to 3 percent of the broad market's annual return. Also, your credited gain, if any, might not resemble stock returns as you know them. They might be calculated over monthly or even daily periods and then averaged, producing returns that don't follow the market at all. The policy's costs are subtracted from your cash value and all the fees are not disclosed. To provide the "no loss" guarantee, the insurance company incurs hedging expenses and invests most of the remaining premium money in bonds. As a result, it's going to be hard for an indexed policy to produce anything better than a bond-like return, if that. If your cash values decline, you might have to pay more money—maybe a lot more money—to keep the coverage going. Of all the overblown and misleading sales pitches in the insurance world, those for indexed universal life might be the worst.

What You Can Do with Existing Universal Life Policies

These policies vary tremendously in the personal choices they offer, depending on the insurance company and the particular contract. It's almost impossible for a consumer to figure out how to get the most

---

7   Like fixed-index annuities—see page 173.

from the money they're spending. I'll say it again: Get the advice of a fee-only insurance adviser or competent fee-only financial planner. For a modest cost you could save (or rescue) tens of thousands of dollars in cash value for yourself or insurance payouts for your heirs. At the very least, get an in-force policy illustration (see page 366) before meeting with an agent. You need to know how much cash you have in the policy and whether or not it's running down. Before making any decision about keeping or canceling universal life, compute the net investment return on your cash value (see page 369). If it's negative or low, chuck the policy with a smile on your face.

In general, here are your options if you own any sort of cash-value universal insurance:

If you're healthy and decide that you don't need life insurance anymore: You can stop paying premiums, cancel the policy, and pocket (or invest) the cash-surrender value. This makes especially good sense if the cash values are shrinking or growing ve-e-ry slowly. If the cash amounts to less than you've paid in premiums, you can walk away clean (but delay your walk until the surrender charges expire, if you're close to that magic year). Alternatively, make use of the loss by transferring the money, temporarily, into a low-cost tax-deferred annuity (see page 371). If the annuity rises in value, the gains can be taken tax free until your loss has been made up. If you'll get back more than you paid in premiums, you'll owe ordinary income taxes on the excess.[8]

If you don't need life insurance but your policy is financially

---

8 Depending on your income, a taxable payout from any type of insurance policy might bump you, temporarily, into a higher income tax bracket, a higher bracket for taxes on Social Security, or even into the lofty bracket for Medicare surcharges.

sound and yielding an attractive return: Some (not many) universal policies might be paying a tax-deferred 4 percent or more after all expenses. That makes them a nice addition to your fixed-income investments. You might want to leave the policy in force and perhaps tap the cash at some future date. Before making this decision, however, scout out the true net investment return, after costs (see page 369). Hint: It's less than the stated interest rate. If you've held the policy for a long time and have a large gain that's potentially taxable, the argument for keeping at least a portion of the policy gets stronger, says fee-only insurance adviser Scott Witt of New Berlin, Wisconsin (WittActuarialServices.com). You might want to hold it until death and pass the entire proceeds to your heirs income tax free.

If you need some insurance for life but not as much as you have now: You can reduce the policy's death benefit. You might bring it down to an amount that can be supported with a smaller annual premium or use the current cash value to create a policy paid up for life. If you're insurable, consider using the current cash value to buy a smaller no-lapse universal policy from another company in a tax-free exchange. Always ask about the surrender charge. If it's still in force, delay the change until the surrender-charge period expires.

If you need full insurance coverage for a few more years but can't afford the premiums: You can stop paying premiums on any type of universal policy at any time. Depending on how the policy is structured, it might stay in force with no reduction in the death benefit until the cash value runs out. Ask the company for an in-force illustration showing what would happen if you stopped paying today. You'll see how many years you'd be covered and what the death benefit would be. If you've been using the policy's earnings to increase your death benefit, tell the company that you now want to use them to reduce the premiums. That would stretch out your coverage for a little bit longer.

If you plan to let the coverage lapse a few years from now, base your end date on your dependents' needs, not on the age you think you'll die: You cannot predict a likely life span based on family history or a health condition that's under control. Better to assume a long life and reduce your policy's death benefit than to keep a high death benefit for a shorter period and hope you die in time.

I've seen this choice up close and personal. Years ago, I had a friend who was seriously ill. His large universal life policy was heading for lapse in a little over three years. Instead of reducing its face value to make it last longer, he gambled his wife's financial security on the guess that he'd die before the coverage ran out. He made it, just four months shy of the lapse date. But what if he hadn't? It's hard to describe that couple's pain and conflicted emotions as he went into a slower-than-expected decline.

If you want to keep at least some coverage for life but need more income now: You can take cash directly out of the policy. It's not a loan, so you don't pay any interest. The withdrawals are income tax free up to the amount of the premiums you paid, which might be substantial. After that, you'll owe current taxes on any additional amounts you take. Be careful not to withdraw too much. You need to keep enough cash in the policy to keep it from falling apart.

Once you've exhausted the cash withdrawals, you could borrow against the policy, income tax free. That's generally not a good idea unless you plan to pay the money back. Besides, there might not be much cash left to borrow against.

If you bought the policy as a way to save for retirement: Supposedly, you can start taking regular withdrawals from your cash value as a form of tax-free retirement income. This will work only if you put plenty of cash into the policy every year, its investments perform like a charm, and you die while there's still some cash value left. If you withdraw too much and live too long, the policy will lapse. You might be left with a big income tax bill and no insurance for your heirs. Before executing this risky strategy, get an in-force policy illustration that shows the effect of your intended withdrawals on your policy's longevity. You might change your mind. If you don't change your mind, put off starting withdrawals. If you live too long, your runaway spending could cannibalize your cash values.

If you still have family obligations and don't want to reduce the size of your policy: Pony up whatever money is needed to keep the current policy going. Or, if you're insurable, consider using its cash value to buy a no-lapse universal policy from another company if it's a better deal.

If you bought variable universal life as a "buy and hold" investment: Why did you choose insurance at all? You'd get better returns from a well-diversified stock and bond portfolio and almost complete tax deferral if you hold for life. At this point, however, that decision is behind you, so take another look at the policy's investment choices. Your helpful salesperson might have steered you into a "diversified portfolio" of 15 or 20 expensive funds, half in stocks and half in bonds. The bond funds probably aren't covering their share of the policy's costs. You'll save money and grow your cash values faster, over many years, by switching most or all of the money to lower-cost stock index funds, if the company offers them. Or choose no more than three broad-based, low-cost stock funds, focused on large and small U.S. stocks and international stocks. (Owning some bond funds and fixed-interest accounts might be appropriate much later in your retirement if a big decline in stocks could wipe out your cash value.)

If you're someone who will switch out of stocks or quit paying premiums when the market falls, you should drop this type of policy. It absolutely will not work out for you.

If you've just discovered that your universal life policy is close to collapse and you still need at least some life insurance: You'll hate this. You were sold the policy as something that would stay in force as long as you paid the recommended premium. You will yell at your insurance agent or financial adviser. After the yelling, you will have to decide what to do.

There are several ways of saving the policy, or at least part of it. You can put in more money to bring the cash value up to a level that will support the current or reduced death benefit. If you have an increasing death benefit, you can switch to a level death benefit. If there's a loan against the policy, tell your insurer to use any payment you send to reduce the loan. Repaying the loan might cost you less than the tax you'd owe if the policy lapsed.

If you're in very, very poor health and your policy has a level death benefit: Quit paying premiums if it's clear that you'll die pretty soon. Put that money into the bank instead. Your heirs will get the insurance and the bank account, too. Morbid, I guess, but good advice. A new policy illustration will show you what the death benefit is likely to be and whether you have enough cash to keep the policy in force. If you need the money yourself, consider selling the policy (see page 372).

If you've just discovered from your annual report or in-force illustration that your policy has enough cash value to last well beyond your likely life span: Here's another case where you should quit paying premiums. With universal life insurance, the bills you get for premiums are optional, not required. Any unneeded money that you put into the policy helps the insurance company, not your survivors.

HOW TO FIND OUT IF A CASH-VALUE POLICY IS FAILING OR SUCCEEDING

You have two ways of checking on your policy's health: the annual statement, which comes to you by mail or email automatically, and the latest in-force policy illustration, which you have to ask for. The information in these free reports not only shows whether your policy needs repairs, it also helps you decide what to do about your coverage going forward.

The annual statement. Opening and reading this statement may be the quickest and easiest way to check on how your universal life policy is doing. It might tell you specifically how much longer your coverage will stay in force if everything remains the same—meaning that you continue to pay the same premium, the insurer levies the same internal policy costs, you receive the same gross rate of interest or investment return that you're receiving now, and the status of any policy loans remains unchanged. For example, the statement might say, "If you continue to pay the planned premium under current charges, your policy will continue until November 2039." At this writing, that would be only 19 years away. If you're 65, you should read that date as a bright red light, flashing "Pay Attention! Fix This Now!" You don't want to reach 84 and discover an insurance fail. By then, your coverage would be *very* expensive to save. If you're in reasonably good health and need a policy that lasts for life, you want the annual statement to show that you're covered to age 110 or more. If you don't find this lifetime estimate in your annual statement, call the company and ask for an in-force policy statement that will give you that information.

The statement also discloses how much you paid in premiums this year, what charges were levied, how much your cash values grew (or shrank), how much you've borrowed (including interest owed), and the size of your death benefit. Some companies provide even more details.

Ignore any projections showing *guaranteed values*. They're misleading and often scary. The "guaranteed" numbers assume that, starting now, the insurer will levy the maximum insurance charge that the policy allows, making the lapse date look pretty close. That's certainly not going to happen right away and is highly unlikely to happen in the future. Concentrate only on the projection of *current* charges. But check every year, because current charges might very well rise.

The annual statement for a whole-life policy contains much less information—generally, the cash value, the death benefit, the current dividend, and the gain in your cash value over the past year. Whole-life is much less risky than universal life because it doesn't depend on investment returns. Its elements are pretty much fixed and guaranteed.

The in-force policy illustration. This is a multipage computer printout supplied by the agent or life insurance company. Like the annual statement, it shows how your policy will perform if nothing changes over the next 30 or 40 years. But here you'll see the potential change in your future cash values year by year. If there's any risk that your coverage will lapse, the in-force illustration will catch it first.

The illustration presents you with several columns of numbers. Some of them show guaranteed values. You should ignore them, as explained above. They overstate your likely costs, which makes the policy look riskier than it actually is.

The columns that matter show your current costs and returns and are known as *nonguaranteed values*.

Here's what to look at:

- **Premiums.** This is the sum the insurance company expects you to pay every year. Holders of universal policies can get illustrations based on paying lower or higher premiums.

- **Current cash value.** In general, your illustrated cash values should rise in every future year. If you're holding a universal life policy and cash values are going down, it means that your policy is gradually running out. A blank or a zero in the cash-value column shows the year that the policy is currently scheduled to lapse.[9] If that zero comes too soon, you should think about raising your premium, restructuring your policy, or dropping it and investing your money somewhere else. If the cash value extends the policy well beyond any reasonable life span, get an illustration showing what happens if you stop paying premiums. You might have paid enough already.

    If you hold a universal life policy, the column showing future cash values is based on the rate of interest currently being credited by the insurer. But the credited rate is not what you're earning on your money. The insurer will deduct policy charges, so your net is less than it appears. Don't believe an agent or financial adviser who tells you that the rate you see is what you get.

    On a variable or indexed universal policy, the cash-value column reflects a future, hypothetical market return, projected at the same rate, year after year. But markets don't perform at steady rates. And you have no idea how the insurance company will apply costs. Finally, on many in-force illustrations, the illustrated future return is, well, *hopeful*. The agent might be projecting, say, 8 percent for 30 years. Ask for a second illustration at a lower rate of return to get a better feel for your risks. The illustration also shows the potential results if your investments earn zero over the years. (No illustration shows the outcome if the value of your investments declines—a bit of a gap, I'd say.)

---

9 Unless you have a no-lapse policy—see page 346. In that case, the cash value can be zero without threatening your coverage.

If you hold a whole-life policy, the illustrated cash value
will normally climb every year. These policies are guaranteed
not to run out. You might lose the guarantee, however, if you
borrow against the policy. A rising loan will send the cash value
down. If the illustration shows it going to zero in the future,
you should restructure the policy or start repaying the loan.

- **Current cash surrender value.** This is the amount of money
  you'll net if you want to cash out of your policy. It's also the
  amount you can use toward buying another policy or restructuring the policy you have. If you've held the policy for a sufficient number of years, the cash value and the cash surrender
  value should be the same.

- **Death benefit.** If you hold a universal life policy, look down
  this column to see how the death benefit changes. If it's rising, you're probably using your policy's earnings to increase
  the payout to your beneficiaries. As you age, this strategy gets
  expensive. Consider using the earnings to build higher cash
  values while keeping the death benefit level. If you hold a
  whole-life policy, the death benefit rises if you're using your
  dividends to buy additional paid-up insurance. Again, you
  can level the death benefit by using your dividends to reduce
  your premiums.

- **Loans**. If you borrowed against the policy, there's a column
  showing how much you've borrowed and the projected annual increase in the loan as the interest compounds. Loans
  reduce your cash value and death benefit. You can get an
  illustration showing what would happen if you paid the loan
  interest out of pocket.

- **Cash withdrawals**. If, as a holder of a universal policy, you
  want to plan for cash withdrawals at some point in the future,
  you can have them illustrated. You'll see the effect on your
  policy's cash value and how the withdrawals would shorten
  your policy's life.

Get a new illustration every year! Small increases in the policy's internal cost of insurance or decreases in credited rates of return can balloon into big reductions in cash values over many years. It's especially important to keep checking a variable or indexed policy. A single illustration won't show what happens to your policy if the stock market falls, let alone how fast or slowly the cash values might recover.

HOW TO CALCULATE YOUR POLICY'S INVESTMENT GAINS (OR LOSSES)

Here's a down-and-dirty way of checking whether an older policy is worth keeping for its investment value.

From the policy's annual statement or in-force illustration, take the cash surrender value at the end of last year. Add the premium you paid this year. Divide that sum into this year's final cash surrender value. Eliminate the "1" before the decimal point. The result is the latest annual percentage return on your investment.

For example, say that last year's cash surrender value was $135,000. You paid $3,700 in premiums this year, so you now have $138,700 into the policy. Your current cash surrender value is $145,000. Dividing $145,000 by $138,700 gives you 1.045. Eliminate the "1" and you get a cash-on-cash investment return of .045, which is 4.5 percent, tax deferred. Compared with the rates on Treasuries and corporate bonds, that's an investment worth keeping for at least another year.

The numbers above come from an actual whole-life policy held for 21 years. In that case, there was no surrender charge. You might get a higher rate of return from a universal policy in a year when the surrender charge declines rapidly.

If you apply this calculation to your own policy and don't get a "1" in front of the result, it's yielding a negative return. You are paying more to the insurance company than you are getting back. That's common in a policy's early years but it shouldn't persist. Note that you can be earning negative returns even if the policy's cash value is going up. If you're losing money on your investment and don't need life insurance, you'd be better off cashing the policy in and investing in mutual funds.

USING YOUR POLICY FOR LONG-TERM CARE EXPENSES

Many whole-life and universal life insurance policies let you use part of the face amount, income-tax free, to cover long-term care expenses. It's called an *accelerated benefit rider* and is usually provided at no extra cost. If you have the rider, you might consider keeping your policy as a health insurance backup (but be sure you understand the restrictions on how much can be advanced, and when).

Alternatively, you might consider an insurance hybrid. Life insurance can be packaged with long-term care insurance worth two or three times the policy's face value. If you enter a nursing home or need continuous home care, you can draw from the LTC portion to help pay the bills. There's a catch, natch. Money you withdraw for care reduces the size of the future insurance payout to your heirs. There may be penalties or limitations. Each company is different, so read the contracts carefully, right down to the footnotes. A plus: You might be able to buy the insurance without a medical exam. A potential plus: If you're in a nursing home for so long that you use up the death benefit, the insurer might continue the payments from its own funds. Not likely to happen, but . . .

You can also find a few deferred fixed annuities packaged with long-term care insurance. These annuities require a health exam.

Hybrids are generally purchased with a large lump sum, with benefits guaranteed. If you're interested, you should buy it with money that you never otherwise intend to touch. If you need long-term care, the product will pay. If you never need care, your heirs will receive the full proceeds of the insurance policy or the money in the annuity.

A TAX-SMART WAY OF HANDLING A CASH-VALUE POLICY THAT YOU DON'T NEED ANYMORE

If you no longer need life insurance, there's no point paying for it. But instead of pocketing the cash, think about switching it into an annuity for a short period of time, using a tax-free 1035 exchange. It has the following valuable tax advantages.

If you'll get more money out of the insurance policy than you paid in premiums: You'll owe ordinary income taxes on the amount of the payout that exceeds the premiums you paid. A large enough payout might bump you into a higher tax bracket. To avoid that cost, don't cash out your policy all at once. Instead, roll it into, say, a five-year immediate-pay annuity, using a tax-free exchange. You'll get regular monthly payments that are partly taxable and partly tax free. If you're in your 60s, the annuity payments might help you put off taking Social Security until you reach 70.

If you'll get less money out of the policy than you paid in: You have a financial loss that can't be deducted on your tax return. But you can transfer the loss to a variable annuity in a tax-free 1035 exchange. Choose a low-cost annuity and put your money into one of its broad-based stock-owning mutual funds. Any investment gains that you make in the future will be income tax free up to the amount of the loss you transferred. Once you've used up the loss, you can cash in the annuity and invest the money in regular mutual funds. Outside the annuity, long-term gains will be taxed at the low capital gains rate.

I have many reservations about variable annuities. But for this purpose, they're ideal. Go for the low-cost annuities offered by Vanguard or, if you qualify, from TIAA. They have no early surrender charge.

SHOULD YOU SELL YOUR POLICY?

Are you 68 to 70 or older? Got a universal life policy? Got no bene-ficiary who could use your policy's payout? Want to pocket its cash? Not feeling too well these days? You might be able to sell the policy to an investor for substantially more than its current cash value. The investor will pay any required premiums while you live and collect the payout when you die. Younger people with short life spans can also apply.

Investors are primarily interested in universal life policies with face values of at least $100,000 to $250,000. They might also con-sider a term policy that's convertible into some form of universal life.

The amount of money you'll be offered will depend on your health (investors like sellers with life expectancies of no more than 10 years and who are already doddering a bit) as well as such things as the premium amount, the cash value, and how old the policy is. The investors will want your medical records and access to your doc-tors. They'll keep checking for your name on Social Security's Death Master File database and might even contact you or your represen-tative from time to time.

Don't sell your policy if you still have heirs who need protection. If you can't afford the current premiums, pay them out of the poli-cy's cash values or ask your beneficiaries to pay. When you die, the beneficiaries will get the payout. If you outlive them, you can sell the policy at a later date and for more money because you'll be that much older. Many insurance companies let you use part of your pol-icy's face amount to cover the costs of a dread disease or long-term care. That's generally better than a desperation sale.

If you want to explore a sale, start with TellUsTheOdds.com. It's a free policy valuation service run by two life insurance experts, Glenn Daily, a fee-only insurance adviser, and Douglas Bennett, a highly re-spected actuary. You enter your policy's details and receive a report, advising you of its probable worth. Fees apply if you want them to handle a sale. Or look for a broker through the Life Insurance Settlement Association (LISA.org), which lists the names of its member brokers and providers on the Web. You might want to go directly to a provider and negotiate the price yourself. If the policy's sale price exceeds the amount you paid in premiums, the excess is taxed as ordinary income. If the sale price is larger than (are you ready?) the greater of the cash value or the amount that you paid in premiums, it can be taxed as a capital gain. If you sell within two years of death, the proceeds might be income tax free.

KEEP TRACK OF YOUR LIFE INSURANCE!

Keep your policies (or the records of them) in a special file for your heirs (if it's an efile, share the password). Some people lose track of their policies, especially if they're paid up and the company is no longer sending bills. No surprise—insurance companies can be, well, let's say, "careless" about finding out whether you've died and your beneficiaries are due some money. It's easy to check. All they have to do is scan Social Security's death records. Instead, they might sit on the money and wait to see if a beneficiary makes a claim. That can happen even when the company knows you're dead.

Some state regulators have started requiring insurance companies to check death records and make serious efforts to locate beneficiaries. New York passed this rule in 2011. Since then, "lost" beneficiaries have received $665.7 million—money they were entitled to but that the insurance companies didn't hustle to pay. New York maintains a free database of unclaimed policies at dfs.ny.gov (enter "Lost Policy Finder" into the Search box). It includes all insurers incorporated in New York State, even if the policy was issued in another state. Unclaimed annuities are listed, too. In other states, there are no lists. Some insurance commissioners are leaning heavily on the companies to look harder for missing beneficiaries, primarily by bringing cases against them and winning settlements. But such pressure isn't universal. It's primarily up to you to see that your family can put its hands on your policies, including old ones, and make a claim. That might surprise you, but it's a fact.

Insurance companies can't hang on to unclaimed policy proceeds forever. After a certain number of years—typically seven—the money is supposed to be sent to the unclaimed property bureau of the state where the policy was purchased. Small policies will never reach the bureau because they'll be eaten up in costs. Nevertheless, potential heirs should check the appropriate state bureaus every few years to see if one of them is holding money in the name of the person who bought the policy. Find the bureau through the National Association of Unclaimed Property Administrators at unclaimed.org. You'll be asked for the person's Social Security number. While you're at it, enter your own name, too. I did that two years ago and found two royalty payments that had never reached me. Claiming was simple; the check came right away.

In another situation, you might simply neglect to pay the premiums because you're losing track of your financial life. These policies could eventually expire unless someone is watching. You might consider automating your payments or having payment notifications sent to a responsible child who will see that the coverage doesn't lapse. Adult children who step in to help with parents' finances should be sure to find out if any life insurance premiums are due. Ask the agent or insurance company for a copy of the most recent annual statement and an in-force policy illustration. The company will send you a copy of the policy and the beneficiary form, too.

READ YOUR MAIL!

Many of you—I'm sorry to have to say this—simply aren't opening the mail or email from your insurance company. Or, if you're reading the annual statement, you aren't necessarily focusing on what it says. Your policy might be programmed to expire. The sooner you repair it, the cheaper and easier the fix will be.

Forget what you thought you knew when you bought your cash-value policy. Life insurance isn't forever anymore.

12

Just Tell Me What to Do

Whew! At last!

Sit back. Relax. Take your shoes off and reflect. Millions of others have passed through these same emotional and financial stages, from "worker" to "retiree," and emerged into a different life. Maybe they prepared for retirement and walked toward it gladly. Maybe not. Either way, time is ticking. Once you get over the surprise of your age (I've been surprised ever since I turned 50), a second surprise comes barreling along behind. You have 20, 30, or even 40 years ahead. What are you going to make of them?

During your journey, your friends and colleagues are your support group and vital source of information. If you're in the preretirement stage, talk to people who have already jumped. If your paycheck has just stopped, talk to fellow retirees about how they found, or are finding, their path. We need our children for love and visits, but at this stage not so much for advice. We learn the most from people like us who share our challenges and hopes.

START WITH A PLAN (YOU KNEW I WAS GOING TO SAY THAT, RIGHT?)

Three numbers matter when you sketch a retirement plan. Which matters most depend on where you stand on the retirement spectrum.

Preretirement. Your number is the gap between the annual income you can count on after you retire and the amount of money you think you'll need to pay your bills. Chapter 2 helps you figure this out. If the gap is wide and your savings small, keep working (if you can). There's no better preretirement plan than to maintain your paycheck, add to your savings, and put off taking Social Security for a few more years. You might also practice living on a retirement budget to see what might have to change.

Retirement. Your number is the amount of cash you decide to hold in your cash reserve (Chapter 9). It should cover any gap between your expected retirement income and your expected expenses for the next two years. That's your financial safety net, so you won't have to worry about what your investments are doing every minute.

Postretirement. Your number is the size of the first withdrawal you take from your invested savings to help pay your bills. If you're 60 to 70, with investments reasonably balanced between stocks and bonds, a typical target is 4 to 5.5 percent. After that, you take annual inflation adjustments (Chapter 8). Revisit your withdrawals every few years. You might want to raise or lower your take, depending on changes in your spending and how your investments performed.

Throughout retirement, write your numbers down, noting any changes in plan as you go along. It's all too easy to lose track of what you "meant" to do. Are you really taking the same amount of money you took last year plus an increment for inflation or are you taking more? If the answer is more, can the current state of your finances support the increase? What are your investments currently worth? It's especially important to note your target asset allocation along with a reminder—in CAPITAL LETTERS—that you intend to rebalance, not sell, when stock or bond prices fall.

YOUR RETIREMENT CHECKLIST

1. If you're still working, jack up your contributions to your company retirement plan or individual retirement account (IRA). The potential for saving more money is exactly what a paycheck is for.

2. If you're married and eligible for a pension, lean toward joint-and-survivor payments that will cover your spouse after your death. It's tempting to take a pension that covers your life only, because you get a larger check. Before making that decision, however, figure out what your spouse's income would be if you were hit by a truck the day after you retire. How well would he or she live on the savings and Social Security you left behind? There has to be a very good reason to choose a pension that ends when you die—for example, your spouse has a pension of his or her own or you married a multimillionaire.

3. Put off taking Social Security. Age 62 is normally too young unless you absolutely have no other choice. Your benefit would be chopped by 25 to 30 percent, reducing your Social Security income now and for the rest of your life. At the very least, hold off until you reach full retirement age—66 to 67—when your full benefit will be paid. If you're in good health, or your spouse is, wait until 70. You earn an additional 8 percent of your full benefit for every year of delay. It's even worth taking money out of savings to live on while you wait. The interest your savings earns is small compared with the delayed retirement credits

that Social Security pays. (See Chapter 3 for explanations and exceptions to the age 70 rule.)

4. Nail down your individual health insurance and revisit the plan every year. New plans are coming into the system all the time and prices change. You can switch plans once a year during Open Enrollment, generally from November 1 to December 15 (longer, in a few states). You can switch or enroll at any time if you meet certain criteria—for example, getting married, losing employer coverage, or moving to a new area. To find your state's plan, go to HealthCare.gov. And keep up with the news about the Affordable Care Act, which may or may not survive.

   You also have annual Medicare choices. Studies show that older people don't do much cost comparison when they sign up for the drug plan, Medicare Part D. Once they've chosen, they rarely switch. That could be an expensive mistake. There are always new plans, many of which will cost you less. Read about your choices in Chapter 4 and then go to Medicare.gov.

5. If you need a major spending cut, look at housing first. That's where the big bucks are and the sooner you harvest them the better. You might sell your house and buy something smaller, sell and rent, or take a reverse mortgage (Chapter 10). Once you've reduced your housing costs, including upkeep, taxes, and insurance, the rest of your budget—including the things you like to do best—might fall into place.

6. Take lifetime annuities seriously if you find that your retirement savings are just enough or a little bit short (Chapter 6). Consider an ordinary immediate-pay annuity. Odds are the monthly payment you receive will be at least comparable to what you'd get by applying the 4 percent withdrawal rule to your savings and investments and you won't have to manage the money. Alternatively, look at a deferred-payout annuity; for a modest investment up front, you can provide yourself and your spouse with a lifetime income starting 10 or 15 years from now. Do not—*do*

not—fall for the costly annuities with lifetime withdrawal benefits. All the reasons start on page 158.

7. Check every one of the beneficiary forms you ever signed to be sure the right person will get the money when you die. Individual retirement accounts are usually paid to the named beneficiary, no matter what it says in your will. In many states, your ex-spouse might inherit if you forgot to take him or her off the form. Also check the forms at your mutual fund company and brokerage firm and the beneficiaries named on your life insurance. If you get married or divorced, do the forms all over again. Immediately. If you took a joint-and-survivor pension, be sure you have a copy of the form just in case the company loses it.

8. Keep a large enough cash reserve—in a bank, credit union, or money market mutual fund—to ensure that your bills will be paid for the next two years. That saves you from worry when you hit a bad stock-market year.

9. For retirement investments, buy index mutual funds. Low-cost index mutual funds. *Only* low-cost index mutual funds, such as those at Fidelity and Vanguard. The high-cost index funds sold by commissioned financial advisers waste your money, reduce your returns, and make it harder to stretch your savings over your lifetime.

10. Buy stock-owning index funds with at least 35 percent of your retirement savings if you or your spouse is likely to live 30 years or more. Choosing 45 to 65 percent would be better. In your bond bucket, put both high-quality short-term and intermediate-term funds. The bond portion of your investments supports your annual withdrawals in years when stock prices decline. Chapter 9 has the details.

11. Choose a withdrawal rule that fits with your stock allocation. If you hold just 30 percent of your money in stock-owning index funds, a reasonable starting place is 3.5 percent in the first year plus annual inflation adjustments. With 45 to 65 percent in

stocks, you can start your withdrawals at 4.5 percent. If you can be flexible about your spending, start with 5.5 percent plus annual inflation adjustments—intending to cut back in a year that stocks turn bad.

12. Remember that it takes just one total market U.S. stock fund and one total market U.S. bond fund to make the 4.5 percent withdrawal rule work.

13. Resist temptation: You *know* there's something wrong with "income investments" promising safe and super-high yields (they're all Venus flytraps).

14. Don't watch your investments every day. Please. It's stressful and a waste of time. Walk the dog, read a book, jump out of a plane—anything but watch the numbers change. You thought carefully about putting your plan in place. Now let it run.

15. If you're holding a life-insurance policy, make sure that it isn't going to lapse (see Chapter 11).

16. Simplify your financial life. Assemble all your traditional IRAs and 401(k)s into a single IRA, if possible. Invest in the fewest possible low-cost index stock and bond mutual funds to make rebalancing easy. Consolidate any stray bank accounts. Gather all your financial records together where your spouse or other heirs can find them. If you're managing rental properties, consider setting up a plan to sell them, over time. They'll become a burden in your older age. Slim down your living quarters and possessions. Clear your mind.

17. Have "the talk" with your spouse. If you've been making most of the family financial decisions, retirement is the time to share. If you're a spouse who's been ducking the money side of life, it's time to wake up. Ditto if you've been spending and saving on separate tracks without knowing what your mate has been doing. Both of you should know what's happening with the bills, the debts, the bank accounts, the retirement savings and investments, the pension, the insurance, the mortgage—everything

that affects your welfare if your spouse dies first. How much income would you have as a widow or widower? Will it be enough? What investment decisions, if any, will you have to make? Where is the title to your car and the deed to your house? Make a master list of all the assets you own, where they're held, and what the account numbers are.

Sometimes a spouse (usually the wife, I'm sorry to say) doesn't bother learning or imagines that she can't. She trusts that everything will be okay. And maybe it will. Then again, maybe not. I've seen widows shocked by the mess their husbands left behind. The day after the funeral is no time to be starting a crash course in personal finance.

Sometimes a spouse (usually the husband, I'm also sorry to say) holds all the financial cards to his chest. He might be playing with stocks, buying cryptocurrencies, or running up debts and doesn't want his wife to know. Or maybe he's just naturally bossy.

These are bad situations for both of you. Talking about money can be challenging, emotionally, but once you get it all on the table, you can make better plans. Take it one subject at a time. Monday, income. Tuesday, bills. Wednesday, insurance. Yum, yum.

18. While you're at it, make a list of your essential passwords. If you're the least bit of a techie, you have home and financial information on your laptop, tablet, smartphone, and other devices. If you died suddenly, could your heirs easily enter your digital world for information they need? Or would they have to hire an Internet safecracker to try to break your codes? Print out the passwords to your devices, financial accounts, personal office accounts, email (for bills sent to you online), and everything else your spouse or kids will need. And keep it current!

19. Update your will (you have one, of course). This isn't a book about estate planning. I'm just checking to make sure you have

a will, a living will that explains the extent of the medical treatment you'd want if you can't decide for yourself, a health-care agent to be sure that your wishes are carried out, and a durable power of attorney (POA). The power gives someone the right to manage your money if (dread thought) your mind turns dim. Please find an attorney to do these jobs. Things can go wrong if you take forms off the Web and fill them in yourself.

THE LAST AND HARDEST PLAN

Readers of this book have their wits about them. You're assessing your options and making decisions. But once you've set up your well-thought-out retirement plan, what happens if you lose your grip?

You might think that you'll need financial protection only if you develop dementia or have a stroke. But you can be perfectly healthy and yet lose the good judgment you had 10 or 20 years ago. You become more suggestible, as all the research on aging shows.

That's when a financial adviser might persuade you to buy unsuitable annuities, trade high-risk stocks, or plunge into risky business ventures. I'm not talking about shady brokers in bucket shops. I'm pointing a finger at the nation's finest. In a 2014 audio recording, secretly made at one of America's largest and most prestigious investment banks, a senior executive is heard to say, "[Our] view was that once clients were wealthy enough, certain consumer laws didn't apply to them." He was talking about you, if you have even a halfway decent net worth. Brokers and "advisers" think it's up to you to figure out if a product they sell carries high hidden risks or isn't worth its price.

I'm also talking about the caregivers hired to help older widows or widowers. Occasionally, one of them becomes "such a loving friend" that the caregive-e becomes a literal give-e—leaving money or property to an unscrupulous usurper. You probably think that can never happen to you. But so did the formerly smart, now vulnerable, people who've signed away money or property, and not necessarily under duress. They might feel glad about making a generous gift to a caretaker they've come to depend on.

So you have one more financial plan to make. You need a defense for your income and assets in case your mental edge gets seriously dulled. Do it now while you're still sharp. The tighter you can draw a circle around yourself the safer you will be.

Primarily, you need to give someone your financial power of attorney. It needs to be a *durable* power, which stays in effect if you become incapable. You can give your agent (or "attorney-in-fact") limited powers—say, to manage your investments—or general powers to handle all your financial matters, including paying your bills.

You might voluntarily hand the reins to your agent if you start feeling uncertain about the decisions you have to make. I know that I'd be happy to be relieved of the burden. Otherwise, your agent steps in only if your family and doctor conclude that you're incompetent. Your family might start this persuasion process if they see your bills piling up unpaid or learn that you're sending money to vultures who cold call with cheating investment pitches. If you resist, they might have to go to court. It's better to have named your own agent than have a court name someone for you.

You're always free to do something dumb with your money as long as you're competent. It's your money, after all. But it's smart to have someone standing by for a second opinion. If you have a living trust, your trustee can fill that role.

There are no rules of thumb for naming an agent. You have to find someone you trust—your spouse, a responsible child or other relative, a business partner, a close and reliable friend. If the friendship fails, you can name someone else as long as you're of sound mind. Or name co-trustees, as a check on each other.

Have a full discussion with your agent about your financial needs and goals. That person has to agree with the program and have the persistence to carry it through. Tell your whole family what your wishes are. If your agent is someone outside the family, they should meet and talk with that person. If one of your children is the agent, your other children should be told why you made that choice.

The potential need for financial protection is yet another good reason to have a written investment plan. You can suggest asset allocations and advise the agent to buy only low-cost index funds, as Warren Buffett did when he instructed his wife's trustee (see page 280). Your future stand-in should also have a general overview of your finances. If you decide to go radically off plan, explain it to your agent first. If you start sneaking around on the person you've chosen to protect you, you're already off the rails.

You can get a durable POA from the attorney who did your will. There are also forms on the Web. Do-it-yourselfers have to be very sure that they execute them correctly, including your agent's name exactly as it appears on the document that he or she will use to prove identity. Your signature has to be notarized and you might need two witnesses. Financial institutions are suspicious of DIY forms. They will refuse to accept your agent if the slightest thing is out of order.

They might even refuse to accept your power of attorney when everything *is* in order. Many institutions worry so much about doing something wrong that they make your agent fight for access to your financial affairs. Some (especially brokerage firms) will say that the POA should have been on their own institutional form (that's wrong; they're required to accept your document if it was properly prepared). Some will stonewall an agent who merely asks for information—for example, a question about what your health insurance covers. (Tip: Call your health insurer now, to add the name of your spouse or agent to the list of people it's allowed to talk to.)

Your agent can't expect to get anything done, financially, with just a phone call. The institution will want to see a copy of the POA. If the customer rep won't help, a supervisor should. Worst case, your agent can ask your lawyer to handle it, but there's no reason to have to pay to assert the right that the POA grants.

Theoretically, your agent can act at any time, but financial institutions will normally check on what happened to you before accepting an agent's word. In some states, you have to execute new powers every five years to prove that your intention holds. You should review them regularly in any event. Maybe you've had a dispute with your agent and need somebody else.

With luck, you'll be able to manage your money right up to the end, in which case the power of attorney will molder in your files, unused. But just as you protect yourself against investment risk, you need to protect against disease or judgment risk. As poet Robert Frost wrote, "Provide, provide!"

YOUR NEW LIFE

Putting together your financial plan will take some time. So will finding your new path. Freedom is daunting when you first encounter it, after a lifetime of being scheduled every day. The common second stage of retirement—disenchantment—might set in. But that's only a way station. Once you start poking around, you'll encounter a world of interesting people like you, engaged in new projects and adventures. There's a vibrancy to life after work, at its slower pace. We let go of who we were and discover who we've become.

Acknowledgments

I owe so much to so many. This book never could have been written without the patient help of a small army of experts in their fields. They generously sat for interviews and reinterviews, corrected and recorrected my drafts, helped me sort through ideas, and gently (or not so gently!) corrected me when I got things wrong. I never cried on the phone to them but sometimes I came close. Any remaining errors of fact or judgment are my own.

For the chapter on Social Security, I'm indebted to Bill Reichenstein, a professor emeritus at Baylor University, in Waco, Texas. He's coauthor, with William Meyer, of the slim and skillful book *Social Security Strategies: How to Optimize Retirement Benefits*. Together they're principals in the firm SocialSecuritySolutions.com, a service that helps you choose your best strategy for taking benefits. A special shout-out to Robin Brewton, formerly the firm's vice president of client services and master of answers to technical questions. Thank you, Robin!

Thanks, too, to economist Russell Settle, now retired from a professorship at the University of Delaware. Russ is a founder of SocialSecurityChoices.com, also a service that helps you collect the maximum from your Social Security account. And yet more thanks to economist Larry Kotlikoff, founder of MaximizeMySocialSecurity .com, a highly detailed service for getting the most from Social Security. Larry is a professor at Boston University and coauthor, with Philip Moeller and Paul Solman, of *Get What's Yours: The Secrets to Maxing Out Your Social Security*. You'll find his lifetime financial planning service, including decisions on investments and retirement accounts, at ESPlanner.com. Retired Social Security expert Jerry Lutz, a consultant to MazimizeMySocialSecurity.com, cleared up many technical questions.

For health-care policy information, there is no better source than the Henry J. Kaiser Family Foundation (kff.org). The health insurance chapter was read by Karen Pollitz, senior fellow for health reform and private insurance at KFF, and Patricia Neuman, senior vice president and director of the foundation's Program on Medicare Policy. They both greatly improved my understanding of how these programs work. Kaiser Health News (khn.org) is the top source on the Web for what's going on with Medicare, Medicaid, medical costs, state health policies, and the Affordable Care Act. I check it every day.

Many eyes scoured the chapter on annuities. My special thanks to Tamiko Toland, head of annuity research for CANNEX USA, the go-to source for annuity pricing data. Her technical expertise is tops, not to mention her kindness while going over and over my sentences to make them clear. Thanks, too, to Moshe Milevsky, associate professor of finance at York University's Schulich School of Business in Toronto and widely recognized as a leader in the field. Mark Cortazzo of the MACRO Consulting Group in Parsippany, New Jersey, has extensive on-the-ground experience with evaluating annuities and helping people make decisions. Hersh Stern, founder of ImmediateAnnuities.com, was my expert reader on immediate-pay annuities.

For life insurance, I had the help of three distinguished fee-only insurance advisers: Glenn Daily (glenndaily.com), based in New York City; Scott Witt (WittActuarialServices.com) in New Berlin, Wisconsin; and James Hunt (EvaluateLifeInsurance.org) in Concord, New Hampshire. They guided me through the pages that provide readers with advice for specific personal situations.

The chapter on retirement plans was vetted by Ed Slott (founder of IRAHelp.com—check out his IRA FAQs), and author of *The*

Retirement Savings Time Bomb . . . and How to Defuse It (2020 edition) and James Lange (PayTaxesLater.com), author of *Retire Secure!: A Guide to Getting the Most Out of What You've Got.*

For advice on tapping home equity, I had the help of the knowledgeable Peter Bell, president and CEO of the National Reverse Mortgage Lenders Association, and Jack Guttentag, professor of finance emeritus at the Wharton School of the University of Pennsylvania. Jack's website, mtgprofessor.com, is the most comprehensive source I know for good consumer information about mortgages of all types.

The investment chapters passed through the hands of the reigning gurus of withdrawal-rate research: Michael Kitces, director of wealth management for the Pinnacle Advisory Group in Columbia, Maryland (kitces.com); Wade Pfau, professor of retirement income at the American College of Financial Services in King of Prussia, Pennsylvania (retirementresearcher.com); Jonathan Guyton of Cornerstone Wealth Advisors in Edina, Minnesota (cornerstone wealthadvisors.com); and financial planner Bill Bengen of El Cajon, California, author of the original 4 percent withdrawal rule (now retired). I highly recommend Michael's and Wade's websites for all the newest information related to retirement income strategies.

These chapters also benefited from the wisdom of retirement researcher and financial planner Joe Tomlinson (josephtomlinson .com); financial planner Harold Evensky, cofounder of Evensky & Katz/Foldes Financial Wealth Management (ek-ff.com) in Coral Gables, Florida; Wesley McCain, founder and chair of Towneley Capital Management, based in Laguna Hills, California; Dave Nadig, managing director of ETF.com, the source of all you need to know about those investments; investment manager William Bernstein (EfficientFrontier.com), author of several thoughtful investment books; Rick Ferri (portfoliosolutions.com), founder of the investment management firm Portfolio Solutions and expert on low-cost index fund investing, and Jack Reed (johntreed.com), whose books are bibles for people investing in rental real estate.

To help me make technical issues clear, I had a test audience— readers who aren't financial professionals: my longtime friend, Judy Hole, who spent her career as an exceptional TV producer for CBS News; my sister, Laurie Young, an expert editor, who, among her many other talents, murders unnecessary commas; and my brother, Bob Bryant, who loves to investigate investment theories. They're all at the stage of life where the issues raised in this book matter to them personally. They read the chapters when I thought they were in finished form. Whenever a sentence or paragraph confused them, I hurried to set it right.

And thanks, extravagantly, to my husband, Carll Tucker, founder of the online local news company DailyVoice.com and author of *The Bear Went Over the Mountain,* about America's presidents and vice presidents. Carll is a splendid reader and editor. This is the third book he has suffered through with me, for which he has earned a Top Husband medal from this author and wife.

Index

About the Author

Jane Bryant Quinn built her career as a trusted commentator on personal finance with books and columns read by millions. She has written a regular column for the *AARP Monthly Bulletin* and AARP .com on issues affecting people in midlife and retirement. She posts on Twitter@JaneBryantQuinn and maintains her own website, JaneBryantQuinn.com. She is also a digital news entrepreneur. In 2010, she cofounded DailyVoice.com, which brings local news to communities online. So far, the company covers 91 communities in New York, New Jersey, and Connecticut.

Jane's bestselling book, *Making the Most of Your Money*, is a comprehensive guide to personal finance, named by Consumers Union as the best personal finance book on the market. It was first published in 1991 and has been in print ever since. The third edition—*Making the Most of Your Money NOW*—was published in January 2010. Her book *Smart and Simple Financial Strategies for Busy People* offers her personal list of the best low-cost ideas for managing money (she uses them herself!). Her career includes one of the country's most successful newspaper columns, published twice weekly and syndicated by the Washington Post Writers Group to more than 250 newspapers. She wrote a biweekly column for *Newsweek* magazine for 30 years. She has also written a biweekly column for Bloomberg .com and long-running monthly columns for *Woman's Day* and *Good Housekeeping* magazines.

Jane has worked extensively in television. She cohosted an investment series, *Beyond Wall Street*, which ran on the Public Broadcasting

System. PBS also ran her own program, a personal-finance series called *Take Charge!* She worked 10 years for CBS News, first on the CBS *Morning News*, appearing twice weekly, then on *The Evening News with Dan Rather*.

Jane is married and has two children, six stepchildren, and eleven grandchildren. She was born in Niagara Falls, New York, and lives in New York City.